SECRETS
OF A
CORPORATE
HEADHUNTER

JOHN WAREHAM

SECRETS OF A CORPORATE HEADHUNTER

NEW YORK ATHENEUM 1980

Library of Congress Cataloging in Publication Data

Wareham, John
  Secrets of a corporate headhunter.

  1. Executives. I. Title.
HF5500.2.W35 1980   658.4'07   79–55603
ISBN 0–689–11059–6

To the nomadic spirit
of my wife and children,
but for whose willingness to share
in my adventures
there might not have been any.

ACKNOWLEDGMENTS

I SHOULD like to thank my directors, colleagues and staff but for whose efforts I should not have had the time to put my thoughts to paper—nor, indeed, as many thoughts. Also Mary Copeland for interpreting my handwriting, and retyping those pieces that didn't quite come out right the first time.

CONTENTS

PART III
SECRETS OF A CORPORATE HEADHUNTER

PART IV
HOW TO TURN A $1,000 IOU INTO A
MULTIMILLION-DOLLAR CORPORATION

SECRETS
OF A
CORPORATE
HEADHUNTER

How to Get Out of a Funeral Parlor Without Being Embalmed

An Introduction and Two Semi-apologies

ABOVE an antipodean funeral parlor sixteen years ago, clutching the proceeds of a $1,000 IOU scrawled upon the back of an envelope, I took my first office and hung my first shingle outside a 200-square-foot walk-up office suite. It boasted ratholes and the solid vista of a decaying brick wall. I was so thrilled not to have a boss, it looked like a clear view of the Swiss Alps.

My credentials included unspectacular careers in banking, advertising, and chartered accounting. I resigned from the bank the day I happened, by accident, to see what the president got paid. I made up my mind to leave the accounting practice the day I saw the senior partner's home; if that was the end of the road, I didn't want to follow the path.

Four years ago, when I left the antipodes for New York, my net audited fees exceeded the magic million-dollar mark and were being calculated in what my banker friends term "the substantial seven figures." On a good day I was employing a full-time staff of fifty-one in five offices spread-eagled across Australasia.

Now my view is framed by Rockefeller Plaza windows and I can see right through this jagged city skyscape to the green green grass of Central Park—and sometimes if I close my eyes, I can see even further.

3

The chattering of the Telex outside my door reminds me that Wareham Associates is now established in four countries on three continents: we have offices in New York, Chicago, London, Sydney, Melbourne, Auckland, Wellington, and Christchurch, where I was born, as I try to tell my disciples, in a manger.

Just to carry the flag to those offices now requires some thirty-six hours of jet travel. I arrived in one office unshaven and so jet-lagged that the receptionist took me for a down-and-outer and would not allow me to impede her entrance.

When I started out and met with modest success, a friend told me that I was living in a fool's paradise. I am. *We* are. I remain in awe of my very presence in New York. Some days I pinch myself just to be sure that I really am dreaming.

My United States chairman, the oracle from Chicago, world renowned psychologist Dr. Robert N. McMurry, once told me that the key to success was very simple: (1) find something you like doing; (2) get good at it. "Do that," he said, "and you can't fail."

Once, in my cups, in a wide-bodied jet forty thousand feet above the earth, I asked my other chairman, Sir Arthur Harper (there are two chairmen and me, a sort of holy trinity), what life was all about. "I don't know that," he said, "but I can tell you what the queen of England thinks it's all about, because she told me."

One morning at Buckingham Palace the queen told Sir Arthur, over a breakfast of mushrooms (which, because he is allergic to the fungus, subsequently gave him food poisoning*) that she had been put on earth, as each of us has been put on earth, "To do our duty." Her duty, she said, was to be the best queen possible.

You and I are luckier than the queen. She inherited her job and has to make the most of it. We are free to set about finding a job we enjoy. Then, perhaps, we have a duty to become good at it.

* Now he says he won't ever eat mushrooms again, not for the queen of England, not for *anyone*.

That's why I'm twelve thousand miles from home. I just fell into headhunting, I liked it, and more or less unconsciously I set out to fulfill my duty of becoming the best (and, therefore, the best-paid) headhunter in town. And when the world shrank to a global village, there seemed no choice but to move to New York.

Before you even turn another page, let me confess that I fear I already owe you at least two semi-apologies.

First, I need to assure half of the human race that I mean no slight by writing most of my material in the masculine mood. You just run out of neuter words after a while, and there also sometimes seems no alternative but to pen either "he" or "she." I chose the former not just because, in spite of many social advances, business still tends to be a masculine sport but equally because it seems easier on the reader. I meditated the point for quite a while and, at the end of it, got the feeling that, if there really is a God, She will forgive me.

Second, I beg to be excused for choosing to see the lighter side of some deadly serious situations. Oscar Wilde said that the gods bestowed upon Max Beerbohm the gift of perpetual old age. I was not so blessed: where a situation is so bad that you could just weep—which is often the way in business—I sometimes laugh instead. I'm terribly sorry.

But, anyway, here I am, sitting atop Manhattan, running my little empire, talking to you, and checking to see that the city lights have not yet been overtaken by the gray-white tendrils of another rising sun. It's a great life, isn't it?

PART ONE

HOW TO UNDERSTAND AND LEAD PEOPLE AND ORGANIZATIONS

1. *How to Manage an International Organization*

It's not the ships but the men that sail in them.

PROVERB

MANAGING an international corporation, or any organization embarked upon a risky pursuit, is like managing an ocean racer.

I got into ocean racing when I went to buy a canoe for my kids and ended up with a thirty-one-foot ocean racer instead. My first experience of an overnight race was in the Aegean some weeks later, aboard a sixty-five-foot black-hulled racer built for Baron Rothschild. There I learned two lessons:

1. A million-dollar yacht is only as good as the people who sail it.
2. Even the money of a Greek tycoon cannot substitute for good organization.

In all there were some fourteen hands on board as we disappeared into the setting Aegean sun. Seven of us spoke English and no Greek. Seven others spoke Greek and no English. The sailing master was bilingual but confined his utterances to universally understood questions of ancestry.

One wild night at around 2 A.M. we attempted to gybe the spinnaker. Among other screams (with which I shall not here assail your sensibilities) was heard the cry *"Laska,"* Greek for "Let it go." In the confusion the wrong line was released, and a fellow called Bob Starret made an indelible impression upon

9

my mind as he was suddenly whipped thirty feet into the air, silhouetted against the dark blue sky like a monkey, with a wire rope imbedded in his crotch.

A lot of corporations, like a lot of yachts, are run in this same haphazard fashion. Everybody talks about getting around to "organizing things," but it seldom happens. Communication is so poor that people might just as well be speaking different languages.

Five hair-raising races and six weeks later I entered my own gleaming and as yet unraced yacht *Chauvinist* in a series of races culminating with the treacherous 650-mile Sydney-to-Hobart Ocean Racing Classic that has attracted such disparate high achievers as former British Prime Minister Edward Heath, America's Cup defender Ted Turner, and newspaper magnate Rupert Murdoch. My intention, loudly proclaimed to anyone who would listen, was to win in my neophyte year. Those few who listened laughed, and coaxing recruits proved difficult.

It seemed that all the big-name navigators and crew members were tied up on big boats with winning reputations, and thus were assured of basking in the reflected glory of the success of the boat, whether they contributed to it or not. Once ensconced on board, some quite incompetent people (as I was in Greece) cling like barnacles, toady up to the owner, and puff their meager knowledge with jargon and tall stories.

It's like that in many of the blue-chip corporations that are a magnet for executives with the ability to keep a clean nose and a covered behind. In such an environment there can be nasty surprises for both crew and skipper.

A fellow I met was the chairman of his country's Admiral's Cup committee, the owner and skipper of a world-famous racer and a consistent winner. He was very proud of keeping the same crew together for five years, and everybody paid homage to his fine powers of leadership and his capacity to inspire loyalty. Then one day he decided to invest in an even better, newer boat. Unfortunately it sailed like a wharf and never looked like winning a race. One by one the crew made their excuses and found berths on hotter boats. The inspiring leader was left to try to inspire a new owner.

The would-be tycoon who thinks his charisma will be more prized than his bank balance may be in for a similar experience.

With only four practice races in as many weeks to the gun that would sound the start of my Impossible Dream, I assembled a crew both confident enough and desperate enough to sail with me.

I recruited a just back from round-the-world-racing "professional," whose jersey proclaimed him "Rick" and from whose belt hung a leather pouch that carried spanner, screwdriver, pliers, and a long, wicked knife. My navigator, the former Irish heavyweight boxing champion, bearded forty-year-old Des McSherry, had been the paid navigator-skipper of a commercial yacht that plied the Pacific. Along too came a twenty-year-old sailmaker and a twenty-five-year-old weekend Walter Mitty sailor, who had never sailed in an overnight race.

It's 8:00 P.M. on a cold, dark, bleak, wet, stormy Friday, and I am in my first long (100-mile) offshore overnight race as skipper of my own boat. It is only a club race with a small fleet, but it's all big time to me. The sky is cloud-filled, black and moonless. Rain whips into my eyes and seeps down my neck. I can't see a thing, and am direly afraid of hitting something . . . another yacht, a steel harbor buoy, rocks . . . anything.

With thirty seconds to the starting gun, wire shrieks on metal as the spinnaker is hoisted: the wheel kicks, we lunge forward surging through the foam at full speed. The starting gun erupts, and we are heading straight out into a pitch-black, white-capped rolling ocean with no moon above it. I am crossing the threshold of my fears, whistling in the dark . . . at both ends.

We seized last position in that race, and we never surrendered it.

At midnight, I went below deck to pour our hot Thermos soup into five mugs. The cabin sole and ceiling moved in a sickening fashion, and my homemade, tasty, thick, fresh green soup proved still to be piping hot as it seared my hands, ran into my clothes, splashed my face. Finally it found a home on the cabin sole, where it wallowed from side to side, cooling to grease as it mingled with the lining of my stomach.

At 6:00 A.M. we rounded the weather mark, a small island jutting up out of the sea, and hoisted our big spinnaker. We lurched drunkenly before the wind at full speed, the gear groaning and shuddering as the last of the fleet disappeared ahead of us. Like Richard Nixon contemplating his resignation speech, I was unhappy and perplexed.

"Relax, John," said Round-the-World Rick, who'd grasped the wheel from me, "we don't need you up here." Sick, cold, shivering, I disappeared to my bunk. Thirty minutes later a big wave surged under us, lifting the boat and letting it drop. There was a loud crack, and I crawled up top to survey the cause. My spinnaker with its beautiful costly red and white stripes was in tatters, blown away, hanging in the air like tired underwear caught on a backyard line in a gale.

At that moment I saw what Ruth Carter Stapleton has been telling her brother for years. My problems were related to my psyche: I needed *inner healing*. I remembered the words of Douglas McGregor:

> I thought I could avoid being a "boss." Unconsciously, I suspect, I hoped to duck the unpleasant necessity of making difficult decisions, of taking responsibility for one course of action among many uncertain alternatives, of making mistakes and taking the consequences. I thought that maybe I could operate so that everyone would like me—that "good human relations" would eliminate all

discord and disappointment. I could not have been more wrong.*

New to the game, I was a reluctant skipper: reluctant to give orders, reluctant to take responsibility for overall performance, reluctant to be shown to be a fool. I was (gasp) emotionally incompetent.

Technically I was relatively competent. I had read and absorbed all the books. I knew, for example, that when my fin keel was tipped over by more than thirty-five degrees the boat slid sideways through the water at an alarming rate. The solution was to change to a smaller sail, thus allowing the boat to sail upright. Yet, when I suggested changing to a smaller sail, Rick, talking like a doctor to a child, said we needed the larger sail to "power us through the slop." It sounded okay to me at the time, but now I know better. You *feel* you are going faster with the water rushing past the windows. But you actually go faster, albeit much less dramatically, sailing upright, on an even keel.

It's like that in any business where the stereotype of a dynamic leader is a manic executive dashing about motivating people and making daring decisions to avert disaster-movie-type crises. In real life, however, the truly efficient executive runs his organization with the noise, drama, and precision of an expensive quartz watch.

As a neophyte I was unwilling to push a common-sense point of view in the face of an apparent expert's view—not one of my common faults. I've since learned that sailors, like executives, make outrageous claims as to their expertise, and use jargon and mystery to cover ignorance.

---

* Professor McGregor achieved fame for his popular "Theory X, Theory Y" analysis of how to motivate people at work. Theory Y, which he recommended, said that if only a "good climate" could be established, everybody would *love* to work hard in order to self-actualize—and they wouldn't need to be "bossed" either. When the professor was subsequently promoted to a senior administrative role, he found he was wrong—and had the courage to admit it. Bravo.

Humiliated and embarrassed, after the race I disappeared to the top of a mountain and emerged with five principles (the commandments had gone):

1. I had to assume responsibility for getting to the front of the fleet.
2. We couldn't break gear and win anything.
3. Beyond 35 degrees of heel, we had to reduce sail.
4. There was a most effective way of performing every task.
5. We were out there primarily to win, but it should be fun also.

I suggested that Round-the-World Rick, who fancied himself a skipper, should find a yacht more deserving of his talents, and recruited in his place my friend from the Aegean highwire, Bob Starret. Our performances immediately improved, reminding me that a beheading is always good for morale.

We switched to prepacked airline-style food, with all meals individually packaged in sealed foil containers and stored in dry ice in the order in which they were to be eaten. At sea, nothing could spill, and oven heating was the only preparation necessary. Careful planning enabled us to effect virtually all sail changes with only three hands. I decided that, for the long race, sleep was our most vital resource, and that it was better to lose a few yards than wake up a sleeping crew member: heresy to most ocean racers. In the last week I installed a sensitive electronic thermometer to check the water temperature and catch the cold southbound current that might add extra knots of boat speed, a tempting thought. Finally, I decided to sail with a smaller crew than comparably sized yachts, reasoning that more people spell more confusion.

I also tempered my ambitions. Reasoning that the bigger boats, in bad weather typical of the Hobart, were bound to win, I decided merely to try to win the class in which I was sailing. It was still an enormously tall order, but my sanity was, nonetheless, gaining on my bravado.

It is 11:30 A.M. on December 26, 1976, and a beautiful day in Sydney harbor, where I am living a fantasy. The air drips with excitement. More than a thousand boats are milling about under the eye of the controlling officials and numerous television cameras. The hills that surround the harbor like a huge amphitheater are lined with tens of thousands of people. Among the international fleet of some hundred racers I see the seventy-footer *Ballyhoo,* holder of the accolade "world's fastest boat"; in front of it, sixty feet in the air, like a great green genie, its massive spinnaker pops open and fills, drawing gasps of pleasure from a nervous fleet.

At noon I see a puff from the starter's yacht. At 12:05 the second warning gun sounds. The last five minutes disappear in a blur and, suddenly, with only fifteen seconds to go, we are perfectly positioned, twenty yards from the line. Grim, sea-hardened faces are demanding room. Where is the gun? Des is counting the seconds . . . "Four . . . three . . . two . . . " The gun, the gun! I see a white puff and know the gun has gone. We cross the line before we hear the explosion. We have made a perfect start. I am thrilled. I know that *you never have to recover from a good start.*

On the second day a fuel blockage makes it impossible for us to start our motor and recharge our batteries. We use the radio sparingly, to give our position and to check that of only the boats in our class. We are both surprised and pleased to find that we are winning our class, and decide to cover the opposition and keep our lead.

At 3:10 P.M. a thin black line appears on the horizon and in a matter of seconds the sky changes from blue to black. We are caught changing from our spinnaker to our smallest jib as the storm strikes. I remember all the broken gear we have suffered in the past and scream to Bob to forget the jib and just get the spinnaker down. "Down! Down, Bob!" I yell. In my mind I see the spinnaker reduced to rags. "Wait till we get the jib up," shouts Bob. "Down! Down!" I scream. Reluctantly he releases the spinnaker, and we lose all momentum as a result of carrying no headsail. I am happy with the decision because I know we will win nothing with broken gear.

> *Some people think that the first goal of a business is to*
> *make a profit. They are wrong. The overriding objective*
> *is to stay in business. Survival first, winning later.*

As the spinnaker disappears below deck, the storm hits. We need a full two minutes just to set the small jib. From that point on until the fifth day, we bash into giant, white-capped waves whipped by a never-abating gale.

Across Bass Strait the full fury of the wind is funneled between the mainland of Australia and the island of Tasmania. Enormous waves beat my tiny boat. It is freezing, and everyone is sick. We sail up the waves and then down the other side like a drunken skier navigating a strange mountain.

On the fourth day I come up at 5:55 A.M. to see that we are well beyond thirty-five degrees of heel. There is no doubt in my mind that we should either take the final reef in our jib or change to our storm gear. I talk it over with Bob Starret, because it is Bob who will be risking his life if we change down. Massive seas are running. I have never been in anything as bad. Though the sky is bright, the brine is black and whipped into foam. Helming requires intense concentration if the boat is not to be dropped off the top of a thirty-foot wave, which could snap the mast. Later we discover that some eight yachts were dismasted, that another half dozen for one reason or another dropped out of the race, and that one inexperienced sailor went berserk.

Bob looks at me. "Whatever you say, John," he asks. I say we have no choice, not if we are trying to win. "Yeah, you're right, let's reef the job—call everyone up." In gale conditions we contemplate the maneuver. In calm weather it would take no more than a minute, but not today. Bob clips his harness to the rail and gingerly inches his way forward. On the foredeck the movement of the boat is greater and more severe. The chance of being washed away by a crashing wave is high. The trick is to shorten the sail while still making top speed. If we allow the sail to flog, then we may stall entirely and run the risk of becoming engulfed by a wave and knocked down, or even turned right over.

> *Such a task is the difference between survival and disaster, winning and losing. In business it might be a spectacular profit or a sickening crash. The mettle of a management team is tested in a crisis. The weak (and sometimes even the wise) reach for the bottle, get ulcers, quit, take a better offer, or rush off to attend a convention. You pay an executive to stay out of trouble but, if it comes, you pay him to stay cool and loyal. And if he wins, you reward him—or you should.*

The exercise takes almost half an hour, and at the end of it Bob returns with white fingers and a hard-won grin. We are sailing upright and almost half a knot faster. Des passes me the helm, and I don the snow goggles that go with the job. Bob ducks beneath the spray dodger and huddles for warmth. Des passes him a container of hot Mexican stew—reward enough in these circumstances.

On the fifth day the heavy seas abate, telling us we have cleared Bass Strait. Midmorning we sight Tasmania, and decide to stay some ten miles offshore to cover the closest boat behind us. At 3:00 P.M. the breeze begins to die. In the clear, crisp air we see, astern and off to our right, a big maroon boat nestled against the cliffs. If it is the boat I think it is, *Ruthless,* a top racer from another class, we are doing very well. I don't quite believe it, and for the next four hours we jostle at a steady five knots on calm seas.

Des reports that we'll be in Hobart for an early morning breakfast. Despite this prediction it seems a long time until we sight Tasman Light. We seem barely to move even though our tachometer shows a steady six knots. Des seems perplexed.

At midnight the freshened breeze drives us along before Tasman Lighthouse, perched on jagged cliffs rising straight out of the sea. The race is drawing to a close. Des prepares coffee and laces it with whiskey. He passes it up, his soft Irish brogue blending with the flavor of warm wheat alcohol racing to my toes and to the tips of my fingers on the wheel.

As we sail the last miles, boats and helicopters greet us. A television crew appears and films us and speeds away. At 11:12 A.M. we cross the finish line. Bob passes up a bottle of champagne. We are towed to an excited crowd and a safe berth. My wife steps aboard. She is quiet. "How did we do," I ask. She looks at me strangely. "Don't you know? You won your class, but you were winning the whole race too." We are disbelieving. "Oh, yes, you've been among the leaders all the way, and if you'd finished three hours ago you would have beaten the entire fleet. All day yesterday you were winning."

My mind races back to our decision a mere sixteen hours ago to stay offshore rather than cling to the cliffs as *Ruthless* had done. We were leading the fleet, but we didn't know it: didn't know because I couldn't conceive of such a possibility, had narrowed our objective to class winner, and shut off radio advice of all other results. World sportscasts had blared all of the last two days that we were winning, and we never heard a word.

Could we have done anything differently if we had known the position? Yes, we could. We lost five hours sailing against an outgoing stream, and this was why Des's prediction—home before breakfast—was unfulfilled. If we had but known the overall position we would almost certainly have paid more attention to the electronic thermometer, and been over against the cliffs with *Ruthless,* which, catching the reverse eddy of the same current, gained seventeen places in that last fifty miles. We lost simply because I was unable to sustain the belief in my impossible dream.

There has to be a moral there for any businessman who ever contemplated his market share.

Nonetheless, we are thrilled to win the class and to discover that we have also beaten the class immediately above us, all but two boats in the class above that, and finished overall with the top ten boats in the entire fleet. "An incredible performance," says the commodore of the Yacht Club, passing me the silver trophies that we have won.

"What will you do now?" asks a reporter. Searching for a suitably epic reply, I find myself paraphrasing the words of Conrad Hilton: "Now I will return to New York," I say, "because if you want to launch big boats you go where there is deep water."

And it was a client of mine, in very deep water here, who confided to me that things would have been better if only he had followed the death-bed advice of his father: "When in charge, ponder; when in trouble, delegate; when in doubt, mumble." Frankly, it's not altogether bad advice. My own experience, both in business and as an ocean racer, affirms that circumspection, delegation, and, on occasion, mystery can be useful qualities when it comes to the five major functions of managing people: Selection, Organization, Communication, Leadership, and Motivation.

SELECTION

It isn't easy to build a team from scratch. Experts make mistakes—even Christ chose Judas, but that, of course, was preordained. A more typical mistake is to assume that executives are mere pieces in a game, *objects* without feelings, that you can hire just an intellect or a pair of hands. You can't, because the whole person and his problems always come along too.

It is for this reason that, at the time of visiting a new client to establish his job specification and the chemistry of his organization, I am fond of pointing him to the following passage from George Eliot's *Felix Holt:*

> Fancy what a game of chess would be if all the chessmen had passions and intellects, more or less small and cunning: if you were not only uncertain about your adversary's men, but a little uncertain also about your own: if your Knight could shuffle himself on to a new square on the sly: if your Bishop, in disgust at your Castling, could

wheedle your Pawns out of their places: and if your Pawns, hating you because they are Pawns, could make away from their appointed posts that you might get checkmate on a sudden. You might be the longest-headed of deductive reasoners, and yet you might be beaten by your own Pawns. You would be especially likely to be beaten, if you depended arrogantly on your mathematical imagination, and regarded your passionate pieces with contempt.

The message that executives are people and that the selection of every executive is therefore vital to the whole seldom escapes the perceptive client. It is a subject we'll look at in detail later, but meantime just let me make these two points:

1. Hesitate before hiring an executive with nothing to prove. Better the hungry, talented amateur than the satisfied fat cat.
2. Be prepared to recruit creatively. To find crew for my yacht I scoured the sailing clubs, and checked more than a hundred leads in three cities. My search for a navigator found me in contact with all of the airlines. The fellow I appointed as my senior helmsman was, in fact, introduced to me as a foredeck hand. I spotted Bob Starret in Greece and filed his name for future reference. The wise leader always has a name or two in the back of his head, "just in case."

For Wareham Associates I have employed Episcopal ministers and Catholic priests (one had been personally ordained by Pope Paul, which was, of course, a significant blessing); a British army colonel who didn't like peace; a naval commander who didn't like boats; several lawyers who didn't like books; an architect who didn't like buildings; and a psychologist who didn't like people (I fired him).

The qualities I look for seldom vary. They are common sense, empathy, honesty, industry, stability, a realistic, rather than idealistic desire to work with people, and a slight abrasiveness tempered with the understanding that business is a team sport.

ORGANIZATION

When told he was a genius, Paderewski replied, "Before I was a genius I was a drudge."

Much of the magic of a winning organization is in the organization: getting everything, down to the last detail, *right*. This means finding the one best way to perform any task and making that best way a matter of *routine* so that energy is focused on *doing* the job rather than dissipated on thinking about it.

Some people denigrate "canned decisionmaking" or "going by the book," as demeaning. But it's difficult to build a house without a blueprint, and you certainly won't build a lasting monument without a plan.

The argument, "It's okay in theory but it won't work in practice," is itself fallacious. A good theory will *always* work in practice. If it doesn't, it isn't a good theory, which means you need a new one. The hard fact is that most people tend to put off finding the one best way to do something because it's easier, short term, to just muddle along without thinking.

A recurring problem indicates a lack of *thinking*: shows that nobody has conceived, implemented, and routinized a workable solution. What then is necessary is that *somebody be assigned to find a solution*. Too often a business's problems, like the shoes of the cobbler's son, just don't get repaired, because Dad is "too busy earning a living."

On my yacht we reduced every task to routine. Finally we were all working to the same blueprint, and there was no screaming, no panic, no confusion: things just happened, as British Airways likes to say, with a minimum of fuss.

I have been able to set up Wareham Associates in four countries, *and leave it running successfully behind me,* because I have brought order to the intuitive chaos that usually surrounds executive appraisal. We know with up to 87 percent accuracy whether or not an executive will fail. By analyzing our own files, we have been able to pinpoint those factors that most markedly render an executive a poor employment risk at the ages of twenty-five, thirty-five, forty-five, and fifty-five. Provided we have enough information about an executive's past, we can place a statistic on the likelihood of his future success. Indeed, we can predict with 71 percent accuracy what will be his earning peak. Of course, it's not possible to reduce all risk: each organization has its own climate, and not all executives can adjust. But still we have been able to routinize the flapping of certain red flags: to identify consciously what I had originally been doing solely by intuition.

Where there are two or more equally efficient ways to handle a task, it is still best to identify a *preferred* procedure and then routinize it. A choir always sounds better when its members are working to the same score, singing in the same key.

And the final piece of organizational alchemy? I think the difference between winning and losing, between being best and being nobody, is *practice*. It's like the new girl in town who asked the cop on a New York corner how to get to Broadway. Back came the surly reply, "Practice, baby, practice."

COMMUNICATION

I made the initial mistake, in ocean racing, of assuming that everyone wanted to do what I wanted to do: get from point A to point B in the shortest possible time. I was wrong. People go to sea for the glamour, to get away from their wives, to order people around, for the camaraderie, and for a whole variety of other reasons. Very few people are *really* out there to win, though everyone *says* that he is.

The disparity between stated conscious aims and *unstated emotional needs* is the major barrier to most corporate communication. So the first commandment to ensure clear communication is this: *recruit people with the same objectives as yourself.*

To be utterly honest, this is next to impossible, and so you will probably have to follow my other commandments instead. They are as follows:

1. Keep in mind that, in business, emotional needs are rarely verbalized. This is partly because they are unconscious and also because you, as skipper, with the power to fire, would be the very last person anyone would want to know about it if those needs were *perceived* to run counter to your expectations.

2. Tell people in clear, simple, unambiguous English what you are doing, what is expected of them, and what constitutes a good job.

3. Get *feedback* on your communications. There are barriers to both upward and downward communication that, if you are not careful, leave you isolated from a true response to your leadership.

4. Make it easy for people at all levels to communicate directly with you. In rigid hierarchical structures the very people whose job it is to give you bad news are precisely those who are most likely to have a vested interest in keeping it from you. Keep in mind Wareham's Paradox of Power: *Power isolates, and absolute power isolates absolutely.* Which is why a box containing anonymous ribald suggestions is more to be prized than an unctuous employee who agrees with everything you say but secretly isolates you from what is happening while worshiping the quicksand upon which you walk.

At Wareham Associates we have a house newsletter, bulletin boards, Telexes, and communicating computers that span the world. I also stay in touch with as many people as possible by way of memo and personal letter. But *nothing* can supplant the Sermon on the Mount. Ideally, it should be delivered by the eminence worthy of deification. I like to pretend I qualify and whenever I call on an office, I get everyone together and explain or reexplain (a good sermon can stand repeating) my business gospel, which runs as follows:

23

• We're in it together and, unlike the undertaker, are privileged that our stock in trade is people who are fully alive. It an honor to be entrusted with the task of restructuring organizations, recruiting executives, helping people. We must always be worthy of that trust, treat people decently, approach our task with reverence, and not become cynical.

• We should aim to be respected and well paid. The two usually go hand in hand and in about that order, but there is no point being well paid if you cannot sleep at night.

• Self-respect comes from knowing that you are doing a good job. The respect of peers and colleagues comes from their recognition that you are *serious* about your work. But you don't need to be solemn to be serious.

• A client is a wonderful person, and a client prepared to pay on time without quibbling is probably divine. A stable of such satisfied clients does more for our name, self-respect, and bank balances than any miracle that a public relations or advertising wizard could ever wreak. And if we keep all our clients satisfied, then we will never need to advertise, so that we can all pay that money to ourselves, or buy our clients extravagant dinners.

• A good client doesn't like extravagant dinners because he knows that, one way or another, he is picking up the tab. He just wants a first-class job, as good as we can do, and better than our competitors.

• Next to a satisfied client, *you* are the person who can do us the most good. You have a duty to develop yourself, to live a creative and enriching life, to enjoy yourself.

• One of the best places to enjoy yourself is at work. Remember the old edict: all work and no play made Jack a rich boy, and pretty girls find him not at all dull. Or, to put it more prosaically, our work, if we are good at it, will be financially rewarding, and as a result we'll have lots of friends.

• If we are both good and fast, we will earn even more

money, so work not only harder but more quickly. *Work
so as to be missed,* then, if you ever leave, you'll become
a legend.

• The tragedian always wants to play comedy, and almost everyone thinks he would be happier doing somebody else's job. If you ever find that you're really not
enjoying yourself at work, then maybe you should be
doing something else. But ninety-nine times out of a
hundred you'll find the grass on the other side of the fence
is only Astro-Turf. So instead of jumping the fence, you
may achieve greater satisfaction by cultivating the pasture
from which you are already taking sustenance. Any job,
after all, is what you make it. Consider the words of
James Thurber:

> There is, of course, a certain amount of drudgery in
> newspaper work, just as there is in teaching classes,
> tunnelling into a bank, or being President of the
> United States. I suppose even the most pleasurable
> of imaginable occupations, that of batting baseballs
> through the windows of the RCA Building, would
> pall a little as the days ran on.

• We have a magic talisman, and that is our good name.
It can attract us clients, open doors, and ease the way in
all manner of means. But, like a brass plate, we must
polish it every day. It tarnishes easily and, if the shine
disappears, so does the magic.

• Speak well of the competitors and respect them, because a worthy opponent sharpens your skills. But do
your level best to beat them just the same.

In addition to these happy homilies, I always, when a new
manager is appointed to one of my offices, give him this
advice:

• You are a leader, not a bureaucrat. Don't waste your
time with paperwork, office housekeeping, or empire
building.

• Get out and see your clients. Talk to them. Press the

flesh. Let them see what a well-dressed, sophisticated, shrewd, dynamic, *trustworthy* individual is taking care of their problems, wisely and prudently guarding their investment in fees.

• You only get one shot at integrity. Our relationship is like a shaving mirror: if it cracks, I'll never be able to concentrate on my beard and will end up cutting my throat. Or yours.

• Profit is a function of time, energy, and thought. The easiest way to increase profits is to get more work done in less time—and *think*.

• It's a mistake to believe that one more employee will make the difference between a profit and a loss. Unless he can create his own work, which few people can, he will just share our existing pie, which means that we shall all have to tighten our belts.

• We all make mistakes, and the more we do, the more mistakes we make. So, when you make a mistake, learn from it. Experience may be the ability to recognize that you have just made the same mistake again, but, after you've gained that experience, further wisdom, at the same cost, may be intolerable.

• It's easier to double income than halve costs, and less painful. So spend money to get money. But don't be stupid. Spend my money as if it were your own and you were a Scotsman.

• You have the authority to do what you want but, where there is a reasonable doubt, it might be both courteous and wise to check.

• Give me the worst picture first. If things go wrong, then let me know about it as early as possible. Don't freeze or put your own self-esteem ahead of the golden goose—it's feeding us both.

• Never write anyone an unpleasant letter on our stationery. Never.

• Never criticize a subordinate in front of anyone else.

- Be on good terms with all of your staff, but be worthy of their respect. They want you to be a leader more than a friend.
- Have the guts to hire people better than yourself.
- Beware of yes-men and flatterers. Your reality changed the day you sat in that chair. Your argumentative employee may be your very best ally, because he may be your only hold on what is *really* happening.
- Work should be a pleasure, and office politics is draining and dissipating. So discourage all politicians. And, since you perpetuate what you reward, don't reward credit-grabbers or coasters either. Reward people who go the extra mile. Soon enough we will all be miles ahead of the fleet.

Having assailed my troops with penny wisdoms, I usually tell them what they may expect of me, and what I expect of myself:

- I am helping you to establish Wareham Associates as the *premier* world-wide executive search and management consulting firm.
- I am prepared to make personal sacrifices to meet that goal.
- I will not place my own interests ahead of yours.
- I will endeavor to create an exciting work climate and to extend us both.
- I will not dodge the tough decisions, but I won't be hasty either: however simple they may seem, some judgments—especially those involving people—command a decent amount of time and thought.
- I am conscious that you want to work for an organization that is professional and serious about its work.
- I will only ever recruit anyone who I think will add luster to our name: someone you would be happy to introduce to your friends as a colleague.
- I promise not to be pompous, have a heart attack, or

become a sad stereotype of the hard-driving workaholic. I want to enjoy my life as much as I want you to enjoy yours.

Where communication is concerned, *brevity* and *clarity* are related virtues, and I do not like to encourage the prodigious memo-writer. If there were no telephones or typists and everybody had to communicate by Telex, a lot of wasted time and effort would be saved. The advantage of a Telex message is that it requires you to go immediately to the heart of your message. "YOUR MOTHER PASSED AWAY TODAY. DEEPEST SYMPATHY," could possibly be improved to read "YR MOTHER DEAD—SORRY." But both are fine examples of what the Telex can do to what would otherwise be an ambiguous, stilted, and long-winded piece of prose.

I receive the results from all my offices by weekly Telex because it permits no room for excuses and prevarications— success requires no explanation, and failure permits no alibi.

LEADERSHIP

A leader cannot delegate the responsibility for having his ship run around—*somebody* must be responsible for winning. Assuming that responsibility is what leadership is all about.

In Greece the owner of the boat chose not to take the helm or lift a line in any race. He took a lot of photos, and spent much time in his stateroom. Looking back, I can see that he was wise to delegate the helm for he was not an experienced helmsman. But he made a mistake—he neither skippered his boat nor delegated the role to anyone else. In consequence, everyone was in charge, and no one was in charge—and chaos reigned.

If you are incompetent and want to cover up, you have two interesting choices. One is to hire people as incompetent as you: that way, if you come last, you can blame them and they won't know any better. Alternatively, you can put the inmates in charge of the asylum, practice democratic-participative management, and pray for a natural leader to appear. I bet he doesn't.

The best course, I think, is to assume responsibility for winning and actually *do* something about it. This may mean delegating authority to a good leader and then getting out of his way. Or you may prefer to assume the mantle of leadership yourself—hoping, of course, that it will not cover your eyes.

Perhaps the simplest way to understand leadership is to look at the *functions* that a leader, whatever his personal qualities, whatever his style, must perform. Capone, Churchill, Napoleon, Kennedy . . . each essentially performed the same three tasks:

1. Satisfied the *individual* needs of his followers
2. Satisfied the needs of his *group*
3. Focused the efforts of the group and the individuals on a *goal*

Satisfying individual needs begins with the recognition that people can and do perform the same task for different reasons. For example, I can drink because I am thirsty, or I can drink because I want to run away from my problems. In a group situation the most important individual needs are:

• A feeling of "belonging"
• Belief in the worth of the task to be performed. The boy scout who wanted to do something big and clean and was sent to wash an elephant probably had a very clever scoutmaster. On an ocean racer, intelligent people will happily perform dull and mundane jobs because everybody recognizes that every task is vital to both survival and winning.
• *Sincere* concern for the individual as a person
• The feeling that someone is in charge who knows what he is doing, and who thus will get us out of here alive

Satisfying group needs involves an appreciation of the fact that a group can be more or less than the sum of its members. If it's more, the extra something is high morale. The members

29

of a group need to feel that it is worth belonging to: that their combined strengths are being used to shape something worthwhile.

Group needs begin with a means of group identification. It may be a company tie and cuff links, or a swastika and armbands, or blue jeans, long hair, and beads. Generally it will be the belief that *we*, as a team, are doing something worthwhile.

When the group ceases to believe in itself, morale disappears, and the group disintegrates. So someone and something have to keep the group together.

Many groups don't want to think about what they are doing or why they exist. They pretend they want to win, but underneath they only want to pass the time. But *way, way* down deep is the yearning for fulfillment that comes from doing something, from being *somebody,* from feeling a part of something that *matters*.

The ability to *focus a group on a goal,* thereby providing meaning and purpose to life, is a key attribute of a strong leader. The very act of fixing a goal tends to inspire people. None of my Hobart crew would, finally, have made the journey had I not somehow been able to hypnotize both myself and my recruits to accept that we were there with a chance of winning. Likewise, business functions most efficiently when it is bottom-line- and target-oriented.

MOTIVATION

Self-made businessmen often ask: "How can I get my staff to service my customers as *I* would service them?" The answer is complex, but can be made to sound simple: *"Involve them as you are involved."*

To ask the question "How do I motivate my team?" is to demean the task and the people because the very language of motivation tends to alienate the best of followers by involuntarily suggesting, as Thomas Fitzgerald so perceptively puts it, that they resemble captive rats in a training box equipped with levers, trick doors, food pellets, and electric grids.* The feeling that anyone wants merely to use us, to play upon our feelings, creates the very state that the questioner seeks to avoid.

Most people *are* dependent, *do* want direction, *enjoy* being helped, *want* to be assured that somebody is in control. But, within that framework, as I have noted, we all like to feel that we are a part of what is happening, that we *matter*. A good leader intuitively understands this fact, and part of his appeal is based upon willingness to share the credit of the group achievements that, as catalyst, he is able to effect.

Let's look at some of the key things that *do* motivate people—and a couple that don't:

Money. On an ocean racer, people are prepared to suffer debilitating seasickness, to risk their lives in terrible conditions, to work for days on end at mundane tasks that would be beneath the dignity of the average corporate employee—*without getting paid a cent.*

We need money to cover our basic needs and wants but, beyond that, money is a poor motivator. The real reward of money is that it provides *recognition* of worth. But there are other more effective ways to achieve that end, which is just as well because the power to give money, once used, is lost. In fact, the *promise* of money may sometimes be a better incentive than the reality.

For example, you are likely to recruit better-motivated people by offering them a lower salary and selling the *value* of the task: many people will give more of themselves for *less* money if other satisfactions are available to them. This was established by a psychologist who paid two groups of students substantially different rates to perform a dull, tiresome research task and then to sell other students on the idea of doing the same work. The highest-paid group was the least effective in finding new recruits. All they could say about the job was

* See "Why Motivation Theory Doesn't Work," Thomas H. Fitzgerald, *Harvard Business Review,* July–August 1971.

that it paid well. The lower-paid students, in order to perform the task and then sell it, first had to sell themselves on the *value* of the research, and this they then communicated to the new recruits.*

Winning. Muhammad Ali, who presumably knows about these things, proclaimed that no one knows what to say in the loser's room. Conversely, morale on a winning boat, I can tell you, is never a problem. Even the *prospect* of winning is a wonderful antidepressant. Practically every problem of morale disappears when a team or a corporation is ahead of the pack or looks as if it will finish with the winners. That's why a martinet who leads his team to victory inevitably enjoys higher group morale than the nice guy who loses. His winningness enables hidden human qualities to be perceived in him, proving that, under it all, he is really a first-class fellow—tough but great—ah, but of course.

A leader must remind his followers that they *can* win, that they *will* win, if they will but work, and believe, and keep on working and believing. And, as long as winning is a distinct possibility, work, practice, and the willingness to accept orders are all very simple.

A major obstacle occurs when a team doing badly is unable to *perceive* that it can win, and these situations need careful analysis because studies show that goals that are thought to be too high act as disincentives: that people would rather give up than struggle toward a goal they believe cannot be reached. So, when morale is low, it can be a good idea to reduce goals until they become credible to everyone, and then gradually lift them when confidence is regained.

But always bear in mind that good leadership can inspire people to do more than they believed possible.

Compatibility. Ocean racing reaffirmed for me that incompatibility cannot be tolerated over the long term. A team of competent compatible people will always defeat a team of

---

* Erudite readers might look at Leon Festinger's book, *Theory of Cognitive Dissonance* (Stanford, Calif.: Stanford University Press, 1957).

brilliant incompatible people. Indeed, a team of incompatible people is not a team, and an executive whose style is incompatible with your own will achieve greater fulfillment within another corporation. And you owe him that alternative.

Elitism. The more difficult it is to gain acceptance to a team, the more membership is valued. Mediocre performance should not be tolerated. It is unfair to those who are competent to let incompetents onto the team, or to keep them there. It is both better for morale and more efficient to sail with a small highly competent crew than to carry passengers. Everybody responds to the increased challenge.

Praise. Praise is like a drug: unless used sparingly, it loses its potency and becomes a pathetic addiction. I am not in favor of praise for the same reason that I am not in favor of "motivation." People confuse it for flattery, and most times it is. Inevitably, also, it carries patronizing overtones: Better than to praise, I think, is to agree in advance upon a standard of excellence worthy of special reward, and then to automatically reward people for achieving that standard.

Of course some people would rather part with their flattery than their money, no matter how great the performance. My hometown friend, the vicar of Fendalton, Bob Lowe, hoping to get a donation for his church, drove sixty miles and gave a magnificent speech to a club of a hundred and fifty women. Giving a vote of thanks the club president said, "We just don't know how to thank you." The reverend leant into the microphone and projected his rich stentorian baritone to inquire "Have you considered *money?*"

"Ooh, Reverend," simpered the president, "we wouldn't want to embarrass you."

"You'd be surprised just how thick-skinned I am when it comes to money," intoned the reverend, as much out of malice as need.

Delegation. Delegation is the great motivator—great because it gets people involved. But effective delegation does presuppose that you have recruited competent people and, additionally, that you're prepared to get out of the way and let them get on with the job. And one thing you learn very quickly on an ocean racer, unless you like the idea of being hoisted thirty feet in the air with wire in your crotch, is to get out of the way.

You also find out that it is literally impossible to supervise everything yourself. Even the martinet has to sleep sometime. And sleep comes easier when you know that there is a whole crew up top who are good at what they do, and who, because they are good, want to give of their best.

Trust. Both you and they will turn in your best performance within an atmosphere of trust, because such an environment enables power to be delegated both downward, and, equally importantly, *upward*. The advice that we should only ask someone to do what we would do ourselves presumes that a leader will possess the skills of his followers. Many times he will not have those skills, and he must depend upon his followers to find him worthy of his orders.

Bob Starret allowed me the power to ask him to go forward and change sail as we crossed Bass Strait in a raging storm. I could not have done it myself, and I would not have tried. In that one moment of crisis, the question of leadership crystallized for me. I wanted to win, and that meant changing sail. I was, on my own, incompetent to the task. I was dependent upon Bob's being prepared to risk *his* life. The key to this exercise lay in our mutual recognition that we were both committed to the same overriding goal of *winning*—but that's not really work, is it? Not if you're really involved in making it all happen—that's fun. Right?

2. *How to Become a Charismatic Leader*

*It often happens that I wake at night and begin to
think about a serious problem and decide I must
tell the Pope about it. Then I wake up completely
and remember that I am the Pope.*

POPE JOHN XXIII

CHARISMA, like beauty, is in the eye of the beholder. It
derives from a Greek word meaning, literally, a magical gift.
Charisma is life's gift to the man of action prepared to risk his
being in a grand undertaking; who takes daring action; who
pursues, gains, and is prepared to wield power. As long as he
is winning, he is charismatic. If he falters, the charismatic
mantle is lost. But that risk is the price of an audience. Napoleon saw it clearly:

> My power is dependent upon my glory, and my glory on
> my victories. My power would fall if I did not base it on
> still more glory and still more victories. Conquest made
> me what I am; conquest alone can keep me there.

Nobody can *give* anybody charisma. It must be seized, and
the individual who aspires to be charismatic must first work
upon his own psyche. If he wants to give great light from his
candle, he must be prepared to burn it at both ends for a while.
But here are nine magical things that anyone who wants to be
charismatic can actually go out and do:

Look like a leader. Writing in *Powers of Mind*, Adam Smith
observed that "if you pass a V-shaped shadow sideways or
backwards over a baby chick in a lab nothing happens, but if
you move the same shadow forward the baby chick goes into

35

panic. The chick has inherited the genetic message—Hawk, danger—for a certain-shaped shadow, even though he is only a couple of days old and has not talked to his mother and may never see a hawk."

The charismatic leader also plays upon such genetic archetypes, triggering unconscious primal responses in his followers. The Freudians tell us that a leader should *look like an authoritarian father figure* by wearing dark suits and virginal white shirts, because we unconsciously infer *moral* judgments from color. Hitler hit the jackpot with the Nazi symbols and uniforms, which still inflame. You probably should not wear an Iron Cross, but a good dark suit could be helpful.

The African witch doctor wisely indulges the unconscious needs of his clientele. Instinctively he knows that most diseases are psychosomatic and can be treated with a chant, a dance, and a three-piece suit. So does his modern counterpart.

A characteristic of the outstanding salesman is his unconscious use of clothes to influence. A survey of gridiron footballers revealed that both winning teams and individual stars took great care over their appearance, while losers kept untidy locker rooms and didn't clean their gear.

Muhammad Ali, in his book *The Greatest,* prides himself on his ability to wear a dark, double-breasted suit and "Look like a United States senator." Charismatic, crowd-pleasing Ali, leader of Black America, never went to leadership training college, but he knows all the tricks.

John F. Kennedy spent fifteen minutes combing his hair before stepping off Air Force One to greet the welcoming crowds during his visit to Berlin in 1961. "It's not Jack Kennedy but the United States that's going to walk off this plane," he explained to protesting aides.

The leader, like the magician, derives power from his cloak and his top hat: no symbols, no magic. The magician may be just an actor, but his illusions must be real enough because the audience applauds. What more do you need?

Have a dream. That prince of darkness, T. E. Lawrence of Arabia, knew about dreaming. All men dream, he said, but not equally. "Those who dream by night in the dusty recesses of their minds wake in the day to find that it was vanity: but the dreamers of the day are dangerous men, for they may act their dream with open eyes, to make it possible."

A dream that is bright enough to stand the light of day is charged with electricity waiting to light anyone who comes in touch with it. A leader without a dream is a bureaucrat.

When a great man talks about a great dream, as did Martin Luther King, Jr., the world stops to listen. A dream invests small words with deep meanings. Information that would otherwise be trite becomes exciting. Rich people have nothing to live for but their money, and are bored. Poor people have nothing to live for but the dream of being rich. Little wonder that John Kennedy, with his dream of Camelot, attracted rich and poor alike: there would have been lots to do and plenty to eat in Camelot—a place as holy and enchanted as the pleasure dome of Kubla Khan.

Set a concrete goal and begin advancing toward it. David was not great when he slew Goliath, but at the moment he decided to try—and fixed the date. Goals and deadlines have a galvanizing effect. Action becomes necessary, and action changes other people. Bystanders who listen to your dream don't really expect you to do anything about it: few people really expect others to lay foundations beneath their castles in the air. The discovery that you are actually embarking, *have embarked,* upon an adventure, will always draw a reaction because your action affects the self-esteem of others: you are doing something, and they are doing nothing. Reaction will be sharply divided. Many will want to jump upon your caravan, to hitch their wagon to your star, to come along for the ride, the thrill, the adventure. Many will become annoyed, angered, cynical, even wish for your failure, because your action highlights their inaction: because you have, in a way, changed their world.

The person who takes action in the pursuit of a dream will inevitably draw strong feelings. Such emotions always follow the daring leader: he draws love or hate, the crown of olives or the assassin's bullet. Perhaps, if he is truly charismatic, his brow will be kissed by both. Lucky him, for the first requirement of immortality is death—and lucky too, while mortal, to have been spared the living death of apathy.

Develop specific knowledge. A leader must know his subject. The better he knows it, the more powerful and charismatic he becomes.

Jack Kennedy was said to have an awesome general knowledge—he read and studied to gain power over his advisers. When he did not have that knowledge or that power, he succumbed to "expert" advice, and the Bay of Pigs debacle was one result.

Hitler boasted that he had read *Clausewitz on War* so often that he knew more than his generals. His spectacular early victories would seem to give some credence to that claim.

Jimmy Carter was able to do what no man has ever done, plan a peace settlement acceptable to both Arabs and Israelis, because he studied every nuance of the Middle East enigma. Premier Begin said that Carter examined and helped structure "every page, every paragraph, every line, every word" of the historic peace settlement. Before Camp David, Carter was said to be incompetent. After it, his followers said that he had worked magic. (His opponents put it down to a sort of Bible-class naïveté.)

Appreciate the value of words and speak to the heart. Syllables govern the world, and the mark of the charismatic leader is his easy command of simple words evoking emotional responses. Words like home, children, love, hate, challenge, enemy, friend—powerful, loaded words. Such words, when charged with a big dream, have the power to reach deep into the heart of all who come in contact with them. Every utterance becomes a piece of prophetic dogma.

Because a leader has given himself the advantage of a big dream, it is almost impossible for him to sound dull. Senator Eugene McCarthy was a poor public speaker yet drew more followers than the Pied Piper of Hamelin. The electricity, the magic, was in his message, heretical at the time, to quit Vietnam.

Mahatma Gandhi had no office, no four-star uniform, no limousine, not even a secretary. He was just a fakir from afar with a reedy voice, a big idea, and an apparently magical choice of words.

Churchill, initially a poor communicator, unable to speak without notes, worked long into the night to hone his words. The results were memorable thoughts and phrases that sliced to the bone. Magic, indeed.

Be mysterious. Somerset Maugham said that it is dangerous to let the public behind the scenes. They are easily disillusioned, he said, "and then they become angry with you, for it was the illusion they loved."

People have an intense need to believe that there is more to life than they know. To be able to fill that void by whatever means is to acquire, in the eyes of many, magical powers.

There are many ways to become mysterious. A good way is to live in a big house and be inaccessible. The pope lives at the Vatican, the queen at Buckingham Palace. The dwelling should be impressive and have big gates that close. When Howard Hughes lived in a private world that absolutely nobody got to see, his mystery and magic were legendary. But when he died and it was revealed that he was just a sick and senile old man who watched old movies, the magic vanished.

An unlisted telephone number used to denote that you were much sought after but unavailable. This ploy is now a little overworked, however, and some very unimportant people now have unlisted telephone numbers. Thus cunning leaders are now listing their numbers but using answering services to intercept unwanted calls.

Unpredictability creates mystery. Never arrive ahead of time: better to be prompt than early. Sometimes fail to arrive at all: your absence can be the talisman of your presence. Arrive where you are least expected or visit the same gathering twice in one day, particularly if you are not expected. Then, when you leave, no one will believe it, and suspect you capable of being in two places at once—and that, I hardly need tell you, would be the beginning of a positively *divine* reputation.

Arriving by limousine is now passé. Jimmy Carter walked to the White House; New York's mayor Ed Koch took the subway to his investiture; Nixon was a master of arriving by helicopter. (The cost/mystery helicopter trade-off is extremely high, making it very popular with aspiring leaders in all walks of life.)

Only show all your cards when your audience is prepared to believe that you are holding something in reserve—and in a way you always are, because only you know when you have played your last card. When faced with an incomprehensible situation, say little or nothing. Or talk in riddles or platitudes. Laugh and walk away.

One of my early employers, a very dull accountant, was blessed with a silver head of hair and a limited vocabulary. At the end of a mundane career spanning forty years, he had parlayed his meager talents into an enviable reputation for sagacity and gotten himself onto the boards of many corporations. He said little but always looked good. Several people commented to me that his advice, so sparing, so trite, so obvious, was actually *inspired*. His power lay in his mysterious silence.

The final mystery of the charismatic leader is his capacity to be honest. If he has first nurtured a reputation for mystery, the truth, however banal, will seem magical when it falls from his lips. People can believe the truth from a leader while simultaneously still suspecting that there must be something more. In a way, there is, and the something more is a mystery.

Be prepared to bend the rules. A boy asked his father if God could make a stone so heavy that no one could lift it. "Yes," said his father. "Ah," said the boy, "but can God lift it then?"

Of course he could. God can do anything. God is magic. The willingness to use power to bend the rules is evidence of magical, godlike powers. In the immortal words of Richard Nixon, "When the president does it, it's not illegal."

A senior financial controller left a bureaucratic corporation to join a client of mine. After one week on the job, he rushed into the president's office to say that the president had violated a policy in the company manual. The president calmly tore the page out of the manual, crumpled it, and threw it in his wastebasket. "Policy," he announced, "has been changed."

"My God," gasped his awe-struck employee—not grasping the irony of his words. And proving too if, of course, proof is needed, that where the power to bend rules is in a leader's hands, the intelligent use of that power can be both good for morale and evidence of godlike power.

Be well organized. If I told you that I could expand time, would you say that was magic? Probably. But the fact is that *anyone* can expand time. You can do it simply by being well organized, by working faster and more effectively. On my yacht I saved valuable hours on food preparation, minutes on sail changes, and vital seconds on the start line. Practice alone can enable you to expand time, yet so few people practice the art. John Kennedy, Richard Nixon, and Jimmy Carter were all superbly, almost awesomely, well organized.

Time spent wondering is lost. "Lost ground we can recover," said Napoleon. "Lost time we can never recover." He was exhorting his troops to be prepared to move more quickly. We must grasp opportunity firmly by the forelock as it approaches—for it is bald from behind. Luck follows the leader who has prepared for all contingencies—luck is preparation meeting opportunity.

Be ruthless without trepidation when necessary. It was Napoleon who also said that nothing is more salutary than a terrible example at the right moment. Maybe he had just read Machiavelli, who advised the prince that it is better to be feared than loved because men "love of their own free will but fear at the will of the prince." A wise prince, he said, "must rely upon what is in his power and not what is in the power of others."

The capacity to take ruthless action is admired because most people have no such ability. Ruthlessness appeals to the darker side of our nature. We feel that we should not admire it, but secretly we do. Secretly we enjoy the smell of blood on the floor: Caesar disliked it only when the blood became his own.

The pursuit of a big dream will necessarily involve some people being hurt. This, in a way, is part of its attraction. The more audacious the idea, the more remorselessly it must be pursued. The recognition and removal of incompetent personnel becomes a necessity. Firing doesn't damage an enterprise at all: it is good for morale, inspiring of loyalty and awe, and exciting to everyone—not least, the person fired.

The paradox is that a ruthless leader is often spared tough decisions because people simply get out of his way. It is the leader who desperately wants to be friends with his followers who is most often faced with the dilemma of hurting them.

At the end of it all, *whether you win* is all that will be remembered, for that is all that will matter to your followers. The wounds of people hurt along the way will heal, and they will come to treasure the scars. Their initial tears and complaints will only enhance your reputation for strong leadership.

It is unnecessary to rule by creating and using naked fear, but if you can get god-fearing respect you should take it with a friendly smile.

3. *What Makes Executives Tic*

> *Man is a brute, only more intelligent than the other brutes, a blind prey to impulses . . . victim to endless illusions, which makes his mental existence a burden, and fills his life with barren toil and trouble.*
>
> H. G. WELLS

AN EXECUTIVE functions within a crucible of intense conflict and stress. He is like a circus performer: at his happiest on a tightrope thirty feet above the ring with half a dozen knives in the air, concentrating so intensely that he is unaware of any other problem. Put him on the ground, take away his knives, and his audience, and he becomes tense and frustrated.

Like the rest of us, an executive is an energy system in pursuit of equilibrium, balancing conflicting tensions in order to attain *homeostasis*—a state of freedom from stress, that contentment we hope will be found on holiday or in retirement.

But even in Florida you still can't send out for happiness, and reclining in an armchair or a wheelchair is no guarantee of psychic equilibrium. Homeostasis is only attainable in the pursuit of life itself: climbing a mountain, painting a picture, raising a family . . . or juggling those shiny sharp knives.

Sources of stress are threefold: in your level of inherited psychic energy: within your environment: and inside your skull. Let's look at each.

PSYCHIC ENERGY

A Greek by the name of Zeno developed the theory, some

two thousand years ago, that there seemed to be a central life force, which he called *physis,* that impelled us to do things: to get better when we are sick, to jog when we are well; to solve puzzles, explore unknown lands; possibly to take up ocean racing. . . .

This force is akin to *psychic energy,* with which some people seem naturally more highly imbued than others. The result is that they are necessarily (some would say unnecessarily) *active,* both liking and needing to be doing things all the time. For example, on vacation they prefer playing tennis to lying on the beach, and frequently they would rather be at work than playing anyway. But these people are really *liveaholics,* not workaholics as they are so often called. H. L. Mencken put it nicely when he wrote: "I go on working for the same reason that a hen goes on laying eggs."

The employee with a high level of psychic energy and an active personality is much prized in business, where profit is a function of time and energy, and the executive whose flywheel spins faster than his colleagues becomes a profit center all of his own.

On the other side of the scale is the passive personality, so well captured in the *Punch* cartoon of the old man who, when asked what he did with his time, replied: "Sometimes I sits and thinks, and other times I just sits."

The passive individual tends to experience and enjoy more of life's subtle pleasures. The active person, if he took an interest in music, would want to conduct the orchestra, whereas his passive companion finds more pleasure in *listening* to the music; or *sitting* on top of a mountain after helping his active friend scale to it.

There is no more inherent value in being active than being passive, but the *outward* rewards of life tend to be seized by the active individual. Basically, he is paid more because he *does* more, but his boardinghouse reach is an asset too.

The greater an executive's psychic energy level, the greater are his stresses. However, this is not at all to say that the stress produces anxiety. The opposite, in fact, is generally nearer the truth—the presence of stress simply propels this type of individual to move faster in order to achieve homeostasis. As one chief executive noted, "I don't get ulcers, I give 'em."

ENVIRONMENTAL STRESS

Lewis Carroll's Red Queen might have been speaking of the pressure that a bottom line exerts upon corporate life when she told Alice:

> Now, *here,* you see, it takes all the running *you* can do to keep in the same place. If you want to get somewhere else, you must run at least twice as fast as that.

Harold Geneen, former chief executive of ITT (where they say his name is pronounced with a hard *G* as in God rather than a soft *G* as in Jesus), refined corporate accounting into an art form and built a world-wide organization of executives dancing to the tattoo of their daily figures.

Management by Objective (MBO) programs intensify this pressure by requiring that an executive publicly pledge himself—like an alcoholic at an AA meeting—to attaining specific, quantifiable goals for his own divisions. Geneen's admonition, delivered after such a session, "No surprises, please," must have been about as tranquilizing as having the Godfather wish you good health.

Sophisticated reporting techniques have also sharpened the juggler's knives, and in some corporations the spotlight is more than an allusion. At the annual ITT executive meetings, according to Anthony Sampson, an executive's actual performance figures really are flashed up onto a big screen alongside those pledges he made while in a manic mood last year. Now he has the pleasure of explaining any shortfalls. An executive in this position might be excused for interpreting Geneen's presence behind the projector, and his needle-sharp insights into the figures, as being reminiscent of the words of Alice's King: "Give your evidence, and don't be nervous or I'll have you executed on the spot."

One chief executive of a sales organization implemented his own *Looking Glass* "incentive" scheme, which he termed "planned insecurity." Each month a listing in order of individual sales results was placed on the bulletin board, and the fellow whose name appeared last was automatically fired.

A more subtle form of pressure was exerted by an insurance organization. The sales competition winner was awarded the down payment on a Mercedes, which was delivered to his home replete with big red ribbon. Unfortunately, to keep the car, along with the esteem of his wife and neighbors, *he* had to pay the installments out of his subsequent commission earnings.

Extreme examples? Not really, because the pressure on executives to "make the team" and retain the respect of peers and colleagues really does pervade modern corporate life.

So too does the problem of coping with accelerating change. Rapid technological advances, coupled with the communications explosion, now require that a corporation, just to survive, move faster than at any time in business history. And as the decision-maker's lead time lessens, the stress upon him correspondingly increases. Running in the same spot may now truly require taking a business lunch in Paris and returning the same day to indigestion in New York.

THE BALANCING ACT INSIDE THE SKULL: A FREUDIAN PRIMER

Freud gave his live to the understanding of how we are continually balancing our inner tensions in the never-ending quest for homeostasis, and a Freudian primer is indispensable in understanding the riddle of what people are doing and why. Very, very briefly, Freud suggested the following.

We like to believe that we act logically and from cool reason, but nothing could be further from the truth. Some 90 percent of our behavior is caused by forces and motivations of which we are unconscious. We are like players reciting lines, unaware that we are in a play or working from a script. Understanding our lines and the purpose of the play requires an appreciation of the human mind.

It is helpful to characterize behavior as being governed by a mind composed of three interacting elements that Freud called *ego, superego,* and *id.* Eric Berne later identified three related *ego modes* that he called *adult, parent,* and *child.* Understanding these elements, and how they interreact is the key to the human drama. Let's look a little closer.

The Ego or Adult

The ego screens, sifts, suppresses, and recalls information in and out of consciousness by causing you to "forget" or "remember" your every experience.

The ego is thus an omnipotent guardian of all your thoughts. Part librarian and part censor, it ensures that the information you need to work with is in your consciousness (on your desk, as it were); that material you might possibly need does not clutter your desk but is nonetheless within easy subconscious reach; and that anything destabilizing—unnecessarily confusing, painful, or X-rated, is *repressed,* hidden in secret corners of a vast archival filing system that Freud called the unconscious.

The ego—your planful, well-organized guardian—thinks like an idealized grown-up adult. It never gets angry like your father did; never does anything childish like drunken Uncle Cecil. Executives are expected to always be operating in this adult mode: to be making hard-headed decisions based upon logic, facts, and computer print-outs. In truth, however, this conscious rational state is but the tip of the mental iceberg, accounting for about only 10 percent of mental capacity. The other unconscious 90 percent is accounted for by your superego and your id.

The Superego or Parent

The superego, or conscience, has been called the still, small voice that tells you someone might be looking. This "someone" is a composite of all the parental "oughts" unconsciously

47

absorbed in childhood that became, finally, a part of your mental equipment—*it is, in fact, your inner parent.*

You may grow up and leave home, or your parents may die, but the *memory* of your parents and all their injunctions lives on, fresh and luminescent in your subconscious. The stern warnings of that parental voice will haunt your head until *you* die. If you disobey your superego, it will punish you, creating guilt and anxiety, just as if your father were still alive and on his way home to frown at you, tell you off, or administer a beating.

The words of one senior executive immediately following his termination were revealing: "I've been a naughty boy," he blubbered into his whiskey-sour, "a very naughty boy." Nobody appeared to be listening, but Daddy was doubtless fulminating inside the poor devil's head, opening the kitchen cupboard again and looking for his stick.

The authoritarian-leader is often effective because he is prepared to play parent to his subordinate's child, exacting blind allegiance in return for the comparative security of childhood. Since most people unconsciously accept that "Father knows best," they are happy with the deal. The irony is that such a leader is often insecure himself and merely acting out the lines and gestures absorbed during an unhappy childhood from his own dominating father.

The Id or Child

Along with the superego, the id comprises the other (and major) part of the unconscious archival library that catalogues every experience you have ever known and "forgotten." It is these forgotten experiences—the good, the bad, and the ugly, hidden from consciousness—that motivate us and determine most of what we call our personality.

The id is more than just a passive library, however; it also represents the force of psychic energy. It is a force comprised of instinctual needs and drives, irrational and conflicting fears, and acquired wishes and wants—all of which continually seek gratification. On its own, this force has no direction. In order to find acceptable expression upon life's stage, this psychic energy must be harnessed and channeled by both the ego and superego.

To understand your moods, your relationships with others, or even why you work at what you do, you must know what has gone into your unconscious. This is easier said than done, and Oscar Wilde was wiser than he knew when he said that only shallow people can know themselves. Locating and analyzing those X-rated secrets are difficult for precisely the same reason the censor first hid them: they could disturb your equilibrium and send you plummeting from your tightrope.

Releasing Id Tensions

Repressed experiences do not just lie dormant, however. They become *id tensions* that need to find an acceptable release, one way or another, in our lives.

Dreams provide such a release and also allow analysis of the unconscious, which Freud, of course, called psychoanalysis. People talk about a dream as if it were a movie, but the dream and the dreamer are one and the same; you are what you dream—you are the screen, the projector, the film, the image, and the audience. A nightmare is a dream that failed to preserve sleep—and clear evidence that the monsters in your mind are merely you.

Tensions that do not find release in dreams must seek it in some other acceptable though subconscious manner, as for example by:

Displacement. My boss gets angry with me. I repress my annoyance but go home in a bad mood and unconsciously pick a fight with my wife who yells at our child, who kicks the dog, who then bites him. Or I stay outwardly cool, internalize my anger, and get a headache or, eventually, an ulcer.

In America many executives attempt to release their frustrations on the golf course, but more commonly displace them onto the golf ball. The story is told of a Japanese business leader returning home from New York. He disembarked his plane at Tokyo, waving a golf club above his head. Grinning

49

to the slightly bewildered disciples who had gathered to meet him, he explained enthusiastically, "Haff just came back from wunnerful U.S. of A., where I learn new game, called *Ah Shit!*"

Sublimation. The Victorian politician William Gladstone sublimated his lascivious desires to socially acceptable behavior by meeting prostitutes on street corners and taking them home to "save" them. His recently published private diaries reveal that these salvations created such guilt that Mr. Gladstone practiced self-flagellation. We don't know the exact source of Mr. Gladstone's demons, but we do know that he was powerfully enough motivated to become prime minister of England. (The moral, of course, is don't keep a diary.)

The tycoon more commonly and acceptably sublimates his repressed sexual tensions into tall buildings, statues, and other monumental erections, which he hopes will gratify him by lasting forever.

Projection. You release id tensions by projection when you subconsciously perceive and point out your own faults (and virtues) in the behavior of a colleague. The fact that your colleague may have *none* of the faults you imagine, will, of course, not hinder your capacity to see "exactly what he is up to": in fact, you will see what you want to see. In business the opportunity to administer "performance appraisals" to subordinates provides an acceptable channel for the projection of just such tensions.

Reaction formation. This is related to projection but is not quite the same thing. It usually means going into paroxysms of wild-eyed righteous anger when you subconsciously perceive someone manifesting *precisely* those faults of your own whose existence you want to bar from your consciousness. It means hating sinners because you don't want anyone to suspect that you are not entirely the holy puritan you claim. Seeing his mother form a reaction pattern Hamlet wryly exclaimed "The lady doth protest too much methinks." Thus do our protestations betray our guilt.

Partial gratification. If you cannot release all of your id tensions you can, perhaps, acceptably show the tip of the iceberg. If, for example, you detest your wife, but are too scared to tell her, you can possibly administer "playful" love pats and accidentally blacken her eye. Or, instead of making love to the numerous nymphets whom you secretly covet, you might instead make do with *Playboy*—but only to read the articles of course. Oh, *of course*. Which leads us to . . .

Rationalization. This is doing as you secretly want and then finding a conscious rational justification for the action. A nice example is the paranoid corporate president who decorated his office in the manner of a Louis XIV palace, but in the center of it all kept a big, ugly black switchboard. He rationalized that only by monitoring all the calls of his staff could he be sure that corporate secrets were not lost.

One way or another, unconscious id tensions are always finding "accidental" expression in the course of everyday life and conversation. The British television broadcaster Michael Barrat tells a nice story: "Back in 1966, I was interviewing two black politicians from Rhodesia, representing the rival Zapu and Zanu parties. It was a live program and one of the politicians put forward what seemed to me a specious argument which led me to round on him. 'That's all very well,' I said, 'but two blacks don't make a white.' " Freud would argue that Barrat's slip of the tongue gratified an unconscious wish to say *exactly* what was on his mind.

I made a similar *faux pas* when a corporate executive told me that he was contemplating starting his own consulting firm. My opinion was that he was not suited to self-employment. I didn't want to tell him that, but I felt obliged to point out the gravity of his risk and found myself explaining: "You'd be either a spectacular failure or a dismal success."

Or take the case of Lewis Carroll, an Anglican deacon who never married but developed instead an interest in little girls, whom he photographed very artistically in the buff. Some psychologists claim that Carroll's repressed sexual cravings also found an acceptable release in his writings, and cite among other pieces the delightful description of Alice and the

King, who seem to be working something out together:

> A sudden thought struck her, and she took hold of the end of the pencil, which came some way over his shoulder, and began writing for him.
>
> The poor King looked puzzled and unhappy, and struggled with the pencil for some time without saying anything but Alice was too strong for him, and at last he panted out "My dear! I really must get a thinner pencil. I can't manage this one a bit: it writes all manner of things that I don't intend—"

The Childlike Nature of the Id

The id is like the child within us. Like all small children, the id is immature and self-centered, always craving immediate gratification of its wishes. A *New Yorker* cartoon showed a woman in Bloomingdale's explaining to the sales clerk, "I have the urge to buy something—I just haven't figured what." What she immediately wanted was assistance in relieving an id tension. Perhaps what she *really* wanted, however, was to punish her husband, or purchase the love she missed in childhood.

Similarly, the story is told of Jacqueline Kennedy (as she then was) just wandering from department to department in the New York stores spending tens of thousands of dollars and buying five of any item that caught her fancy. Had her husband been a psychologist, he might not have been at a loss to explain the childlike behavior of his loved one.

But then again, he might have been. The story is told that Freud got testy when a colleague observed that his cigar might be symbolic of, perhaps, an oral fixation or a death wish. "Sometimes," said the great man, "a cigar is just a cigar." Maybe, but Freud's addiction to cigars—he smoked up to twenty a day—gave him cancer of the mouth, which finally killed him.

The charm of the supersalesman—enthusiastic, spontaneous, bright—is the child at its most engaging. And, notoriously, the best natural salesmen need constant discipline, lavish praise, and special attention.

One no-nonsense sales organization devised a unique "incentive scheme" that rewarded its top salesmen by allowing the release of childlike id tensions and repressed hostilities. At a special dinner, the sales competition winners sat at one table and ate steak, while the losers sat at another and ate beans. And, as an after-dinner treat, the winners were allowed to tear the shirts from the losers' backs. What could be nicer?

Kenneth Graham's Toad, from *The Wind in the Willows,* is pure id. He sights a bright red sportscar and cannot deny himself the pleasure of "taking it for a spin." He doesn't see this as stealing: he just "had" to sit at the wheel, feel the wind in his face, his foot on the accelerator, the sound of the horn at full blast. Toad's existence is one of perpetual trouble with the authorities, who despair of being able to "fix" his personality.

Executives with poor control of their "child" are like Toad, getting themselves into debt, in trouble with the law, losing their jobs, until people wonder if they will ever lose their immaturity and "grow up."

The Interaction of the Ego and the Id

The role of the ego is to make the child grow up: to curb those childish excesses and get us operating in an adult mode. So this librarian-censor is always at work, sifting and suppressing any information that might be destabilizing.

The paradox is that, in order to be consigned to the dark archives of the id, threatening information must first be *subconsciously* perceived as threatening; then immediately suppressed. Thus *every* experience is absorbed, whether we know it or not, into the psyche.

A virtue of alcohol, especially for the immature salesman who doesn't want to grow up (and couldn't even if he did), is that it intoxicates both ego and superego, relieving anxiety and allowing his child to play whatever games it likes. But, whether you are a salesman, a seer, or whatever, it would surely be a shame to go to a party and not allow your child to take part in charades, which is why they serve those consciousness-altering drugs called cocktails.

THE CHEMISTRY OF AN EXECUTIVE: HIS VALUES

Bernard Shaw said that getting married is like buying a gramophone that plays only six records. The mind, in a way, is like the gramophone, producing a certain quality of sound depending upon how well it functions. And your responses to people and problems are like the records you play. On those records are your value constellations—the sets of emotional beliefs and responses you have absorbed into your unconscious during the course of your life.

Values pervade both the id and the superego and make up most of an executive's chemistry. Values are the beliefs and attitudes that fix the way he perceives and responds to the world around him. They determine his choice of clothes, home, suburb, accent, political allegiance, social expectations, choice of career and corporation.

Birds of a feather enjoy each other's company because they share the same values, and in corporate life the unconscious perception of an executive's emotional plumage determines whether he will become a trusted member of the management team—someone to be relied on under pressure because he shares the values of the flock and is, as they say, "one of us."

And since attaining and succeeding in that exalted status is determined by an executive's values, you can often predict how high the bird will fly—or whether it will fly at all—by appreciating the following ten key points about values:

1. Values are beliefs that are not subject to proof—indeed, cannot be proven. "Man's judgments of value," said Freud, "follow directly his wishes for happiness—they are an attempt to support his illusions with arguments."

Some people believe in communism, some in

capitalism, while most of the balance are starving to death and will believe anyone carrying a loaf of bread. Nobody can *prove* that either capitalism or communism is a "better" philosophy than the other, yet the beliefs are so deep as to be capable of causing whole nations—not to mention very intelligent individuals—to go to war.

2. Constellations of related values repose in the unconscious, where they are like books of opinions in our archival library (or records for that gramophone) to be retrieved as needed. Some books are more important than others but you *have* a book and an opinion—and often to your way of seeing things, the *only* opinion—on every subject.

Because values come in these related clusters, you can often predict a great deal about an executive's personality from just one or two pieces of information. If, for example, an executive tells you he is a Republican, you could guess with a good chance of being accurate that he may also believe in the inherent value of the profit motive, initiative based upon self-interest, taking out a mortgage, and aspiring to own a yacht. Obviously, the more information you have about a particular value constellation, the more accurate will be your predictions.

3. Values, not technical qualifications, are the prime determinants of both life goals and competence. If you don't believe in capital punishment, you probably won't make a happy executioner no matter how sharp your axe.

4. The values that most determine personality are unconsciously absorbed from whoever happened to be closest during infancy. The Jesuits have long said, "Give us the child till seven, and we will give you the man." B. F. Skinner, who argues that human behavior is conditioned in exactly the same manner as that of white rats, takes it a little further: "Give me the child," he says, "and I will give you anything."

5. Because values are absorbed unconsciously, we are

rarely aware of why we believe what we believe: there are, as the saying goes, "Some things that you just know without needing to be told."

6. The earlier a value is acquired, the less it is subject to change. Parental values acquired in infancy are the foundation of personality. Important values are also acquired from subsequent authority figures: school teachers, teenage heroes, professors, silver-haired news anchormen. But, finally, as William James observed: "The ideas gained by men before they are twenty-five are practically the only ideas they shall have in their lives."

7. The more important a value is to your psychic equilibrium, the more fiercely you will espouse it. If you find it vital you may, like Reverend Jim Jones, want to convert everyone with whom you come in contact—perhaps the entire world. Jones was a little extreme, but Thomas Watson, former chief executive of IBM, was virtually a Messiah, a missionary who got his salesmen to sing hymns before going onto the business battlefield. Even today, IBM represents a special set of values—a whole way of life—to its employees.

8. Values need not be, and seldom are, consistent. A person can be a week-long swindler and a Sunday Christian utterly devoted to both callings, and be unaware of any conflict or hypocrisy. In a related way, President Jimmy Carter could with absolute sincerity instruct a weekly Bible class and yet see absolutely no problem in keeping as his chief of White House staff a fellow whose ways with women and wine are a matter of public record.

9. Such conflicts in values are resolved by your librarian-censor, who only lets you take one book out at a time, thereby keeping conflicting values out of your consciousness. Thus you are only conscious of values appropriate to the environment in which you find yourself. For example, an executive can be a pious family man over morning coffee, tell you what he did in Las Vegas over a three-martini lunch, and possibly allow himself a sexual

peccadillo on the way home from the office. If, as he functions in each of these roles, his censor is efficient, the others will be blocked out, so that he can be industrious on the job, pleasant and amusing over lunch, and a bundle of fun in bed.

Al Capone saw through the social rationalization that prohibited the sale of alcohol while tolerating its consumption. "When I sell liquor," he said, "it's called bootlegging. When my patrons serve it on silver trays on Lake Shore Drive, they call it hospitality."

10. When a stranger insists on bringing conflicting values into my consciousness, I usually resolve the conflict by:

• Getting prickly, rednecked, and hostile. Possibly I may punch his nose.

• Refusing to discuss the matter, like the old man who settled arguments with his wife by turning off his hearing aid.

• Explaining the conflict away to my own satisfaction with rationalizations. Most people think they're thinking when, in fact, they're only rearranging their prejudices— like Aesop's fox when he explained that the grapes he couldn't reach were sour. *And the more intelligent you are, the more sophisticated will be your ability to rearrange your prejudices and marshal clever arguments.* This is why intellectuals like William Buckley and John Kenneth Galbraith can assail each other with opposite arguments literally for hours on end with neither yielding an inch.

The moral is that, since value beliefs and value judgments are virtually unshakable, it is usually imprudent to get into heated arguments on values-oriented subjects. Unless you're on a talk show and getting paid, you can't win. And even when you seem to win, you never do, for in the words of Robbie Burns: "A man convinced against his will is of the same opinion still."

Two other key concepts that are related to an executive's ability to function while still maintaining sometimes violently opposing beliefs are *ambivalence,* and *the executive mask.*

AMBIVALENCE

Life insurance actuarial tables reflect the somewhat daunting fact that getting married significantly increases the likelihood that you will die a violent death.

The reason is that you and your loved one are entering into a *dependent* relationship, and not even true love always compensates for the fact that dependency tends to create anxiety—and with it first resentment and then hostility. This is why Frankie sent Johnny to the graveyard: not because he was cheating on her, but because she depended upon him to provide her with love—she shot him precisely because she loved him.

The capacity to experience, simultaneously, conflicting emotions of love and hate—and the deeper the love, the greater the hate—is called ambivalence, and it pervades, to a greater or lesser degree, *any* dependent relationship.

Thus since almost every executive is dependent not only for his salary but also for his self-esteem upon the corporation to which he has pledged his troth, he inevitably experiences feelings of ambivalence toward the hand that feeds him. He may both resent and admire his boss, or the board of directors—and they, of course, since they are also dependent upon him to perform his job well, may also enjoy mixed feelings about him, especially, oddly enough, if he is good at his job. Ambivalence, in short, pervades every level of corporate life.

THE EXECUTIVE MASK

Whereas hostility may be more or less openly expressed within the bonds of holy matrimony, it is seldom openly displayed upon the corporate stage. The reason for the apparent harmony is that, while at work, an executive suppresses and *masks* his hostile feelings in order not to jeopardize his paycheck or his prospects of promotion. But those hostile feelings do not, as we have already noted, just go away. They are suppressed—both consciously and unconsciously—into the id: they are hidden behind a mask (or more technically a persona), but they will seek and, one way or another, find expression.

As well as hiding ambivalence, the executive mask serves and is chosen by its wearer to perform one more vital purpose—to project an idealized self-image of the person behind it. An executive often chooses a particular mask for the same reason that an aging Casanova may wear a corset; precisely because he is hoping to project a deception and cover up an unappetizing reality.

The executive assumes that his public will only find him attractive if he seems to be what in fact he is not—which may, indeed, be true. But *he,* of course, must live with the knowledge that he is not what he seems; consequently he may live in terror of ever having his true self revealed. And so, to ensure that no one gets to suspect that a jelly-like creature is hiding behind the mask (or within the corset), the executive will commonly *overcompensate,* exaggerating the outward behavior that masks his true self—which is why the bully is proverbially a coward.

The lesson to be drawn is that, if you want to determine the truth about an executive, you often need only to assume that *precisely those qualities that he takes the greatest care to project represent the exact opposite of his true self.* In corporate life this often means that the apparently macho executive may be a pussy cat, or that the seemingly loyal and trusted confidant is not unlikely to *really* be a veritable Uriah Heep, an Iago, a one-eyed Jack or a fawning Janus-faced lackey.

Ambivalence and the masking of hostile feelings are intrinsic causes of many corporate problems—and also, as we shall presently see, the reason that many executives become incompetent.

TWO THEORIES THAT COMPLEMENT FREUD

The insights of two modern psychologists complement Freud and are of relevance in contemplating what an executive is unconsciously pursuing in his work.

Satisfying a Hierachy of Needs

> *Men have moral as well as physical needs.*
> NAPOLEON
> *Every fulfillment is slavery. It drives us to a higher fulfillment.*
> ALBERT CAMUS

A. H. Maslow said that, in finding homeostasis, we must satisfy a hierarchy of needs, beginning with food and shelter, progressing to friendship, sex (not always in that order), and material comfort. After that we attempt to *self-actualize*—to express our full human individuality—and then, finally, to satisfy our spiritual needs.

A company president who earns enough money to satisfy his material needs may self-actualize by collecting paintings, as did J. Paul Getty. Or, he may find spiritual satisfaction, like the Rockefellers, by expanding his corporation and using its profits to make him a philanthropist.

Individuals may be satisfying different needs yet still perform the same task. The story is told of three men breaking rocks on a building site. A stranger approached and asked each of them what he was doing. "I'm earning a living by cracking rocks," said the first. "I break and trim these rocks to fit them into that wall over there," said the second. "I'm helping to build a cathedral for Christopher Wren," said the third. On a top ocean racer, everyone is winning the race. Every job is vital and everybody knows it.

The term *job enrichment* means making a task satisfy a higher level of need. The man who breaks rocks to build a cathedral is obviously going to do a better job than someone

60

whose only motivation is a weekly paycheck. On an ocean racer, seasickness (not to mention the risk of loss of life) is tolerable because the need for self-actualization is being satisfied.

Affiliation, Achievement and Power Needs

David McClelland said that different executives seek to satisfy basically one, more than another, of three needs: affiliation, achievement, or power.

Affiliation-seekers join tennis clubs to play tennis and make friends. High-achievers join to play tennis, develop their games, and win championships. Power-seekers join to get elected to the club committee and become president.

In a business context, the affiliation-seeker organizes the social club and makes friends of his colleagues. The high-achiever is a results-oriented loner who wants to show outstanding growth, an expanded bottom line, and new and better ways of doing things. The power-seeker wants to be in charge: he gets his satisfaction from using or threatening to use his power. He likes the idea that he has power. If he does not have it, he will try to get it.

The high-achiever takes risks only when he can control the outcome. He dislikes gambling on horses or at roulette. If he had to gamble, his choice would be poker or backgammon. The high-achiever sets himself goals and works toward them. Commonly he dislikes affection, and has a chip on his shoulder or a strong need to "prove himself." Because he likes to rely on his own efforts, he will often be a bad judge of people. Basically he wants to do the job himself. Put in charge of a group, he does not like training people or having to explain things to slow learners, and will usually just leave people to get along, as he would get along, without supervision.

The power-seeker, however, enjoys the political ramifications of corporate life. He is good at stroking, influencing, and manipulating people. He likes being at the center of things. That for him is more of a reward than actually setting high goals and trying to achieve them. Good managers tend to be motivated by power and can derive continual satisfaction from directing a relatively static organization. The high-achiever gains no such reward and simply wants to show high growth or increased effectiveness. If he cannot do this he may quit and go somewhere else. Former Ford chairman Henry Ford II was certainly motivated by power: his former president Lee Iacocca possibly by achievement: "I thought," said Iacocca, "that if the bottom line was good, I was secure." But Ford perceived Iacocca as a power threat and fired him.

One final point on power-seekers is worth some thought. A recent survey of men in political life revealed the pervasiveness of a *power-sex syndrome* whereby:

> The exercise of power is a headier experience even than orgasm. It *is* orgasmic, since in him (the power-seeker) the sex drive and the power drive are identical. Sex pervades his life. If he had to choose between sex and political power he would certainly give up sex.*

Or, in the memorable words of Mathew Troy, the former Democrat boss of Queens, New York: "Politics is men who kiss your ass and women who . . ."

And that, dear reader, is what it takes for some hard-headed businessmen to maintain psychic equilibrium.

*Sam Janus, Barbara Bess, and Carol Saltus, *A Sexual Profile of Men in Power* (New York: Warner Books, 1977).

4. *How to Predict What an Executive Will Do with His Life —and When*

"Would you please tell me which way I ought to go from here?"

"That depends a great deal on where you want to get to," said the Cat.

"I don't much care where—" said Alice.

"Then it doesn't matter which way you go," said the Cat.

"—so long as I get somewhere," Alice added as an explanation.

"Oh, you're sure to do that," said the Cat. "If you only walk long enough."

LEWIS CARROLL

W H E N it comes to determining the path to walk, and how far to go to before arriving somewhere, the executive doesn't have to rely upon the Cheshire Cat. Compass, map, and timetable are imprinted within his unconscious, and he journeys through life fulfilling a discernible, predictable, *family destiny.* He works, subconsciously, to what Eric Berne called *life scripts:* in a sort of preordained flesh-and-blood Punch and Judy show within which the drama, the role, the words are, for the most part, fixed with an almost frightening precision. Indeed, it is not uncommon to see a fifty-year-old executive, in his parent mode, affect the tone, words, and demeanor that admonished *him* in his childhood, right down to the hostile flashing eyes and sharply pointing finger.

In the unresolved debate as to whether behavioral traits are the result of genetic inheritance or environmental conditioning, one fact should never be overlooked: *parents provide*

63

both. And in so doing they determine the destiny of their progeny, the Kismet of their kith and kin. Just as the child of a circus performer may be destined to walk the high wire, so are we all destined to walk another high wire in another circus that we carry around in our heads.

It is not by accident, then, that Liza Minelli sings her soul away on Broadway as did her mother, Judy Garland; that Joe Frazier's oldest son is training to become heavyweight champion of the world; that seven generations of Bachs were distinguished musicians; that Lyndon Johnson's grandfather, on the day of LBJ's birth, rode along the Texas hill country proclaiming that a U.S. senator had been born; that Jerry Brown walked away from his Jesuit vocation to become governor of California just like his dad. And the question is not whether Edward Kennedy will ever become president of the United States, but whether he will succumb to a more chilling family destiny and follow his brothers to an early grave.

Carl Jung wrote: "The more one sees of human fate and the more one examines its secret springs, the more one is impressed by the strength of unconscious motives and by the limitations of free choice." Oscar Wilde said: "My past and not my future lies before me." And in nearly twenty years of executive appraisal, I have learned that family background is the *dominating influence* of an individual's life, so that, if I want to determine what an executive will do, then I must examine the invisible threads that tie him, like a puppet, to his past.

The theory of family destiny goes some way toward explaining why executives are drawn to, and sometimes turn away from, certain careers, and at what level of achievement they may burn out, or reach a "comfort zone" and ease up. The theory derives from Freud and complements the insights of Berne. But my own need to predict an executive's likelihood of success has compelled me to give thought to my own successes no less than my failures at that task. In so doing I have also drawn upon statistical analyses of Wareham Associates' detailed computer files containing biographical data on literally tens of thousands of executives, and also on an ongoing research project we undertook in America, Australia, and New Zealand with Professor George Hines, an American who currently heads the School of Business Administration at Massey University in New Zealand.

It would be nice to offer you from all this a theory that was 100 percent accurate, but, when the product is people, it's difficult to be dogmatic. Nonetheless, application of the following concepts, together with my other advice on interviewing, should enable you to outguess at least one corporate president, whose proud boast was that he enjoyed a 51 percent success rate simply by using his powers of intuition. You can't really do too much worse than that tossing coins.

People attending our executive selection seminars have reported a reduction in hiring errors typically averaging up to 67 percent. My own batting average is higher, but then I get paid for being right and so I tend to be careful.

Basically, the theory of family destiny says that *choice of career and level of motivation is absorbed during childhood; that parents and home environment leave an indelible imprint upon the subconscious, determining, often extremely precisely, the path upon which an executive will embark, the level of society to which he will gravitate, and the destination at which he will feel that he has arrived.*

Even at the moment of conception, the destiny of a fetus is already determined, to a great extent. If unwanted it may be terminated as soon as the bad news is discovered: its destiny determined entirely by the circumstances of conception and the caprice of its procreators. But, assuming it survives that first appraisal (no small task these days), the impact of parents and their existing world will make an impression virtually impossible to erase. For, at the moment of birth, or soon after, the following elements will have been largely or wholly fixed: geography, sex, place within the family unit, name, religion, education, and familial expectations. These are the threads from which—until one day it is put back in its box—the puppet will dance, and each of these threads repays at least a few moments of consideration:

Geography. The location of the pillow upon which a child lays its head—country, city, suburb, and home—will determine both the dreams of childhood and much of the reality of childhood's end.

Children in Manhattan *are* different from those in Boise, Idaho, because, as Andy Warhol noted, "Just living in New York gives people real incentives to want things that nobody else wants." But within Manhattan the children in Harlem are shaped by a different culture than is to be experienced on Central Park West. To be born in Leningrad is to embrace an altogether different philosophy again. And an Arab boy may be destined by his geography to become a sodomite, a girl to filter her perceptions through a veil. Schools attended, friends, neighbors, childhood heroes—all are functions of the geography of birth, and primary sources of lifelong values.

Sex and place within the family unit. Obviously, a boy who is the last-born in a family with six sisters will develop a different personality from a first-born child, a son, who has only one sister. More is expected of the oldest child, especially a boy. As a result he tends to expect more of himself. If he is an only child, much of his time will be spent with adults. The oldest child is usually the most ambitious and the most hostile. The youngest child, however, tends to have a sunny disposition, to be playful, rather more passive, and dependent.

Name. The surname Vanderbilt might bring more good luck than baptism. And "Joseph P. Kennedy IV" (or V, VI, or VII) would also carry a special set of expectations to trail that individual and shape his lifelong behavior. Hitler commented that, had his family name not been changed, he might not have led his country. "Heil, Schicklgruber," he said, sounded mildly humorous. If you doubt that the name of an individual affects the perception of his peers, and therefore his own responses, then reflect upon the advertising industry that spends millions of dollars researching the names of soap powders. Likewise, a quick scan of the list of American presidents will reveal that every name is easy to memorize and clean to the tongue.

You can see that when Henry Ford said, "It is all one to me if a man comes from Sing Sing or Harvard. We hire a man, not his history," he displayed a very poor understanding of human nature. Just ask his son, who a generation later observed that, for the good of the corporation, there should always be a board member whose surname was Ford: and preferably, said Henry Ford II, that uniquely qualified and superbly groomed young fellow who had already displayed such promise as the chief of Ford in Australia—*his* own son.

Religion. The roads of a Buddhist, a Christian, or a Jew may, finally, lead to the same place, but they rarely cross until that destination is reached. Even if no religion, either by accident or design, is assigned, that omission may also be far-reaching, since atheism and agnosticism carry their own values. "God," observed Mahatma Gandhi, "is even the atheism of the atheist." Even nihilism is just another window through which to view the world, and to embrace such a philosophy is necessarily to act in accord with that perspective.

Education. A child seldom chooses its own school, this being either a function of geography or the wallet of its parent, or both. And early schooling very largely determines whether or not the child will "make it" (or even want to make it) into the cloisters of an Ivy League college. However, the advantage of attending such an institution is not in the curriculum—but in the opportunity to become, in one's own head, part of an elite, and able therefore to move easily in what otherwise seem socially stressful situations. Life's high wire, from such a vantage point, is likely to be perceived as a clear, wide path to opportunity, and not terribly far off the ground at all.

Familial expectations. A well-known artist demonstrated the power of familial expectations with this remark: "When I was a child my mother said to me, 'If you become a soldier you'll be a General. If you become a monk you'll end up the Pope.' Instead, I became a painter and wound up as Picasso."

Rich children develop an attitude of "entitlement": they subconsciously expect to do well in high-status careers, this being their birthright, their launching pad to life. They do not have to be upwardly mobile, needing only to mix with those about them to be already "up." They are not awed by important people. The son of a rich man has values that automatically enable him to mix with others similarly blessed, rendering it unlikely that he will earn less than a certain figure. If he ever works with his hands, it will be as a surgeon.

Downward mobility is about as rare as upward mobility, and the industrious upwardly mobile individual from a poor family is still likely to happily settle for a niche in life *below* anything acceptable to the indolent child of rich and powerful parents.

With these threads in mind we can go on to understand, at least in part, what is happening in life's Punch and Judy show. Basically there are ten points to remember:

We spend our lives paying back our parents. You can either pay your parents back by obeying their injunctions and fulfilling their expectations and *rewarding* them, or, if you didn't like them, you can pay them back by disobeying their injunctions, disappointing their expectations and *punishing* them. Alternatively, you can punish a domineering father by taking the values he holds so dearly, adopting them as your own, and *beating him at his own game.*

Consider Franz Strauss, the finest horn player in Munich and a bitter enemy of Richard Wagner, whose music, under Wagner's baton, he played with open contempt. When the news of Wagner's death was announced to the orchestra, every musician rose in tribute—except Franz Strauss. Richard Strauss knew of his father's dislike of Wagner and shared it until one day, in what his biographer called a "blinding flash," Wagner's genius was revealed to him. Thereafter he "worshipped only one musical God, Richard Wagner," convinced of a "destiny to be his most passionate advocate and brilliant interpreter." And poor old Father Franz lived to see it happen. What an absolutely exquisite way to torture an old man.

How we choose to repay our parents will depend upon the relationship we shared with them in childhood. I was talking to the founder of one of the world's largest classified-space advertising agencies, who quite heatedly denied that any family destiny had affected his life in any way at all. He was a self-made man, he said, who had fallen into advertising "quite by chance."

The father whom he admired and said that, as a child, he had always wanted to help, was poor, and the son had to leave school early and take a job to make ends meet. The job the son got was on the advertising side of a big newspaper. When the war came, the son went overseas to fight. After the war there were no jobs so he began a small newsagency selling cigarettes and newspapers. In a drive for business the local newspaper offered all newsagents a commission on any advertisements referred. Soon the son was making more money from placing classified advertising than from selling newspapers. From that small beginning he built a unique multimillion-dollar classified advertising agency.

And what did his father do for his daily bread? His father, all his life, had been a typesetter with the local newspaper —*setting only classified advertisements.*

The son had unconsciously spent his life in the fulfillment of a destiny to provide his father with work. (That his father had long since died does not matter.) His first job was on the revenue-producing side of his *father*'s paper, and then, after the war, he again gravitated to the newspaper industry, first selling his father's newspapers and then, even more directly, sending him type to set. The grandson is now employed with the classified advertising agency.

The typical executive pays back his father by adopting his values, walking in his footsteps, and marginally improving upon the father's status as it was perceived in childhood at about age five. Jerry Brown, governor of California and the son of a former governor of California, put it this way: "As I look back on my life, and the fact that I became a lawyer and a governor, I don't see that I've done anything more complicated than a son following the thoughts and gestures and patterns of his father."

Freud called this motivation to marginally improve upon the father's status an id wish to "kill the father." Perhaps you could call it an id wish to repay the subconscious memory of a psychic debt to the father. Our analysis at Wareham Associates suggests that some 73 to 79 percent of executives redeem that childhood loan with about a 10 percent interest rate.

Even where an individual does not follow the general direction of his father, the parental voice provides the criteria of success. Actor Bruce Dern said that his father "never forgave me for becoming an actor, and even though he died right after I became an actor I've spent twenty-two years proving that I could be a good actor, right?" Exactly so, Mr. Dern.

The greater an executive perceives his father's success to have been, the greater will be his own goals. Winston Churchill, son of the eminent cabinet minister Randolph Churchill, endured a poor relationship with his father, who was dominant, overbearing, and contemptful of his progeny. Winston Churchill eclipsed his father by becoming *prime* minister. The well-spring, both of Winston's initial failure in politics (his caustic insults and blunt manner caused him to be called the most hated man in Parliament) and his subsequent success as a warlord, both seem to derive from the expression of repressed childhood hostility.

Churchill's venomous nature was very well known, though the memory of his excesses has faded. But one story illustrates at least two facets of his personality—his flight into alcohol and his easy command of a nasty rejoinder. He was sharing an elevator late one evening with a group of cabinet colleagues and Lady Astor, who remarked, with justification, "Churchill, you are drunk."

"Yesh, Madam," he replied, "and you are ugly. But tomorrow I'll be sober."*

---

* He treated the good lady to another memorable reply when she interrupted him during the course of a speech to Parliament. "If you were my husband," she said, "I would put arsenic in your tea." Churchill smiled at her and said, "And if you were my wife, Madam, I would drink it."

Or take the case of an Australian who achieved fame in an earlier generation. His business was publishing, at which he was very successful, becoming chief executive of a powerful newspaper empire. He wielded that influence to great political effect, earning the title "kingmaker." He was also awarded a knighthood and took a place on the international scene by, among other things, becoming one of the founders of the American-Australian Association in New York.

However, when he died prematurely of a heart attack, it became necessary for most of his newspaper holdings to be sold in order for his estate duties to be paid. In consequence the inheritance of his eldest child and only son, in terms of what might have been, was very modest: one small, ailing newspaper, an Oxford education, and his father's name—Keith Murdoch.

That son, adopting his middle name, Rupert (after his grandfather), has, of course, gone on to spectacularly eclipse the success of his illustrious father. He has not only built a world-wide publishing empire, but also enjoys the same reputation for being able to wield the power that his papers command, and even the most powerful politicians in the world are careful to court his favor.

The Rockefeller family also illustrates the fact that life goals are possibly the most important part of any child's inheritance. Nelson Rockefeller set his sights beyond banking to what must have seemed a greater prize than money—political power; and came, as vice president, within kissing distance of the best chair in the Oval Office.

It would be a mistake however to suppose that simply because a fellow is born with a silver spoon in his mouth, he will go on to make a stir in the world.

Life for the oldest child of a famous parent is rarely easy. Sometimes, when the child perceives that it may be impossible to get even by succeeding, he may settle the debt by failing, and thereby subconsciously destroying the father's monument. He can do this simply by becoming either a highly public ne'er-do-well or a criminal: or, perhaps even more cruelly, by investing the family fortune on speculations that any outsider could see are "destined" to turn sour.

Each executive tends to fix a "culminating achievement" as the talisman of his success. Unlike Alice, the average executive can tell when he has "arrived" because a particular milestone will be emblematic of journey's end. This event is normally linked to an inner clock—*the status which, as a child, he perceived his father to hold.*

"A man feels," says Professor Daniel Levinson, "that by about forty he can no longer be a promising young man." Accordingly, success delayed is success denied, because an angel in heaven is nobody in particular.

Levinson's research was entirely separate from our own but that age, "about forty," correlates quite precisely with the average age of an executive's father, as perceived by the son in childhood.

The milestone event itself may be a particular promotion, say to vice-president, headmaster, congressman, senator, or professor. Or it may be an event such as the publication of a book, becoming self-employed, or taking ownership of a piece of property such as a farm.

Realization of a culminating achievement will probably reduce an executive's motivation to go on performing the same task with the same intensity. The id tensions that propel an executive to seek a goal will be eased by a culminating achievement, and this may free him to some extent of the need to prove himself to his superego. He may then be able, for the first time in his life, to set about becoming his own man. On the other hand, some children spend their lives despising their parents until age forty, when they suddenly become just like them.

But the removal of a specific life goal may also be disappointing and disorienting, like seeing the Cheshire Cat vanish, leaving behind only the memory of an enigmatic grin to light the way. Then it will be a time to ponder what to do now: to set about finding a higher level of self-actualization, another circus, another tightrope—another audience, perhaps.

Failure to attain the culminating achievement increases the level of an executive's internal stress, possibly causing psychosomatic illness. Any unresolved unconscious tension must find expression. Where it is not successfully channeled into a career, it may be internalized and may then appear as any one of a number of symptoms: a heart condition, or an ulcer, or simply a sense of bitterness.

In about three-quarters of the cases in which an executive felt that he had failed, feelings of depression (melancholy minus its charms) were experienced. One executive memorably noted that: "The two most important influences in my life have been my father and my asthma." His asthma, he explained, had denied him the chance to equal the success of his father. The reverse, of course, is nearer to the truth.

Another executive, depressed at being passed over for a promotion that represented his culminating achievement, plaintively asked: "Will I ever be comfortable?" When asked to define *comfortable* he replied, "Like my father." He subsequently became an alcoholic and was fired by what he sourly claimed was a callous employer. Bertrand Russell's perception that bitterness is a sure sign of emotional failure eluded him.

Above 90 percent of apparently successful executives believe that they have equalled or surpassed the status of their father as they perceived him in childhood. In one batch of answers from two hundred successful executives, only one said that he had failed to equal or surpass his father—and that executive had been fired just two weeks earlier.

The reason for this high self-esteem possibly lies in the fact that the ego tends not to allow a well-adjusted individual to seriously contemplate an impossible dream. Most times our ambitions are within reach or the ego would, literally, not tolerate thought of them. Additionally, your ego may allow you to fudge a little, so that, whether or not you really did, in fact, pay back your father, you will *think* that you did. And, since the whole deal is recorded in your own unconscious, who, outside of your own head, is to argue?

A characteristic of the successful executive from a low-

status background is childhood identification with a high-achieving role model, or mentor. Jimmy Carter is reported to have realized that he could become president, only when, in the course of his duties as governor of Georgia, he met the other presidential aspirants and was unimpressed. Most people do not get to meet such figures of influence and, accordingly, never realize the extent of what is possible. The bars remain firmly fixed behind their eyes.

The role of the mentor is to adjust those bars and inculcate into the id of the protégé new values, higher goals, fresh ideas, enhanced self-esteem. According to one American survey, *all* successful female executives had been given a leg up the corporate ladder by a mentor. Our own finding was that above 90 percent of all upwardly mobile executives, male and female, had been influenced by a mentor. Significantly, the earlier a mentor is acquired, the greater is his influence. Past a certain age (twenty-five or so) a mentor's magic tends to lose its potency.

Usually the mentor is a school teacher or a first boss. Tennis star Evonne Goolagong might still be unknown were it not for her first coach, Vic Edwards, who saw her talent and presided over her initial stardom. Richard Nixon identified with Dwight Eisenhower (though the reverse is not so certain): the subsequent opportunity for Nixon to observe Eisenhower firsthand undoubtedly enabled Nixon to perceive that the role of president was within his capacity.

The exceptions are exceptional. Since most people are like living puppets being moved by invisible threads, any piece that appears to be initiating its own moves repays close examination.

Because Norton Simon chief David Mahoney, Bronx-born son of a crane operator, has evidenced an extraordinary upward mobility, you don't need to be terribly smart to realize that he is a remarkable individual, possibly a self-motivating Mr. Punch. You can either guess that Mr. Mahoney is proving something to the demons in his head (as we all are) or you can say that it doesn't really matter: that what does matter is the clear evidence of his uniqueness and strong motivation.

Either way, research reveals that even this kind of drive can be detected relatively early in an executive's career—certainly before age thirty—and that there is a discernible, *predictable* set of characteristics exhibited by million-dollar executives like Mr. Mahoney: that even the vaunted "winners" in life's puppet show are simply performing ritual roles, oblivious to the threads that never let them rest.

Perhaps we could let Omar Khayyám have the last word on the subject:

'Tis all a Checkerboard of Nights and Days
Where Destiny with Men for Pieces plays
Hither and thither moves and mates and slays
And one by one back in the Closet lays.

5. The Midcareer Crisis, Executive Menopause, and the Man on the Flying Trapeze

How did I get here? Somebody pushed me. Somebody must have set me off in this direction and clusters of other hands must have touched themselves to the controls at various times, for I would not have picked this way for the world.

JOSEPH HELLER

O N E day a man wakes up and realizes, for the first time, that he is old. But more poignant than the realization of autumn is the mourning for spring. Executive menopause is a state of grief, a lament for the loss of precious youth. It is characterized by deeply depressive feelings, and psychosomatic, though nonetheless real, physical symptoms. Marked loss or gain of weight may be experienced, and severe personality disorientation may occur.

Business aspirations are suddenly perceived with bewilderment and ambivalence. The menopausal executive feels cheated. In a way, he has *been* cheated. He did not know, could not have known, when he pledged his precious youth to a business enterprise, that it was the only youth he would ever have. In our twenties we believe we will live forever.

It is only in the most traumatic of life's milestones—birth, marriage, death—that the pain of the old Persian tent-maker's lines is fully perceived:

> The Moving Finger writes; and, having writ,
> Moves on: nor all your Piety nor Wit
> Shall lure it back to cancel half a Line
> Nor all your Tears wash out a Word of it.

We weep at the weddings of our children not because we are gaining a wastrel son-in-law nor even losing a daughter: we weep because we are losing a part of ourselves—it is our own childhood that is walking down that aisle and out of our lives. We grieve at a father's funeral not so much because we loved our father but because our own role is now finally and irrevocably changed. Our own childhood has been laid to rest in that coffin.

The midcareer crisis is related to the attainment of an executive's culminating achievement. By age thirty-five or so, time is pressing and the executive begins to know the bitterness of failure, or the emptiness of success. Either way he explores his options, seriously considers his future directions. He may have equaled the success of his father and now feel free "to become his own man." But his past and not his future lies ahead of him. His future options very largely depend upon what his past has suited him to become. The crisis may be handled, and homeostasis maintained, by changing employers, joining a service organization, developing a hobby, drawing closer to his family.

But sometimes the adjustment may be more spectacular. Once a thirty-seven-year-old born-again Chicago clergyman wanted to talk to me about "new directions" for his life.

He confided that when he was twenty years old a spectacular conversion at an evangelical meeting had "saved" him from a life of debauchery, and he several times mentioned that he was deeply in love with his wife.

Yet curiously, when introducing himself to my receptionist, he had been unable to restrain himself from laying his hands upon her (only to show his Christian love, of course), and he also confessed that he suffered an ulcer.

It did not take special insight to espy a roué trapped behind the mask of a clergyman: he was both living a lie and paying the price—not that I told him that, of course; we just chatted generally.

But, I was not surprised to subsequently learn that, immediately after leaving me to fly home, he resolved his midcareer crisis by simply calling his wife from an airport phone to say that he wouldn't be in for breakfast in the morning—nor any other morning. Ever. And he quit the church too. And now that he's hell-bent on enjoying himself, his ulcer is healing.*

Menopause at fifty. Executive menopause is a deeper malaise than the midcareer crisis and is experienced in the years forty-five through fifty-five. The transition from thirty-nine to forty is not particularly traumatic. At forty a man may have neither the power nor the money for which he had wished, but he usually still has his dreams. He may choose to attend Dale Carnegie classes and "improve" his personality, or he may take to the jogging track in the hope of finding his former sylph.

Not only that, but fifty seems far away. And sixty . . . well, who could think that far ahead with the icing of a fortieth birthday cake still clinging to the corners of his mouth?

But at fifty? Fifty can be a cruel, difficult, and disappointing landmark. As the half century approaches and then recedes, men who were jaunty at forty get lost in a depression that can last for years.

Lee Iacocca, talking of transition just before he was fired from Ford, put it this way: "If I had to pick a day, I'd say it was when I turned fifty. It was a milestone. All of a sudden, you say, 'Let's review the bidding.' If finances aren't your problem, whaddya wanna do?"

A mistress, a sports car, heavy drink, a new wife—these are some ways that the "self-sufficient" executive copes with the threat of early dismissal, or the suddenly all-too-imminent approach of mandatory retirement at age sixty or sixty-five.

For, at fifty, there is a sudden realization that the race is drawing to a close, that the finish line offers not honor but death; that youth, family life, precious dreams have been sacrificed. And in the pursuit of what? A monetary success that came too late; an aging wife unconsciously preparing herself for widowhood; children long since gone off to live their own

---

* Some details changed to protect the innocent.

lives; freshly minted vice-presidents who respect nobody's laurels; instead of a bright red sports car, a black limousine chauffeured by a heavy-set ambivalent young driver with tight stomach muscles. Alfred Prufrock sounds the unspoken dread of many a great man:

> I have seen the moment of my greatness flicker,
> And I have seen the eternal Footman hold my
>   coat and snicker,
> And in short, I was afraid.*

At age fifty, a man's children have left home or are leaving home. A man's father, and possibly both his parents, have died. If he is successful, in a business sense, he will have few friends. Is it too late to change? Is it possible to drop out of the system? Or, in the words of Peggy Lee, "Is that all there is?"

The conventional wisdom of the business psychologists is that, in order to cope with executive menopause, the high-achiever must slow down and restructure his life: that he should make a conscious choice between family or business; that he should realize that he has the option to live out his sunset years in a leisurely fashion and find comfort in the fragrance of flowers or the sweet sight and sounds of children playing.

Many of the business executives I have known would be more likely to find greater comfort in the sentiment of W. C. Fields that "any man who hates kids and loves whiskey can't be all bad."

The orthodox advice might be sound for an academic, but I think it may be too simplistic for the million-dollar executive or anyone like him who is locked into a love affair with his work. For this type of person, work is wife, mistress, lover: a sort of corporate black widow spider, the delicious intensity of whose lovemaking imparts magic to every moment—even, and perhaps especially, the last.

It is often easier for the six-figure executive to cope with

---

* T. S. Eliot, *The Love Song of J. Alfred Prufrock.*

death than the fact that the little boy inside him is all grown up and has nothing to do and no one to play with. A hard-driving, highly successful banker friend of mine retired at age sixty with a gold watch and a ticket to a retirement village. "I'll be on easy street now, John," he told me, "I'm home free." Exactly twelve months later he threw himself off a bridge to his death.

In his fifties, Iacocca, after being axed by Ford, considered the question of what to do with the remainder of his life. True to form he plunged back into the fray and took the Chrysler presidency. "So what the hell more would you want to do to end an auto career?" he asked. "The only other option, I guess, was to take all my money and run."

But did that option *really* exist for Iacocca? Where could he run to? What would he do? Who would give him praise? "An energy crisis," observed Johnny Carson, with more wisdom than wit, "will be when the applause sign goes out."

Another fifty-year-old company president, a friend of mine, was stricken with a heart attack and rushed to a hospital. Two days later he had two phones by his bed, and his secretary was at work in a makeshift office outside his door. The angel of death had issued his calling card, but my friend was just too busy to acknowledge the Great Headhunter with his final offer. "If I can't take it with me," he said to his wife, who had made an appointment to speak with him, "then I'm not going."

In appraising the six-figure executive, it is important to consider how he will adjust (or has adjusted) to the passage of time. A man whose father is still alive has a trauma ahead of him. An executive whose children are soon to be leaving home, unless he is particularly happy at home, may be preparing to take a mistress.

Alternatively, as Elliot Jaques has observed,* he may be about to embark upon the most productive period of his life. Old wine in old bottles has a body, color, and bouquet—a

---

* "Death and the Mid-Life Crisis," *The International Journal of Psychoanalysis,* October 1965: 502.

character—that time alone can impart, and, contrary to popular belief, the period of greatest creativity can begin at age forty. Shakespeare wrote his comedies before age thirty-five, but his greatest works, his tragedies, came later. Benjamin Duggar was removed at age seventy by compulsory retirement; he then joined the research staff of Lederle Laboratories and gave the world aureomycin. Pablo Casals, I am reminded, played the cello as no man ever has at ninety. Carl Sandburg chiseled *Remembrance Rock* at seventy. Canadian Lord Thompson at sixty, when many men are accepting a gold retirement watch, emigrated to England to establish a whole new publishing empire there: then, in his eighties, set out to find North Sea oil for England—and the venture succeeded. There may even be hope for some in the lecherous late-life observation of Groucho Marx that a man is only as old as the woman he feels.

Nobody can really tell you or me or anyone exactly what we should be doing with our lives, but if I had to choose a personal philosophy I'd be hard-pressed to pass up the advice of that one-time world-weary preacher Ecclesiastes, who advised:

Go thy way, eat thy bread with joy, and drink thy wine with a merry heart.
Let my garments always be white; and let thy head lack no ointment.
Live joyfully with the wife whom thou lovest all the days of the life which he hath given thee under the sun.
Whatsoever thy hand findeth to do, do it with all thy might,
For there is no work, nor knowledge, nor wisdom, in the grave whither thou goest.

By which I guess he means to live a balanced life—but live it to the full. Anyway, he wasn't telling anyone to slow down—least of all the hard-driving executive for whom life begins anew every day when he performs his death-defying act on the flying trapeze: For him, the worst kind of death would probably be a seat in the audience.

But, of course, such people are rare and, in hiring a middle-aged executive, the shrewd interviewer will want answers to several questions:

1. Is it likely that upcoming menopausal conflicts will adversely affect his work?
2. Will he continue to be a "dynamic," driven performer—like Sisyphus, will he continue to roll heavy stones up treacherous mountains?
3. Should he reach a "mature" decision to "slow down," will he continue to make a significant corporate contribution?

In a business context, the six-figure executive, whatever his personal problems, is paid to go on taking risks, to produce results, to meet targets. Becoming a "worthwhile individual" at the expense of business output may devalue his corporate currency.

Appraising such an individual is not a matter to be taken lightly over lunch.

6. *Why Executives Become Incompetent*

Bureaucracy is a giant mechanism operated by pygmies.

HONORÉ DE BALZAC

THE key to understanding the incompetent executive is to recognize that he is rarely incompetent for technical or intellectual reasons, but that his condition is almost invariably *emotional, and caused by stress.* He is like a neophyte highwire artist whose safety net has just been removed: suddenly he experiences emotional pressures that may be totally paralyzing. Technically the task is exactly the same—but the id releases vivid pictures of an untimely demise that overwhelm the consciousness, rendering the executive frozen in his tracks, frightened, insecure, and incompetent.

He freezes because of tensions inside his skull. *Failure has gone to his head.* He is unable, under pressure, to imagine anything but failure. Playing in the big league requires internal adjustments that some people—most people, in fact—are unable to effect.

SEVEN COMMON CONDITIONS SURROUNDING INCOMPETENCE

Seven of the most common conditions surrounding incompetence are these:

The syndrome of the emotional pygmy. Weakness begets weakness, and an incompetent leader instinctively recruits

83

subordinates less competent than himself, who in turn do likewise.

I call this phenomenon the syndrome of the emotional pygmy and first observed its physical manifestation when I visited a construction company and was introduced to a production manager standing five feet three inches tall. Beside him stood a five-feet two-inch marketing manager, and next to him a treasurer of barely five feet. Feeling like Snow White, I was ushered in to meet the corporate president, who looked down on me from behind a fat desk. During the course of the discussion I noticed that his feet did not touch the floor. When he jumped down to bid me goodbye, he stood some five feet four inches, on the top of platform soles.

The tendency to recruit subordinates who are *emotionally* two inches shorter is common, and in consequence some corporations become almost entirely composed of emotional pygmies whose business education has been akin to that of Alice's Mock Turtle:

> Reeling and writhing, of course, to begin with, and then the different branches of Arithmetic—Ambition, Distraction, Uglification, and Derision.

An unconscious desire to fail. Eric Berne observed that "the id seems 'lazy' and set in its habits, and tries again and again to obtain gratification in the same old unprofitable ways." If the ego doesn't have a watchful eye, Berne said, "the id compels the individual to repeat the same imprudent or ignoble mistakes over and over."

The reason, then, that some executives are kissed with a mirror-Midas personality, ensuring that everything they touch finally turns to scrap metal, is that staying on the wire inside of their skulls requires failing and being returned to a social level that does not engender guilt. This is not an uncommon problem for the self-made tycoon of humble origins. It could be argued that one very eminent rags-to-riches corporate president unconsciously sought the demise of his own empire: that in a final much publicized attempt to attain psychic equilibrium he was compelled to become downwardly mobile and depart his high-floor office via the window.

Shakespeare saw the problem very clearly:

> And oftentimes, to win us to our harm,
> The instruments of darkness tell us truths,
> Win us with honest trifles, to betray 's
> In deepest consequence.

Executives with a history of "bad luck"—of joining corporations about to bust, of continually getting themselves fired—are commonly gratifying childish id wishes: sometimes to get even with their parents, sometimes to return to childhood and once more experience the pleasure of being forgiven, sometimes just to get attention.

Lynette (Squeaky) Fromme put it very nicely when explaining why she attempted—with terrifying near-success—to assassinate President Gerald Ford: "When people around you treat you like a child and pay no attention to the things you say, you have to do something."

Lack of vital personal qualities. A bag of tricks is only as good as its magician. He keeps his act together through his ability to pick up and immediately respond to subtle audience reactions. This requires acute powers of perception, especially in corporate life, where the audience is acting too.

But, however dazzling the magician, success in some other role may require an entirely different, though deceptively similar, set of innate personal qualities. Promoting a sales wizard to manager because he is "good with people" can be like calling the magician a lion-tamer, giving him a whip, and pushing him into the lion's cage. The audience might, for a while, believe in his act (he might even believe in it himself), but sooner or later the lions will eat him alive—and usually sooner.

Lack of mature judgment. There are some tricks only old dogs can learn, and I remember a sage Parisian chairman turning thumbs down on a technically well-qualified executive because, at thirty-four, he was six years too young. "At twenty," said the chairman, "we have the enthusiasm, at thirty, the will power, at forty, the judgment. We must wait for the judgment."

How right he was. A college degree is a wonderful thing, but it takes life's traumas to remind us that nothing worth knowing can be taught. The experience of despair allows insights that happiness denies, and pain is indispensable to the seasoning of an executive's capacity to empathize, influence, and reach mature decisions. Judgment is usually enhanced by such predictable traumas as:

- The death of a parent, with its realization that nothing lasts forever.
- Marriage and the necessary disciplines that it may impose on an otherwise self-centered life.
- The arrival of a child to both stabilize and instruct a willful parent.
- The galling successes of old school friends.
- Seeing a child leave home to make its own way in the world, quite unaware of the travail that went into the preparation for just such a moment.
- The acquisition of unwanted intimates through the marriage of an offspring.

The cult of masculinity and the curious condition of the heartless lion. When Vince Lombardi observed that "Winning isn't everything: it's the only thing," he spoke for the American nation, for the most lionized of all American idols is the "winner." The behavior of such an individual is usually characterized by supposedly "masculine" traits such as dominance, aggression, tough-mindedness, and the insensitive pursuit of victory. The expression "Nice guys finish last" usually carries the disparaging suggestion that nice guys are *weak* and deserving of no more than they get. One sportsman observed, "You don't die in America, you underachieve."

In consequence, the business world is inhabited by large numbers of essentially passive and insecure individuals who feel compelled to exhibit the outward characteristics of the winner. Alfred Adler perceived the syndrome back in 1911, noting that "some patients fear the feminine role and react with masculine protest."

Such a person is like the lion on his way to Oz: outwardly hostile and tough, yet inwardly terrified and insecure; unable to do anything but jump through hoops; likely, if the going gets rough, to fall apart. Yet still he feels compelled to seek a position requiring the heart of a real lion, and, because he usually looks the part, may well land it.

Ironically, such an appointment may exactly represent his life's culminating achievement, and the pursuit of it is therefore necessary to the maintenance of psychic equilibrium. But attainment of the prize, instead of lobotomizing his past, suddenly subjects him instead to unexpected tensions, rendering him incompetent.

However, in the corporate jungle not every executive is a sheep in lion's clothing, and when the pie cannot be cut to give everyone the lion's share, mere survival may become particularly stressful for the lion who bleats.

Lack of structure. Give a bureaucrat a book of rules and he will take it to bed with him and learn it by heart because he knows that, if he obeys the rule book, his job is secure. Thus a company manual relieves stress by providing automatic, routine answers to what would otherwise require thought and the inner courage to make a decision.

But ascension in a profit-seeking organization brings an executive face to face with a hard fact of corporate life: the higher he goes, the fewer the guidelines, until finally there is no book and no one of authority to guide him.

There can be no manual for the high-wire walker, no one to hold onto—because even the advice of an understudy who secretly craves the spotlight carries both the green edge of envy and a tension all its own. And then, of course, they take away the safety net . . .

The self-esteem syndrome. The incompetent executive is frequently a victim of a vicious circle called the Self-esteem Syndrome: preservation of his self-esteem denies him the capacity to admit his incompetence. His problems might melt if only he could utter the words of Mark Twain, who once said: "I was gratified to answer promptly, and I did. I said I didn't know." But the executive suffering from the Self-esteem Syndrome is too insecure to make such an admission, afraid that people might laugh at him, or patronize him. His *greatest* fear, however, is that they may *pay him less money,* thereby rendering him unable to keep his children at expensive private schools, or make the payments on his big house, or retain his country club memberships—all of which are also pivotal to his self-esteem.

You could almost say that he has climbed the ladder to the high-wire in order to be able to acquire and put into the air more knives than he can juggle. And now his hands are beginning to bleed, and the audience is more attentive than ever. However will he cope?

HOW INCOMPETENT EXECUTIVES COPE

> *You can take your stomach with you, but not your money. Yet too often a man elects to keep his name on the door and let the surgeons have his stomach.*
>
> ERIC BERNE

The incompetent executive copes by developing a psychogenic illness such as a heart condition, blinding migraine headaches, or ulcers. As if by magic, his ailment invariably satisfies five criteria:

1. *Removes him from the scene of the stress.* He will be too ill to work, and his doctor will require that he take a protracted holiday.
2. *Shields him from the realization of his incompetence.* The essence of a defense mechanism is that the perception that it *is* a defense mechanism is denied to the sufferer. Thus the incompetent executive believes that his ulcer is rendering him unable to do his job. The truth is

the exact opposite: he has the ulcer because he is incompetent.

3. *Commands sympathy and attention from his colleagues.* He does not expect to be held responsible for getting an ulcer. What he does expect is understanding and special treatment.

4. *Punishes him.* The superego that punished him with *anxiety* now *substitutes* ulcers for anxiety. This is part of the price that the incompetent executive *exacts of himself* for being away from work.

5. *Punishes his superiors.* This punishment is relatively subtle. The words may be unspoken, but the message is unmistakable: "You've made me work so damned hard for you, and now look at what you've done to me." One corporate vice-president parlayed the corporate guilt into an international transfer, a long holiday, and a cash bonus.

Fifteen other face-savers for incompetent executives have been detailed by Dr. McMurry,* and I wouldn't try to improve on his words:

1. Take flight into detail; be too busy to consider the problem. (Perhaps it will dry up and blow away after a while.)

2. Counsel indefinite delay of action: "We must crawl before we walk and walk before we run," and "Haste makes waste." (Conditions may change and eliminate the problem.)

3. Delegate the problem to a committee and wait for its recommendations. (Committees usually take a long time to make a report.)

4. Look for the answer in the "book." (If no answer is to be found, no action can, of course, be taken.)

5. Induce the boss to commit himself on how to handle

* Appeared most recently in *Nations Business,* U.S. Chamber of Commerce, February 1980. Reproduced by permission.

the problem. (If the solution is the wrong one, the responsibility is his.)

6. Give an answer in double-talk: "If this is true, we do this, except under this or that circumstance, when we do the opposite." (If enough confusion can be created, perhaps the problem will be forgotten.)

7. Delegate the problem to a subordinate; practice "democratic-participative" management. (Perhaps *he* can come up with a workable solution.)

8. Indicate that all problems must be considered in serial order; it's not fair to show any one precedence. (By the time this problem is reached, perhaps the whole issue will have been forgotten.)

9. Have a research "study" made to "get all the facts." (Most such studies require at least six months to complete.)

10. Arrange to be called out of town or into a series of urgent meetings until the crisis is past. (Then come back and carry on as if nothing had happened.)

11. Call in the consultant, the accountant, the lawyer, or some other type of expert to "make sure we're on solid ground." (If his recommendations are wrong, he can be made the scapegoat.)

12. Deny that any problem exists. (Insist that the issue is unimportant or that it was settled long ago.)

13. Take flight into the bottle; find courage in the bottle to reach a decision. (After a few drinks most problems get easier to solve, anyway.)

14. State that this problem belongs in someone else's province; he has jurisdiction and can give an answer. (If it is kicked around enough perhaps someone will find an answer.)

15. Simply walk out on the problem; put on one's hat and go home. (Someone will find a solution somehow.)

7. *How to Salvage an Incompetent Executive*

Whenever a man's failure can be traced to management's mistakes, he has to be kept on the payroll.

PETER DRUCKER

THE MYTH OF PERFECTIBILITY

M O S T attempts to salvage incompetent executives are doomed from the outset because they are founded upon the false premise that *people are perfectible;* that an executive's personality can somehow be "fixed"; that if his personality "weaknesses" can be revealed to him he will Pull His Socks Up.

Unfortunately, "fixing" an executive's personality is akin to making a silk purse out of a sow's ear: a dubious exercise, the success of which depends upon maiming the pig.

So-called weaknesses are usually defense mechanisms, and, by definition, the perception of them is repressed from consciousness by the ego: both the weakness and the denial of it may, in fact, be balancing the executive on his high-wire.

One corporation wanting to fix an executive sent him to a "sensitivity class" (described by a cynic as a place where sensitive people go to be insulted). As a result of the unqualified help he received there, he hanged himself.

An inexperienced prison psychologist I knew once also attempted to "fix" an inmate's personality by regressing him under hypnosis. Unfortunately, the result was that the poor devil went insane and had to be transferred to a mental institution (the prisoner, not the psychologist).

A problem common to all these approaches is that the gift to see ourselves as others see us would probably just confirm our suspicion that their perceptions were wrong. It is, in fact, virtually impossible for the average executive to objectively appraise a *valid* insight into a quirk of his own behavior. The classic case is that of the corporate executive who was advised by the company psychologist that his tests and appraisals revealed him to be indecisive. When asked, "Is that true?" he gave the question a few moments thought and then carefully replied, "Maybe yes, maybe no."

Psychological testing as a means of making an incompetent executive face his weaknesses has enjoyed a checkered history, and Ross Stagner probably sounded its first death knell in 1954 when:

A legitimately published personality inventory was administered to a group of personnel managers attending a conference. Subsequently, each received a "personality analysis," ostensibly based upon his responses to the inventory. Each participant received identically the same report, but each believed that he had received an individualized analysis of his personality based upon the results of the inventory. Actually this "analysis" consisted of 13 glittering generalities collected from dream books and astrology charts. The report included such statements as these:

- "You have a great need for other people to like and admire you."
- "You have a great deal of unused capacity which you have not turned to your advantage."
- "Disciplined and self-controlled outside, you tend to be worrisome and insecure inside."
- "You pride yourself as an independent thinker and do not accept others' statements without satisfactory proof."
- "At times you are extroverted, affable, sociable,

while at other times you are introverted, wary, re-
served."

Following this, each recipient was asked to read the fake
analysis of his qualifications and rate its accuracy as a
measure of his own personality make-up. *Fifty per cent of
the men characterized the description as "amazingly accurate" and an additional 40 per cent thought it was
"rather good."* *

It's not just that people are frightened to tell the emperor that
he is naked, but that the whole exercise is akin to reading tea
leaves, where whatever you believe may be partially true and
people will believe, quite literally, anything. "What," after
all, "is truth?" asked Pilate, never getting an answer.

One other short-lived panacea involved "fixing" an executive by getting him to believe that "I'm okay, and you're
okay." Closer to the truth, where executives are allowed to
operate at their level of incompetence, is that very little is
likely to be okay. The okay litmus test may, anyway, be the
perception of a paranoid employer. It's not comforting, either,
to reflect that psychologists are reputed to enjoy the highest
suicide rate of any of the professions: *Quis custodiet ipsos
custodes?* "Who shall guard the guards themselves?"

Transcendental meditation is the latest discovery in the long
search for a panacea to make people perfect, and one airline
was reported to be subjecting its pilots to this discipline as a
part of their training. As Sir Arthur Harper remarked to me, "I
wouldn't care to fly in such a plane."

There *is* a cure for incompetence, but the Catch-22 is that
the patient may prefer the disease to the medicine. But here,
anyway, is the medicine: *instead of trying to change the individual, change his job*—like this:

Get him down from the tightrope or give him back his safety

* Robert N. McMurry and James S. Arnold, *How to Build a Dynamic
Sales Organization* (New York: McGraw-Hill, 1966).

net. You do this by transferring him to a position of less stress. Most commonly an executive is transferred from a line to a staff position, which is generally less stressful. Or he may be "kicked upstairs" to ruminate the truth of the old German proverb, "Too soon we grow old, too late we grow smart." Indeed, from such a position he could possibly attain psychic equilibrium by passing such pearls to a protégé.

Restructure his job. Change his role so that it involves less decisionmaking, more structure, or a combination of both. In this manner, even a very insecure individual is faced with the happy prospect of only having to dread one day at a time.

Play to the inherent strength in his weakness. Allocate him a role that will, as the song says, accentuate the positive and eliminate the negative. A dollop of paranoia, for example, makes for a happy auditor, prepared to go on looking, suspecting, never relaxing for a moment. Innocent findings confirm his suspicion that something is being hidden. Finally, if everything balances, he derives satisfaction from the suspicion that, but for his eagle eye, something *would* have been hidden.

Or an abrasive, petty, obsessive person can find fulfillment as a credit manager. Since the job demands persistence and a readiness to be nasty if need be, it acceptably channels otherwise troublesome id tensions, and produces peer-respect as a valuable team member able to handle tasks that others prefer to dodge.

Understand the sanity of the Mad Hatter approach. Just as a good conjurer diverts the attention of his audience from the mechanics of his deceptions, the best way to painlessly remove an incompetent executive is to preserve some of his self-esteem by misdirecting the corporation-watchers. The easiest way to do this is to coincide the transfer with a wider restructuring in which a number of titles, hats, and chairs are also moved around.

The regular use of this Mad-Hatter's-Tea-Party approach can sometimes even *prevent* an executive from becoming incompetent. The prospect of temporarily losing his chair is less stressful if it seems likely that he can get it back, or if the prospect of having to stand for a while is not particularly ignominious. However, in a rigid hierarchy where What Is Really Going On may be readily apparent to everyone, any move tends to reflect a more traumatic adjustment.

Recognize the end of the road. If these Machiavellian moves do not work—and, by the nature of the beast with which you are dealing, they may not—then it may be time to reflect that you have given the fellow more thought than he deserves: that if he were halfway decent he would have offered to stand aside, step down, or even quit.

The shrewd executive will, indeed, have done just that because he will not care to linger in any arena where his performance invites down-turned thumbs. It is the executive with innately poor judgment who gets himself in over his head. He craves what he cannot justify—the respect, status, prestige, and money of a job that he cannot handle.

Salvaging such a person is practically impossible because he is unrealistic in his self-expectations. And, if you transfer him to a job that *he* feels is beneath his abilities, you may be nursing a viper in the corporate bosom—which is, I hardly need tell you, almost the worst possible place for such a creature to be carried.

Thus the time may be at hand for him to gain first-hand experience of Regan's advice to King Lear:

> *To willful men*
> *The injuries that they themselves procure*
> *Must be their schoolmasters*

Or, as my friend Peter Reid, New York vice-president of the international insurance brokerage house Alexander & Alexander, remarked to me at a Manhattan lunch overlooking a collage of corporate headquarters: "You know what happens in the beehive? They kill those drones."

8. *How to Fire and Still Be Friends*

"Off with his head," said the Red Queen.

LEWIS CARROLL

I REMEMBER asking the fifty-one-year-old founder-president of an advertising agency on the day he went broke, after seven years in business, whether he had any regrets. "Yes," he said, "Two. I should have followed up on more of my client prospects. And I just wish I'd been quicker to fire some people. I was always too slow. I procrastinated, hoped, prayed they'd improve, but nobody ever did."

I have never yet met an executive who didn't procrastinate over a firing. The reason for the delay is threefold. It's an unpleasant task, it involves an admission of your own earlier poor judgment, and you tend to worry about how it will affect other employees.

Well, yes, it *is* an unpleasant task and, of course, it *is* a reflection on your earlier judgment. But that is not the problem at hand. Console yourself that everybody makes mistakes but that it takes special courage to admit to them. This may not make the task ahead of you any more palatable, but at least it will make you feel better.

As to how termination will affect your other employees, let me set your mind at rest. Properly handled, done with dignity and poise, a firing can be an excellent public-relations exercise, providing stimulation and relieving the tension of repressed hostilities. Your staff would rather believe you courageous than cowardly: they will respect and admire you for accepting the full burden of your responsibility as leader. But if you dodge your duty, then you invite the sneaky suspicion that you are weak.

When a decision to terminate is dragged out and duck-shoved, it becomes the subject of corridor whisperings and poisonous jokes. The prospective terminee becomes vested with all the appeal of a cadaver, and the office atmosphere begins, as a result, to take on a distinctly unpleasant aroma. It was all very clear to Macbeth in the days before refrigeration:

> If it were done when 'tis done, then 'twere well
> It were done quickly.

But first, reflect on your objective. This is not just to terminate, but to terminate with the least possible rancor; without an argument, loud words, or unnecessary pain. There is only one way to do it—quickly and with as little dialogue as possible. If you feel guilty and want to help the terminee get another job, then pay for him to go to an outplacement firm. Don't even *attempt* to run your own outplacement program—your kindness could very badly backfire on you.

Whether the final handshake is to be of gold, bronze, or clay will be determined by the circumstances of the termination. You can be very merciful in your judgments of those who fail in some ways, and very unmerciful on those who fail in others.

But before you attempt to assuage any corporate guilt with the payment of more money than is legally owing, you should reflect that people seldom forgive us the favors that we bestow upon them because of their weaknesses. Unless I were an undertaker, I frankly would not put gold handles on pine coffins.

However, if that is your want, then your kindness should be tempered with common sense, and the payment of any conscience money delayed until you have determined that nothing is missing, and that your investment will not be used to fund a suit against you.

The Friday 4:45 P.M. *shuffle.* The day and the time are significant. The office will be emptying (emptying very fast on this particular day) and there is an implied 5:00 P.M. deadline, at which time the terminee will be spared the indignity, at this delicate moment, of having to face his colleagues.

When the fifteen minutes are up—and, frankly, it should take less—the deed, the day, and the week will be over. There will be an enforced two-day cooling-off period: no hasty calls to a hungry lawyer; less chance of upsetting other employees whose minds will be turning to weekend activities. Instead, a time to unwind, readjust, stay in bed, maybe. Two long days to fully contemplate the repercussions of any hostile act.

The venue. One corporate president I know likes to terminate out of the office. On the Thursday before an execution he drives his wife's station wagon to the office, leaves it in the parking lot, and catches the train home. On the Friday he drives his Rolls-Royce to the office and after lunch explains to the terminee that he has the problem of getting two cars home, and could he please help. They each drive separately to the president's home and then return together in the Rolls at about 4:30 P.M. On the way in, the president announces the termination, timing his last words to coincide with journey's end at a subway station, where he allows his former employee to alight. "It's the best way," he told me, "and I don't need to see their eyes." In fact, all eyes in the organization become a little wider whenever his wife's car appears in the parking lot.

Former British Prime Minister Harold Macmillan is reported to have ushered an incompetent cabinet minister into an old-fashioned elevator and held his announcement of termination until he had slammed the cage doors and seen the fellow push the Down button. Slowly the victim descended into the bowels of oblivion blubbering, "But why? *Why?*" Watching the head symbolically disappear beneath his feet, Macmillan harrumphed, "Not good enough."

My suggestion of venue, however, is your office, with you in place behind your desk. This is a time to be formal, to accord the terminee the dignity of a proper ceremony. The desk between you serves an emblematic purpose and may also be an impediment to the (remote, I am sure) possibility of physical hostility. But, however remote that possibility may seem, this is a task that always calls for discretion; it is a time to heed the wisdom inherent in the American Indian folklore, which cautions that when poking an old bear in the eye with a stick, you should be sure that the stick is longer than the arm of the bear. I have only known one president to be physically assailed as a result of a termination: significantly, the eruption came in the week following the announcement that the terminee would be assigned to an outplacement program, and allowed to follow up new job leads from his old office. Had my advice to immediately sever all contact been followed, the incident would not have occurred.

The dialogue. The essence of the "Friday 4:45 P.M. Shuffle" is summarized in four words reportedly uttered by Henry Ford II when he was stopped late one night driving with a lady apparently not his wife and advised that he was violating the speed limit, and also that he seemed to have imbibed a little freely. Did he have anything to say? he was later asked in his prison cell by reporters. Ford's answer was to the point, and memorable: "Never complain—never explain."

You could do worse than remember this advice as you survey your terminee. If he assumes that you've invited him to drop by for a leisurely review of current market trands, sweetened by an end-of-the-week cocktail, you will very quickly indicate that the bonhomie is inappropriate. It is more likely, however, that he will suspect *exactly* the purpose of your meeting and greet your words with inevitability.

At this moment he will be attempting to cope with the conflicting emotions of relief, anger, shock, and shame: he will want both to stay and to go. But what he really wants is for you to play your role with dignity and decency: for you to realize that this is a moment of ritual significance in the continuum of human life: for you to honor your obligation not to relent, but to be cool, and not to allow him to make an unnecessary fool of himself.

Turn quickly to the matter at hand. Tell him quietly but firmly that you're quite sure that it's in his own long-term interests that he and your organization part company. Tell him he's a fine man, that you have the greatest respect and admiration for him as an individual—but refuse to give him any reasons for the termination. Tell him that you've thought it through extremely carefully, that naturally the decision was not made without considerable pain on your part, and that you deeply value the contribution he's made.

Your tone at this moment should be that of a well-heeled mortician: bereaved but in control. Don't at any time be lured into criticism or explanation of your reasons: the moment is inappropriate, the day is late, and, *jacta est alia*, the die is irrevocably cast. Stick with Ford's advice.

Although the terminee may tell you it would help him if he knew why you were acting this way, rest assured that it won't. Far better for him to invent any rationalization he likes to fill the vacuum of your silence in the days to come. Any words of "explanation" at this particular moment will all too easily develop into discussion, and then degenerate into an argument that both of you will afterwards very much regret—and which will do far more harm to your long-term relationship than your silence. Words unspoken cause least offense.

If you want to soften the blow and feel compelled to give a reason then it should be something with which there can be no argument whatsoever. But choose your words with care. You may wish to use this soothing approach: "I've lain awake and been right through this whole thing, and I'm now certain in my heart that God never intended you to spend the rest of your days with the XYZ corporation—you were made for better things."

Well, God has spoken, and who are you, indeed who is anyone, to question the Almighty. The essence of such a homily is *not* that it should make sense—for nothing will make sense at this moment, but that it should be anodyne, while intrinsically inarguable.

Be warned that one of the surest ways to have *successful* legal action brought against you by a vengeful terminee claiming unfair discrimination is to try to justify yourself at this moment. Any rope you give him by way of "logical" explanation may be taken by his lawyer and woven into a noose for *your* neck. Give him nothing. Certainly at the blue collar level you will want to be sure that a terminee's *indisputable* past misdemeanors have been duly noted in his personnel file. An executive however usually fails for reasons that are gray indeed, and which can rarely be put to paper: he fails because the "chemistry" is not right, or because his judgment is bad.

But actually trying to persuade an unwilling terminee for reasons based upon sound logic, that his judgment is bad, will be virtually impossible. And so, your best course, morally, ethically, and legally, is to draw upon your fine command of the English language and say nothing.

What you both need is a cooling-off period: a chance for emotions to settle and for rationality to emerge. Offer him your help, your unstinting support. Let him have an immediate check to finalize whatever severance monies your lawyer says are owing. Suggest, quietly, that he may prefer to clear his office right away, and that you see little point in his coming into the office on Monday morning. Far better to be thinking in terms of what lies ahead, rather than returning to what is now over.

Treat him not unlike a party guest who has tippled too freely and is now proposing to drive himself home—a proposal that you, as host, have to regard with some misgivings. You know he is not quite in full control of his faculties, and his judgment may well be impaired. Treat him with tact and discretion: assure him of your support, your loyalty, and, if he chooses to accept it, your friendship—but don't at this moment suggest dinner or even a drink. It could possibly be construed as the final insult. Even worse, he might just accept.

Shake hands with him as men who have shared both the rough and the smooth (as you now assuredly have), and who know how to handle a difficult moment with grace and dignity. It is on that basis that you have the best chance of retaining your previous friendship—a friendship to be subsequently based upon what Sir Robert Menzies once called "the pearl of countless price: mutual self-respect."

PART TWO

FIVE ARCHETYPAL EXECUTIVES: WHAT MAKES THEM RUN—AND WHY SOME OF THEM DON'T

9. *The Million-Dollar Executive—the Midex*

Money is the symbol of duty, it is the sacrament of having done for mankind that which mankind wanted.

SAMUEL BUTLER

T H E age of the million-dollar executive—the "Midex"—is upon us, but some people are still wondering what an executive can do to justify a seven-figure salary. Is he worth it?

How could you ask? Celluloid heroes who never completed school get paid a million dollars to walk in front of a camera. So what price can you put upon a person who not only excites people, gives meaning to their lives, distracts them, amuses them, but *gainfully employs them in the creation of wealth and progress: who welds them into an empire?* And there never was a *great* empire without a *great* (and possibly unreasonable) man behind it.

If, indeed, as Shaw observed, all progress depends upon the unreasonable man, then the Midex earns his money by being unreasonable to the point of insanity: for becoming obsessed with a vision and bringing it into existence.

The special characteristics of the Midex are these:

Fingerspitzengefühl. This is a wonderful German word meaning sensitivity—a synthesis of intuition, creativity and judgment—in the tips of the fingers: the Midex touch.

Intuition is a faculty of the unconscious that comes very close to clairvoyance or extrasensory perception: it is the ability to *divine* an insight into reality without using rational thought.

Intuition is a particular faculty of the Midex, who invariably makes his decisions on the basis of what he may call his "gut reactions." Since the whole process is subconscious, he is unable to tell you why he is doing what he is doing. He only knows, *feels,* that he is right.

In fact, he is drawing upon the archives of his subconscious that, rich with ideas as the result of an active life, enables him to sift, compare, and synthesize a rich pattern of perceptions in order to solve complex problems that cannot be comprehended rationally.

Rupert Murdoch hovers about the presses that produce the *New York Post* to see the front page as it appears. If he doesn't "like the look of it," he will stop the presses and change it, again and again, *without quite knowing why.* He is a litmus, a conduit, a membrane between his paper and his public. As a result, circulation expands.

Whether people like Mr. Murdoch are solely tapping their own id, or by some mystic process also that of their public, is a question upon which Jung and Freud argued. Jung liked the idea of a collective unconscious. I like it myself. Look at how it relates to the peculiar accomplishments of Cornelius Vanderbilt:

> In his big transactions he seemed to act almost on impulse and intuition. He could never explain the mental processes by which he arrived at important decisions, though these decisions themselves were invariably sound. He seems to have had, as he himself frequently said, almost a seer-like faculty. He saw visions, and he believed in dreams and signs. The greatest practical genius of his time was a frequent attendant at spiritualistic seances; he cultivated personally the society of mediums, and in sickness he usually resorted to mental healers, mesmerists, and clairvoyants. Before making investments or embarking on his great railroad ventures, Vanderbilt visited spiritualists; we have one circumstantial picture of

his summoning the wraith of Jim Fiske to advise him in stock operations.*

And David Ogilvy, who built an advertising empire based upon the premise that statistical marketing research was the key to creating good advertising, paradoxically records that in an attempt to create a "miracle" campaign for Hathaway shirts, "I ducked into a drugstore and bought an eyepatch for $1.50. Exactly why it turned out to be so successful I shall never know. What struck me as a moderately good idea for a wet Tuesday morning made me famous. . . ."†

Creativity and intuition are double edges of the same sword, and a particular trait of the creative individual is his ability to disappear inside his head. A creative executive can sometimes seem as deaf and distraught as Beethoven when, stone deaf, he created the Ninth Symphony.

Such a gift is not always endearing or recognized, and the early life of the Midex commonly reveals a history of "delinquency": an unwillingness, sometimes an inability, to submit to authority or to conform. For example, Churchill, not bright enough, was rejected for Eton. Verdi was adjudged *privo di talento musicale*—"lacking in musical talent"—by the Conservatory of Milan. Einstein "showed little scholastic ability," and finished school at the age of fifteen with poor grades and no diploma. David Ogilvy, by his own admission, was "almost incapable of logical thought," and his poor scholastic performance got him sent down from Oxford.

People trained to think only rationally sometimes seem to lose all power of intuition, and become unable to comprehend it in others. Oscar Wilde noted that "Ignorance is like a delicate exotic fruit; touch it and the bloom is gone." That happened to a fellow I knew who took an MBA, and lost the rest

* Burton J. Hendrick, *The Big Age of Business: A Chronicle of the Captains of Industry* (New Haven: Yale University Press, 1921).

† David Ogilvy, *Confessions of an Advertising Man* (New York: Atheneum, 1963).

of his bloom completing a doctorate at Harvard. He forsook his business career after suffering frustration as the personal assistant to the CEO (chief executive officer) of a great international corporation. Just before quitting, he told me:

> I take months to prepare him detailed reports and then when I present my findings I have to chase him around his desk to get his attention. He *never listens,* is always distracted, never seems to read anything. Frankly, the man has *no intellect,* possesses no reasoning processes that we can discuss. But somehow, almost by magic, he always comes up with precise answers to complex questions. *It's as if he is three people each living double lives,* and I just never know which of them I'm talking to.

Which is very close to the truth. The Midex functions at several layers of consciousness, works while sleeping, and, in the ballroom that we all share, always dances in double time.

An abnormally high level of psychic energy. The Midex mostly functions in the manic phase of the manic-depressive cycle and sometimes seems to be on a "high." Gail Sheehy saw it in Lee Iacocca, noting that "he becomes palpably, almost erotically excited when talking about his cars."

The Midex can maintain several conversations on different levels more or less simultaneously, his words coming in torrents, his thoughts cascading in a stream of consciousness. He seldom seems to listen to what people are saying. In fact, he absorbs almost every idea into his id, which may process an answer for him to spit out later during the same conversation but on another subject.

When not simultaneously carrying on several conversations (some of them with himself) he likes to be doing several things simultaneously: one of them, very frequently, is traveling. The Midex likes to call on his disciples in the field. He is mercurial and rarely plans his journeys—one CEO I knew always kept an overnight bag in his office, packed and ready to go. The Midex's traveling companion is a dictaphone, and he may sleep with it beneath his pillow. On his deathbed he is likely to echo the words of industrialist Cecil Rhodes: "So much to do, so little time."

An almost desperate need to prove something. Someone said that Yves St. Laurent was born having a nervous breakdown, which may or may not be true: what is true is that while the Midex functions almost perfectly under stress, he is commonly boxing unconscious childhood shadows, surpassing the achievement of an outstanding father; or, if he is one of those rare animals who feels he began from the wrong side of the tracks, erasing the humiliation, a spur that often impels illegitimate children to great achievement.

Our research reveals that between these two extremes there are very few individuals with a deep enough *need* to become a Midex. The middle classes simply perpetuate themselves.

You can readily detect an aggressive "edge" to the personality of the Midex in the chip on his shoulder, a free-floating hostility that may attach itself to anything or anyone seeming to represent a threat, however slight.

Usually this hostility finds acceptable release in the great battleground of business, but sometimes it may be directed against his own employees. One Midex I knew was so annoyed when the forklift drivers at his plant went on strike that he ordered their demands to be immediately met: then, at great expense, he reorganized the entire plant so materials handling no longer required forklifts, and summarily fired all the forklift drivers. "The exercise was good for morale," he explained. It was. His.

Yesterday's performance, however great, is never enough for him, and his quest for new ideas, new techniques, improved methods, never ends. He is unhappy with the status quo because he is unhappy with himself. To build his own self-image he must forever improve everything.

His work becomes a monument to what might be called a weakness in his psyche. That weakness is like the grit an oyster needs to produce a pearl, or the rich manure that feeds a luxuriant rose.

Balancing this great need to produce a monument is a corresponding sense of emotional security, an apparently massive ego that enables the Midex to contemplate and take apparently gargantuan risks. Possible failure will not faze his public presentation, for temporary failure, to him, is the necessary corollary of future success and thus a necessary part of proving his own worth. This willingness to countenance failure, and still proceed, can pass for courage. In fact, however, beneath the façade, the Midex seldom gambles on a heavenly roll of the dice: rather he takes calculated risks based upon sound marketplace hunches, and then works at making them come true. Like a duck he appears to glide across the water, but in fact is paddling like hell underneath.

Persuasive powers. The persuasiveness of the Midex stems from his ability to invest in his followers the same sense of special significance that *he* feels for his work.

Salvador Dali remarked, "I don't take drugs, I *am* drugs." The Midex too is a kind of drug, with the capacity to intoxicate anyone who comes within his influence. He has a commanding, sometimes overpowering, almost animal presence, and he communicates on several levels, intuitively choosing words to stroke the unconscious needs of his followers. He is not so much a politician as an evangelist. He offers not a job and a paycheck but *fulfillment.*

At the end of the day, it might not matter one jot or tittle whether Chrysler sells more motor cars than Ford. But it is a matter of almost spiritual significance to our old friend Lee Iacocca, who said in an interview: "I really believe that if we can turn this company around I will have helped 200,000 people in their livelihoods."

But could it be that this is just a rationalization? Could it be that Mr. Iacocca's persuasiveness stems from the fact that he may still be sparring with the unconscious memory of a similarly dynamic father who used to command a fleet of rental cars?

10. *The Gilt-Edged Bureaucrat— the Gilbric*

An official man is always an official man, and he has a wild belief in the value of reports.

SIR ARTHUR HELPS

A GILT-EDGED bureaucratic executive—let's call him "Gilbric"—can command a handsome six-figure salary through his capacity to straighten out the mess that the Midex left behind.

Unlike the Midex, the Gilbric's talent is rarely creative or intuitive. If asked how he rose to the top, he may choose the immortal words of J. S. Bach: "I worked hard." And the Gilbric's contribution is not unlike that of Bach: within a classical pattern he can, by dint of hard work and the painstaking analysis of alternatives, produce a rich tapestry—an organization that is tightly woven, efficient, and cost effective. To a connoisseur of management, the Gilbric's work may indeed be a thing of beauty.

The Gilbric is accustomed to thinking in terms of millions, usually other people's. Shareholders make him their custodian because of his transparent integrity. He usually ascends the corporate hierarchy by making a first-class job of any task assigned to him. He possesses the conformist corporate values: *savoir-faire,* the ability to compromise, and the capacity to work harmoniously.

The Gilbric is thoughtful, careful, conservative, and functions in his rational adult mode most of his life. He has common sense, plus blinkers to protect him from taking a wrong turning. He runs his empire like a clock. He believes in good management and an up-to-date set of books. At his most magnificent, he is ITT's Harold Geneen, who weaved a spell with figures, literally playing the percentages in everything he did.

Usually the Gilbric is drawn from a comfortable upper-middle-class background, attended good schools and colleges, and aspires to do an excellent job, as did his father before him. He is happily married and there is only a 4 percent chance that he will divorce.

His strengths are the other side of those weaknesses that impelled the Midex to found an empire and to shape it. But, whereas the Midex is often inherently unsuited to *running* an organization after it is up and going, the Gilbric revels in that role. He enjoys the power and savors the opportunity to mix as an equal with heads of other corporations. The Midex, on the other hand, commonly *hates* the opposition because they represent the enemy.

The bureaucrat appoints his subordinates within a hierarchical framework after careful deliberation. The Midex *anoints* his *disciples,* and tends to select them on the basis of his intuitions. He expects personal loyalty to him to be more important than job title.

The Gilbric rarely possesses the ability to invest the *work* of his followers with special significance because the work itself, to him, is not special. He derives his greatest satisfaction from his *position* and his power base.

The Gilbric is nonetheless good at influencing people because the act of stroking gives him pleasure. And he especially likes the idea that he has the *power* to stroke.

Under pressure, the Gilbric copes by closing his door and working harder, or putting in longer hours. He believes that "our systems and sound management will save us." Though he is not an inspiring leader, he can be a comforting figure of authority. He looks, talks and thinks like a grownup, which is his strength and his weakness. However, if it is not a great strength, it is certainly not a great weakness, either.

11. *The Amazing Female Executive— the Amazex*

The great question that has never been answered, and which I have not yet been able to answer despite my thirty years of research into the feminine soul is: what does a woman want?

SIGMUND FREUD

Instead of this absurd division of the sexes into masculine and feminine, they ought to class people as static and dynamic.

EVELYN WAUGH

THE key to identifying the amazing female executive—the Amazex—that one in approximately ten thousand women who really does make it to the top of the corporate ladder—is to appreciate that she succeeds because her temperament is virtually identical to that of the Midex or the Gilbric.

What this means is that the Amazex exhibits the classic characteristics of the winner. She is imbued with Horatio Alger values and a burning drive to succeed. In consequence she is persuasive, bold, extroverted, self-reliant, competitive, and concerned with power, status, and reward.

And it is precisely because she manifests these qualities that some people get confused and wonder what she is *really* like. The confusion arises because these very traits that bring about her success have traditionally been assumed to be more or less exclusively male, masculine, macho. In consequence most attempts to analyze either the behavior or the business success of the Amazex are inevitably clouded by a possibly well-meaning, but nonetheless inane question: *Is she feminine?*

This question is the reddest of all herrings. She is neither masculine nor feminine, she is dynamic.

How did she get that way, and what is she doing?

She is doing what each of us is doing, which is fulfilling our family destiny. That destiny, based upon our own survey of the CEOs in the *Business Week* survey of "100 Top Corporate Women," together with the other data in our files, evidences the following characteristics.

The Amazex is the eldest or only child or the only daughter, and she thus has a strong positive identification with her father, accepting his values and becoming, in effect, his emotional clone. This was true in above 78 percent of all cases where women had powerful line management positions.

In a country where women are traditionally regarded as inferior or chattels, Indira Gandhi rose to become prime minister, and was commonly referred to as the "Only man in a cabinet of old women." Whether or not this accolade had anything to do with her decision to enforce a program of mass vasectomies upon her subjects, I cannot say, but Freud might have perceived Indira as the ultimate castrating female. However, her father and grandfather were, of course, both former Indian prime ministers, and she was her parents' only child: clearly she was fulfilling her family destiny. Mary Wells, president of the prestigious advertising agency Wells Rich Greene, was also an only child.

Margaret Thatcher, the first woman to become prime minister of England, is an exception in that she was the second daughter, but it is significant that her middle-class father, touted by the press as a grocer, in fact presided on a magisterial bench as justice of the peace when his daughter was only sixteen years old—and then went on to become town mayor. But even being only a grocer—a capitalist, after all—in what Napoleon called "a nation of shopkeepers" is hardly working with one's hands. And Tricia Murray, in her biography of Margaret Thatcher, records the well-spring of her motivations: "I was closer to my father than my mother . . . he [never] tolerated the words 'I can't' or 'it's too difficult' . . . duty was strongly ingrained in us . . . *he [tried] to realize his ambitions in me."* And, of course, the father's ambitions were political.

Jean Schoonover, president of the oldest extant public relations agency in the United States, and one of the female CEOs on the *Business Week* list, chose to begin an important address in Chicago in 1974 not by talking about her present billings but about her past life as a little girl, "in glasses and dreams, growing up in Westport, Connecticut, and wishing I had been born a boy." She drew particular attention to her parents, "who made the parent in me," and especially her dad, "tall and gaunt with overwork, a country veterinarian, a hell of a man in a man's world; a man who wanted sons, lots of them—a man who got a daughter, me, another daughter, my sister, and then, finally, my brother."

Probably in the interest of modesty, Ms. Schoonover chose not to dwell on the link between the decisive influence of her father and her own subsequent success, but the connection may reasonably be inferred. Her desire to have been born a boy clearly derived from her desire to win her father's approval, to achieve recognition in his eyes, and to prove that, despite the apparent liability of her female sex, she too could make it within a highly competitive environment.

Similar strong father identification was apparent in virtually every case we surveyed, and it is intriguing to note that, whereas most men dedicate their books to their wives, Marcille Gray Williams, author of *The New Executive Woman,* inscribes hers to " . . . my Dad, who taught me never to accept second best."

This subconscious response to the psychic sculpting of the father negates the cynical observation of Alfred Jarry: "O' the despair of Pygmalion, who might have created a statue and made only a woman!" The Amazex would seem to be both a monument to her father and a living flesh and blood Pygmalion.

Like her male counterpart, the Amazex very rarely comes from a humble background. She is well bred, well educated, and inculcated with the middle- and upper-class mores. Upward mobility is so rare as to be virtually nonexistent. Most typical of the Amazex is the riches-to-rags story of Gloria Vanderbilt, who literally spins her family name in gold on the pockets of the jeans she designs. And, as I said earlier, a name like Vanderbilt carries a whole set of responses as well as expectations: exactly what women think they are buying when they purchase that label might be hard to say.

If the Amazex has a husband, he is supportive of her career. If he is not, she divorces him and takes one that is or lives alone. Divorces were significantly high among the Amazexes surveyed: 23 percent were single and 31 percent divorced—a striking contrast with the male CEO divorce rate of only 5 percent.

The social status of the Amazex's husband tended to be equal to that of the wife. No Amazex was married to a working-class husband. It was difficult to get an answer to the question of who was the dominant person in the home, but the Amazex definitely seemed to receive more support from her husband than is the norm for a "traditional" marriage.

The sexuality of the Amazex is not an issue, any more than for the Midex or the Gilbric. We didn't run a survey on sexual behavior, but everyone we spoke with agreed that the Amazex does not send out the sexual signals that typify some women, and, of course, some men. Her mind, her energy, are focused on doing a good job. She operates almost exclusively in her parent and adult modes, and is nobody's little girl but Daddy's.

The Amazex is imbued with a high level of psychic energy. Margaret Thatcher, to gain entrance to Oxford, crammed five years of Latin into one year and came first in her class. This is an extraordinary feat, but every Amazex evidenced the ability to channel a powerful, dynamic psychic force.

One characteristic did seem to set the Amazex apart from her male counterpart: she tended to be drawn to historically "feminine" industries such as publishing, advertising, public relations, and cosmetics. This was true in above 75 percent of all cases.

The Amazex is a rare breed—a minute elite of the total

female executive work force, which itself represents only 1 percent of all executives. Thus she is no more typical of the female work force than the Midex or the Gilbric is of the "normal" male work force. Unfortunately, there is still a tendency for women in business to be overpraised for very modest successes. Marcille Gray Williams's publishers describe the one-million-dollar annual turnover of her advertising agency as an "impressive business triumph." The triumph, while commendable, is hardly likely to cause much lost sleep on Madison Avenue, and such hyperbole tends to cloud the issue of whether or not, as Jung suggested, any "buried womanhood" will assert itself in the more static female executive attempting to wear a "masculine" mask. Even if Jung was on the wrong track, it will still take, I suggest, at least two more generations of "liberation" to undo the programing that makes the average woman a relatively passive creature.

In America, where that deprograming is an issue very much to the fore, the Equal Employment Opportunity Commission (EEOC) guidelines now require that women be advanced into the hierarchies of management. However, the women who are pushed up the ladder are almost invariably given "soft" roles, generally in personnel or public relations. They should not be confused with the Amazex, who is a thoroughly unique and dynamic character—dubbed the Queen Bee by one authority—who herself pushes her way to the top in clear fulfillment of her family destiny.

12. *The Super Sales Persuader— the Wooer*

All charming people have something to conceal, usually their dependence on the appreciation of others.

CYRIL CONNOLLY

You know what charm is: a way of getting the answer yes without having asked any clear question.

ALBERT CAMUS

T H E solution to the riddle of what makes a super sales persuader—that one in a thousand performer whom *nobody* can refuse—is contained in the answer to another intriguing question: what was Don Juan doing in all those beds? The answer is that he was proving to the world that he loved it, that it loved him, and that he was a man.

The superpersuader is doing exactly the same. He is not really just a salesperson. He is a star. He is a *superstar*. He is a prima donna who just happens to have somehow fallen into selling instead of serenading. Yet in a way he *really* is a romantic troubadour—for he is a *wooer*, who stays on the high wire inside his head by seducing his clients.

The wooer is no more a typical salesperson than Muhammad Ali is a typical boxer, or Henry Kissinger a typical diplomat. The wooer is special, rare, and delightfully maladjusted. He is *compelled* to go on selling, and selling, and selling, but never merely life insurance, or real estate, or mutual funds or whatever it is that he carries in his briefcase. The wooer, only and forever, really sells but one commodity: himself.

The wooer must love and *be loved* by a "client," who is

prepared to prove that love by surrendering both his signature *and* his psyche. Quite simply, to stay on his mental high wire the wooer needs, craves, *must have* both the money *and* the admiration of his prospect.

Telling the wooer that you like him, without buying from him, is akin to a beautiful woman's telling Don Juan she loves him while attempting to deny him the final intimacy: it will simply inflame his passions. Even if, at the outset, the wooer is rudely rebuffed, he will simply not believe that his prospect means what she says, and thus he will go on relentlessly pushing . . . and pushing . . . and pushing. . . .

For, the ruder the rejection by the prospect, the more tantalizing she becomes; and, in turn, the more charming, persuasive and, ultimately, penetrating, becomes the sycophantic struggle of the wooer. The wooer believes that he knows what the prospect *really* wants, and accordingly his every tango must be the tango of love—complete only when the prospect has succumbed. He must woo and he must win, and the client must love him for it.

HOW THE WOOER MAKES THE SALE

How does the wooer actually bring all this about—how does he make it happen? Frankly, he doesn't know. Wooers are unable to explain any rational sales process that could account for their outstanding sales performances. They may point to the lines they have rehearsed or the many calls they have made—but so too can their colleagues who fail. The wooer's results are achieved as if by magic. But the alchemy is contained, as usual, within the unconscious. And since the whole process is subconscious, it cannot be explained logically by its perpetrator.

By operating in his child mode—which for him is "normality"—the wooer employs the charm, innocence, intuition, guile (and perhaps the evil too) of a wise child. He is able to perceive and respond to the subconscious needs of his prospect. He may even shift temporarily into his adult mode to rationally explain a point, or into his parent mode to play a father-figure such as a lawyer, doctor, policeman, or financial adviser. But, in order to *charm,* he always returns to the state of a *vulnerable* child exposing, as it were, the membranes of his delicate id. In this mode he is sensitive, innocent, playful, sincere, childlike . . . so engaging and so persuasive that you could just hug him.

WHY THE WOOER SO BADLY NEEDS
TO MAKE THE SALE
BUT WHAT IS HE REALLY *DOING? AND WHY*
IS HE SO DESPERATE *TO MAKE THE SALE?*

The driving force of the wooer rests in an unhappy childhood, usually a denial of love, that produces a failure to mature emotionally. As a result, the wooer functions almost exclusively in his child mode, unconsciously doing two things: pursuing the missing childhood love, and, in the process, getting even with those who denied it.

In pursuing love, the wooer intuitively and compulsively charms, strokes, and compliments, in order to make people like and admire him. He is bright and engaging with the childlike capacity to inspire empathy and intimacy. Unfortunately for him, he seldom gets *all* the admiration he needs, but these characteristics do usually get him *liked*. And he possesses his childlike charm precisely because, as we have noted, he is, emotionally, still a child. Behind the charming mask he remains an anguished child, needing desperately to draw attention to himself in order to prove, almost paradoxically, that he is a man.

Getting even requires that the wooer *simultaneously punish and charm his prospect.* To achieve this he gives a part of himself—the only thing he has, his childlike charm—in order to exact *both* a premium and a smile from his "client." However, this charm invariably masks a high level of aggression. Listen to a group of salesmen talking among themselves about both the job and the customer, and you'll often hear the language of the bordello. The need to seduce, to conquer—to *screw,* if you will excuse the indelicacy—is the wooer's way of revenging himself upon those who denied him childhood love.

THE TRAGEDY OF THE WOOER

The tragedy of the wooer is that in order to prove himself a man, he must behave as a child. This, to an extent, he intuitively knows, but that knowledge is continually suppressed for him by his ego.

The desperate need to prove that he is *someone* makes the wooer lust for status, hanker after a "proper job" with an office and a desk, seek a position where people are reporting to him. Unfortunately, these are exactly the business situations for which he is the least suited.

The wooer is unpromotable to an executive role because he cannot function as an adult: discipline, organization, a cool head, are "adult" qualities that he just does not possess. His magical empathy is virtually his only strength—and, in an executive role, it is only of marginal significance. In fact, the executive who has a deep inner need to be liked has a major problem right there.

In frustration, the wooer frequently seeks to draw attention to himself in more distracting ways than merely producing sales. Often he is a chronic hypochondriac with a symptom for every season and every organ. Frequently he literally *leans* upon his supervisor (whom, incidentally, he also resents), refusing to be left to get on with the job alone, and demanding, like a willful child, to be continually stroked, praised, congratulated, rewarded.

A shrewd employer recognizes all these psychic deficiencies and counts them as part of the wooer's total overhead to be offset against the income he produces. And, of course, the shrewd employer continually focuses the wooer on "winning" sales: and since the wooer has an intense need *to be seen to win,* thereby proving his virility, he is readily susceptible to such bait.

He feels *compelled* to beat all the salespeople in his own corporation, but after having done so still cannot rest and must push himself to even more exclusive sales elites where the prime (and usually only) qualification is the capacity to produce high-volume sales. The first of these targets might be something like a "million-dollar round-table club," followed by the "president's table," and so on and on. And then, when the summit is seemingly finally reached, to preserve his self-esteem and retain his place among the elite he must do it all again next year. And he *can* too!—and, by golly, he will! . . . again and again and again.

These are, of course, all blessings for the wooer's employer. But there are risks too. The need to be seen to win, or to preserve his place among the elite of selling, is so great that the wooer will sometimes be forced to "fudge a little." Then he may either sign himself up as a client or simply invent clients who do not exist, paying the premiums out of his own commissions, or subsequently canceling or lapsing the "sale" from the proceeds of a bonanza week—or so he hopes.

The wooer goes on running because he knows that, as long as he sells big, he commands some sort of respect. While his volume stays up it does not matter if his company administrators joke about him behind his back: he is both earning more than they and, in his mind, paying their salaries into the bargain, so they must treat him deferentially in the corridors of power. And, of course, if he is selling big, he has big money too: money that can be turned into a large house, high-status cars, a pool . . . and perhaps even the power to demand a little genuine respect. Usually the true superwooer has all the self-esteem that his money can possibly buy because he commits his every last cent—and often dollars not yet earned—to conspicuous consumption for the purpose of impressing anyone and everyone with whom he comes in contact.

Secretly, however, way down deep, the wooer is often a frightened individual, fearful that neither of the items that he is so intensely purveying—himself and his briefcase of papers—have any real worth.

I remember a fifty-five-year-old wooer intimately confiding to me over lunch that "When I quit schoolteaching twenty years ago to sell life insurance, a dramatist friend begged me not to sell my soul for thirty pieces of silver—he said I'd become a pathetic Willy Loman-like salesman. But I was making more money inside three months than I'd ever seen before—and I'm as good as anyone." His words actually were not a statement but a question. Across the table I could see that he was asking *me* for approval . . . to put the *Good Housekeeping* seal of approval on his manhood, as it were.

It was a difficult moment, as such moments always are, because the truth is that if you wear a mask, any mask— doctor, lawyer, headhunter, politician—long enough, there comes a time when you can't get it off. And, even if you can, you'll find that the face underneath has grown to look exactly like the mask. I know that happens to all of us, and so do you, and so did he. He was Willy Loman, all right, but making more money than Willy, so he didn't have to die that day. Only sell another policy.

THE MAGIC TREADMILL

The wooer is like a rat caught within a magic treadmill. If he runs fast enough, the world changes and he becomes Prince Charming sharing a ballroom with Cinderella. But if he slows down, perceptions change, the ballroom disappears, and suddenly he is just a rat in a cage again. And so he runs and runs and runs, and the ballroom keeps coming back and everyone keeps telling him he is Prince Charming. And, in a way, he is, because, while his world is spinning, he swirls with his fairytale princess into the palace boudoir every time he makes a sale—which is how he knows, as well as everyone else, that he really is a proper prince.

If the wooer's inner censor ever allowed him to seriously question his motives, to realize that he is satisfying an unconscious need to both win love *and* punish his "clients"— then he would probably fall from his high wire.

That will rarely happen, however. I once shared a platform with a gentleman billed as the "world's greatest life insurance agent," a fellow whose annual commissions ran into millions of dollars. Someone in the audience asked, "Isn't it unethical to sell someone more insurance than he needs?" The wooer had no trouble answering that question. "No widow ever complained about having too much money," was his charming reply.

I doubt that I need tell you that the purpose of the answer was to preserve the sanity of the wooer rather than to enlighten the questioner. The fact is that it is virtually impossible for a wooer to consciously accept that a sale—any sale—doesn't need to be made, because *for him it always does.*

EXIT FROM THE MAGIC TREADMILL

Not every wooer runs himself into oblivion on the magic treadmill, and there is one exit that holds him in particular thrall: that which leads out of the boudoir and onto the public platform.

Wooers love going to sales seminars, but most specially they like to be in front of the audience up on the stage regaling protégés with tall tales: describing the thrill of the chase and exciting the sensitive psyches of younger wooers with intimate details of seductions past; of glorious conquests in sales competitions; of fat commission checks that commanded the world's respect.

Upon a public platform, in the guise of a wise and revered authority-figure imparting knowledge, the wooer is able to enhance his self-esteem, and, at the same time, gratify the childish id wishes within him that crave attention, affection, and, of course, the spotlight.

See him up there on the stage now—look at him, what is *really* going on? You are looking at a child who has caught the attention of his parents by making an attractive exhibition of himself. He is crying out, "Look at me, Mom! No hands!" He is usually a *superb* public speaker precisely because he is a spoilt child virtually trained to become an exhibitionist. He is happy on the stage too, because there he can be funny and charming and childish and, in the process, *make a whole audience fall in love with him.*

And his stories are usually intended to do just that. I vividly remember one somewhat inebriated wooer who had escaped from the magic treadmill and onto the speaking circuit as he wound up his address. "Ladies and gentlemen," he said, momentarily adopting his parent mode and affecting the tone and demeanor of a stern professor lecturing a freshman class: "Today we need sales *professionals*—for the day of the hard sell, and of the fast-talking, dirty-story-telling salesman is over. . . . " And then, as his own words suddenly triggered him back into his child mode, his eyes began to gleam, and he smiled his intimate smile. "By the way," he chuckled, "did you hear the one about the farmer's daughter who. . . . " And on he went to tell one of the smuttiest stories that I have ever enjoyed. And, of course, the audience just *loved* him.

THE "PROFESSION" OF WOOING

The wooer is usually drawn to what he often calls the "profession" of selling intangibles for three reasons:

1. Such sales carry very high commission-earning possibilities.
2. He can make believe that, by selling people, he is helping them.
3. He elevates his art (at least in his own mind) to that of a "proper" professional, thereby enhancing his own self-esteem.

The word *professional* becomes terribly important to the wooer precisely because he subconsciously fears that he may be cheating his customers. All the sales seminars he attends are *professional* seminars; he calls himself a *professional* persuader, and all his customers get *professional* treatment. Actually what they really get is seduced by a regular Don Juan—and what, while it lasts, could be nicer?

THE SELF-DESTRUCT SYNDROME

Unfortunately, the wooer's love affair with his client seldom lasts for long. For, like Don Juan, the last thing on the wooer's mind is loyalty to last week's conquest. He can only slake his need for love by seeking out attractive *new* prospects and getting even all over again by penetrating their pocketbooks and making them like it—*but only on a temporary basis*. For, paradoxically, the wooer has an unconscious need to break up the very relationships that he so assiduously courts—and in the process to destroy himself as well.

The wooer achieves these twin objectives by unconsciously inflicting more punishment than his client is prepared, in the long term, to go on accepting: the wooer sells the client until it hurts—hurts them both.

This is precisely why the wooer rarely—very rarely indeed—establishes a coterie of satisfied clients upon whom he can rely for either a steady income or even useful referrals—nobody, after all, intentionally gives his sister's phone number to Don Juan.

The wooer also often turns his aggression even more directly upon his own being: he may attempt to dissolve his frustrations, his psyche, and himself in alcohol: he may set about converting his company car into a hearse; or he may create such havoc for his employers that they will have no final choice but to fire him. As part of the same syndrome, the wooer may also be compelled to unconsciously bring about the breakup of any marital relationship to which he becomes a party.

At the end of his career the wooer's empathetic powers commonly degenerate into, quite simply, pathetic behavior. And when the wooer has imported his last embracing fleshy handshake and exchanged the last sliver of his charming soul, he may, like any sagging Don Juan, simply be a tragic parody of his former self. When that happens, the ball will be forever over, and Prince Charming may look rather like one of Cinderella's horses upon the twelfth stroke of the clock.

At such a time the wooer's personal finances are usually more chaotic than ever before, his money spent in the vain pursuit of illusions long since faded. He may have endured several unhappy marriages and vaguely recall a blur of one-night stands. The "clients" whom he seduced and abandoned will almost certainly now have abandoned him and settled down with less entertaining but more reliable suitors. Thus does the world of the wooer most commonly dissolve, finally leaving him to charm no one but his creditors.

How to Spot a Wooer

If you want to recruit a wooer, and a lot of people do, look for these characteristics:

- The capacity to create empathy
- Signs of instant intimacy: gets on first-name terms quickly, congratulates you on your office furniture, your suit, your tie, anything: tells your receptionist jokes
- Obviously anxious that you should *like* him
- Responds to any questions in a beguiling childlike manner
- Shows signs of a desperate need to win or to achieve—draws attention to prizes he won or special achievements mastered
- A troubled or moderately troubled childhood
- Verbal fluency, a lively way with words, and a desire to influence others
- Membership past or present of a debating or drama club
- Previous jobs that put him in front of people or on stage—as, say, in school teaching
- Attention-getting clothes (often gaudy) or, possibly, studied sartorial elegance
- Financial insecurity—the wooer automatically over-commits himself because he believes that he can always sell his way out of debt
- A childlike lust, greed, or hunger for money, status, and prestige: a concern with status-conferring objects
- Evidence of hypochrondia. Suggest to him that he looks a little off color and be prepared to listen.

13. *The Dreaded Tap-Dancer*—Le Poseur

When you go to dance, take heed whom you take by the hand.

PROVERB

A TAP-DANCING executive is not really an executive at all, for, though he appears to be the very quintessence of effectiveness, hurrying earnestly from meeting to meeting and memo to memo, the truth is that he never gets anything done. It is difficult—impossible, in fact, for a casual observer—to differentiate between a tap-dancer and the television version of a tycoon. However, the very similarity between the two provides a valuable clue to serious organization-watchers, for the tap-dancer is above all else a "performer." He is a song-and-dance man with the capacity to hold an audience. He looks, acts, talks, commutes, eats, breathes, and laughs like an executive. But he is not an executive. Rarely if ever—and our own experience would say never—does he contribute to the bottom line.

The tap-dancer is unconcerned with results, but almost totally absorbed with appearances. On a purely existential plane the life of a tap-dancer probably has a lot to commend it: most of them are happy, whereas some apparently "successful" executives are driven by a sense of inadequacy. But if it assumed that the role of an executive is to get a job done, to show a profit, to make decisions, to direct the work of subordinates toward meaningful goals, to be the catalyst for an expanding bottom line, then the tap-dancer has no place in business.

Notwithstanding this fact, some organizations almost systematically recruit tap-dancers to some 30 per cent of middle-management positions. This is not because of a desire to build an organization of song-and-dance men, but simply because it is very difficult to spot a tap-dancer at an employment interview. You can understand the problem by understanding the personality of the tap-dancer.

PERSONALITY

The personality of the tap-dancing executive is characterized by good-natured extroversion and bland charm. Without exception, tap-dancers are affable, friendly, bright, enthusiastic, surgent, role-aware people. They are at ease in the interview situation because they have the capacity to relax and to talk fluently while saying very little. They are engaging, likeable individuals who quite naturally involve the interviewer, leading him to forget his professional objectivity. A good tap-dancer moves effortlessly on to first-name terms, though he will not do so until the atmosphere is suitable.

The tap-dancer is pleasantly ingratiating, spontaneously flattering, and has the gift of making instant friendships. The extroversion is not an act: it is real, and springs from a desire to be liked and a deep-seated wish to please. One clear characteristic of tap-dancers is that they never become hostile or unreasonable, even in situations that a capable executive would find stressful. The tap-dancer acquits himself superbly at job interviews. This is usually because he has had more experience of the interview situation than most interviewers, and he knows the role expectations. He has also probably often been in far tighter situations than an employment interview, so that the situation is not a particularly difficult one for him. Many interviewers mistake the tap-dancer's bland manner as a capacity for self-control, but it is merely a mask, and behind that mask there is nothing.

The abstract intelligence of a tap-dancer is usually quite low, and his IQ level is unlikely to exceed 115. However, he *does* possess apparently excellent verbal skills, together with a level of social awareness that can give him the polish (veneer might be a better word) that is normally associated with an above-average intellect. This awareness might pass for cunning with the spite removed. Tap-dancers have a capacity for survival born of a long need to justify their place on stage, and have diverse ways of distracting the onlooker. It is upon the dance and not the dancer that the spotlight must fall.

People normally assume that the tap-dancer is intelligent because he *seems* intelligent: they mistake extroversion and charm for a genuine command of logic. But a careful interviewer will notice that a tap-dancer has difficulty in pursuing a discussion to any logical conclusion. Indeed, a careful tap-dancer will steer the interviewer away from such a discussion. The well-known "halo" effect, whereby an interviewee is rated highly on all skills because the interviewer likes him, always operates in favor of the tap-dancer. He knows that he has the knack of "handling interviews," and so his confidence is quite well founded.

The tap-dancer is not a *conscious* manipulator of people, for often he does not possess the raw intelligence to set about logical deception. His skills are brought into play by the id, and the process of influencing is unconscious. If the tap-dancer knew exactly how he achieved his results, he might move into the realm of being an effective executive. But he does not know. There is no center to his personality. You seek for the center, and it is hollow: there is no core, no edge, no bite, no sting—just a bland charm and friendliness that is very easily mistaken for the assurance of a competent executive on top of his job.

Tap-dancers are not uncovered by objective psychological temperament tests, which reveal them to be extroverted and showing little or no anxiety. The very shallowness of the tap-dancer personality enables them to seem well-adjusted, and, indeed, many tap-dancers achieve above-average scores on other factors normally associated with executive success, i.e., good team member, flexible, able to exhibit social dominance.

In extreme cases, tap-dancers may be compulsive liars, psychotics, or sociopaths.

APPEARANCE

Tap-dancers are well-dressed, socially-aware people, quite fastidious about their appearance. Their clothes usually evince a sound appreciation of trends and styles while not reflecting high fashion. They wear the clothes expected of an executive and are often well aware of particular totems and taboos. They may wear trenchcoats and carry attaché cases.

Suits are pressed, and shirts are clean. A particular flash of style may be noted, but this is never overdone. The whole effect will normally inspire initial confidence in the heart of any interviewer. There is no malice to a tap-dancer—he is concerned merely to please and to be safely employed. Consequently, he impresses as a good team person, someone well able to be part of an organization. Not a boat-rocker. Not a credit-grabber.

When actually employed, the tap-dancer takes his tone from the corporate personality. If it is a shirtsleeves organization, he is a shirtsleeves individual. There is a chameleon quality to the tap-dancer that again makes him very easily mistaken for a sound "organization man" in the sense that William Whyte used the term.

WORK HABITS

As noted, the single most important trait of the tap-dancer is that he *never* makes a valid contribution to profit—although he never appears far from pulling off a quite spectacular "deal," or devising a wonderful marketing plan. He has the capacity to dazzle superiors—especially superiors once or twice removed—with jargon and impressive-sounding ideas and concepts.

The tap-dancer's desk displays symbols of his importance: a name plate, notepaper headed "From the desk of . . . ," impressive trays of gold or silver, company emblems, and the like. He normally works in marketing, advertising, public relations, or personnel. He is attracted to quasi-professional organizations such as insurance brokers, or big blue-chip companies that carry surplus fat. In these organizations he is able to disguise the fact that he is achieving nothing by writing memos, conducting interviews, "handling loose ends," or establishing good public relations.

Most tap-dancers are drawn to what they call "public relations" as a fly to compost for two very simple reasons. They have the capacity to make idle time good fun, and it is impossible to quantify the results of their "work." Indeed, many tap-dancers are given high-visibility positions because of their appearance and demeanor, and their own natural desire to be included in this function. In this role the tap-dancer is able to wine and dine clients in expensive restaurants, which is something he very much enjoys and which at the same time frees him of the need to actually *do* something. Out-of-town clients tend to admire tap-dancers for their easy command of jargon and their usually very astute appreciation of the organizational pecking order.

However, it should be noted that a tap-dancer rarely if ever sells anyone anything, or uses his otherwise quite remarkable charm to clinch a solid deal. This is because the desire to ingratiate himself with whomever he is currently talking to is greater than any desire or capacity (the two are linked) to "close" on anyone. This total lack of an effective cutting edge is central to the personality and, therefore, the work capacity of the tap-dancer.

When a tap-dancer is not attending conferences or meetings, he is often organizing them. He enjoys meetings because they provide a relatively fruitful use for his time. He is able to talk, to shine, to agree, to go along with the conventional wisdom, all the time acting out his role to the full in front of a live audience. His command of jargon and buzz-words is usually greater than that of other participants, and, among the usual red herrings that are raised at every meeting, his lack of intellect or sharp focus passes unnoticed. A meeting to him is just another interview, but with more people present; and he may, since he never constitutes a threat, be highly regarded as a "meeting man." However, although he could at different times happily support two opposing views, he will always come down on the side of the majority, or the chief executive, whichever finally predominates.

For the very reason that the tap-dancer likes meetings, he is also fond of "democratic-participative" management styles. He likes "open, free-ranging discussions" of "options," "viable alternatives," "marketing strategies," and "trade-offs." He never suggests conclusions or strong, positive action. Thus in a decision-making-by-consensus environment a tap-dancer is almost impossible to spot, and many quite sound people would even go so far as to say that he is doing a good job.

The tap-dancer writes memos and, on occasion, lightweight articles for trade journals. Where such articles are published, his name and photograph are prominent, and copies are quickly brought to the attention of management. Close examination will usually reveal that absolutely nothing is being said, and that jargon is proffered as wisdom. The point is that tap-dancers quite like to see their names in print, but lack the intellect to thread together any set of ideas along a common theme. Indeed, it is not unusual for such articles to be a paraphrasing of some other lightweight article, or even straight plagiarism.

Tap-dancers are prone to absenteeism, irregular hours, and procrastination. In every case this is a means of coping with the conflict inherent in the work situation. The conflict is a simple one. The tap-dancer cannot function as an effective executive because he lacks the cutting edge, the focus, and the intelligence. Thus he copes by dazzling his colleagues with charm, guile, jargon, and the promise of pie in the sky. It is an act that will finally always be exposed, but in a large organization this may take time. When pressure is applied for him to show results, he will become ill or absent for any number of reasons. He will arrive late and leave early, and spend even more time on "valuable public relations exercises" that entail being out of the office.

A common ploy of the tap-dancer is to join numerous professional and trade organizations and get elected to their committees. This, he will then advise, is "good PR" for his employer, who thus cannot deny him time out of the office (or even in the office) to serve these worthy causes.

Similarly, he will enroll in management programs for which the only entry qualification is the ability to pay a fee (which he may collect from his employer), and at the end of which he will receive a diploma to hang on his office wall or to display at future interviews.

Tap-dancers are particularly fond of public-speaking groups because these provide an almost perfect vehicle for self-advancement while at the same time producing applause. Tap-dancers are *not* outstanding speakers because they lack depth of feeling and logical thinking processes, but they will nonetheless acquit themselves far better than the average stage-shy executive. It is always impossible for a member of the audience to relate any *message* from the speech of a tap-dancer, even though the speech will have been well received. This is because the tap-dancer, like the politician who pleases everybody, must say nothing.

INCOME AND LIFESTYLE

With few exceptions, the tap-dancer is *not* highly paid. He fails to achieve an outstanding salary because of his inability to show results. Nonetheless, his income is not slight, usually falling in the lower third quartile. His rewards reflect an estimated "potential," plus the fact that he may get to be a member of a management team or committee and, therefore, "justify" a salary similar to his colleagues.

The tap-dancer's lifestyle is well described as transient. He is rarely "settled," and his private life is characterized by an inability to maintain any sort of deep relationship. It is likely that he has never married, or, if he has, that the marriage has broken up. Where a marriage is claimed or does in fact exist, the partner is usually a well-bred, socially desirable person not without substance in the way of family wealth. The tap-dancer generally does not have children, but if he does he will not take the responsibility seriously.

The tap-dancer is normally in the process of moving residence, and lives in rented premises or with friends, or even in a private hotel. He will speak of buying a home, and it may even be assumed by his colleagues that he is a normal suburban commuter. Such, however, is not usually the case.

He may be seen around airports, international hotels, and the more fashionable parts of town because his social awareness gives him an appreciation of these places, and he enjoys the glamour. He realizes that other people are impressed by his ease in dealing with the personnel of high-status clubs, bars, and restaurants, and by his genuine ability to be at home in these surroundings. His comparatively low income does not permit him to spend heavily in such haunts, but he will order well if buying a client lunch.

Mobility is a keynote of the tap-dancer, for finally his inability to perform will necessitate his leaving most employers. His search for a new job will very often entail travel to cities and countries far from his home or his previous employer. There is a double value in this mobility: the tap-dancer enjoys the travel, and it provides an entirely new set of people for him to charm. He will use the very fact that he is from some glamorous far-off place to gain interviews with relatively unsuspecting employers. His transience and lack of apparent roots will be explained by the fact of his emigration.

The tap-dancer is part of a traveling vaudeville show that must roll on from town to town and from corporation to corporation—and, very often, country to country. One particularly charming tap-dancer completed documentation at Wareham offices in three countries—and not one job on any set of forms was the same. Nonetheless, one telephone reference check from a previous employer whom he served for six months was quite favorable, and he was described as "pleasant, easy-going, good team man with a ton of potential."

The moral is that the tap-dancer has excellent survival skills, developed over many years, and, as distinct from run-of-the-mill incompetents, is seldom fired. He moves before the axe falls making a polished departure that may include a pretty speech and a polite note. For this reason it is difficult to establish his effectiveness with past employers. If he is ever "found out" and fired, the embarrassment of his incompetency is such that the previous employer will seldom want to discuss the matter.

The tap-dancer reads light, popular novels and simplified business texts. There is no depth to any of his interests, although he will be well acquainted with films, celebrities, and cult figures. Similarly, he has no interest in music or art save for a smattering of "useful" names.

IDENTIFYING THE TAP-DANCER AT AN EMPLOYMENT INTERVIEW

This is no easy task for, by definition, the tap-dancer is extremely plausible, likeable, and disarming. His major assets at an interview are that he seems to make good sense and has the capacity to evoke a "suspension of disbelief."

You should also note that tap-dancers are exquisitely good liars. Lies seem to conjure no guilt, and where an interviewer points to an inconsistency, or even produces evidence of a lie, the tap-dancer is able to explain away the "error" in a bland and plausible manner.

Because he feels at liberty to "massage" his life history, the tap-dancer's resumé can never be taken at face value. In the final analysis, the only way to nail him to the wall is to insist upon a month-by-month account of every job since leaving school. However, he will often produce a defense even to this approach by explaining that large chunks of his work history have been in distant lands and have become, with the passage of time, difficult to verify.

Some companies, he will explain, have changed or merged,

or simply faded into oblivion. Addresses and contacts will be proffered, however, and written references might even be available. In some cases the contacts may exist, but usually they do not. Reality and fantasy merge, and it becomes impossible to check all leads without investing an inordinate amount of time. We have seen fictitious references both on bogus and genuine letterheads. The rule is not to trust *any* piece of information that cannot easily be verified, and preferably from two sources.

Recognition of the genre is the prime weapon of the interviewer, and it must begin with the ability to suspect executives who at first blush seem too good to be true.

How to Spot a Tap-Dancer

A useful technique for identification of the tap-dancer is to compare all biodata with the following check list:

- Currently between jobs for what appears to be a very sound reason
- Salary expectations *less* than might be expected
- Seeking job in marketing, advertising, public relations, personnel, or any staff role
- Born in a city or country other than that in which currently seeking employment
- Worked in more than one city
- Worked in more than one country
- Gives work history in terms of years only and is reluctant about or "cannot remember" exact dates of beginning and finishing employment
- Socially aware
- Charming, engaging, and socially dominant
- At ease in the interview situation. Answers questions in a manner calculated to please the interviewer. Good use of jargon and "managementese"
- Good results on psychological temperament test but only average IQ

- No university or *bona fide* professional qualifications
- Two or more university degrees claimed—possibly including a Ph.D.
- Affiliation with a number of management organizations and quasi-educational bodies
- Is single, separated, divorced, or twice married
- Evidence of transient dwelling
- Age around middle thirties or so
- Seems eminently employable.

PART THREE

SECRETS OF A CORPORATE HEADHUNTER

14. *The Art and Alchemy of the Corporate Headhunter*

There are only the pursued, the pursuing, the busy and the tired.

F. SCOTT FITZGERALD

WHAT IS EXECUTIVE SEARCH?

THE difference between executive search and any other form of recruitment is that a search consultant—a headhunter—is retained to go out into the marketplace and actively solicit—reach in, touch, turn around, and tempt—the top talent of his client's most successful competitors.

In so doing, the headhunter produces "candidates" who would otherwise remain unavailable—rare flowers who might otherwise have been born to blush unseen and waste their sweetness on only one employer.

By sifting and unsettling the *crème de la crème* of the competition, the headhunter delivers to his client the head, the hands, the psyche, the drive, and the dynamism of, at that moment, the one *best* available candidate in all of the marketplace.

WHEN TO USE A HEADHUNTER

Headhunting services and fees are justified when the executive sought will be capable of making a significant contribution to a corporate bottom line: when it is vitally important to recruit a candidate of impeccable caliber, someone who can step aboard and command the immediate respect of clients, colleagues, and subordinates. In other words, to find someone capable of filling "Brown's Job," still empty since the day the specification was written in 1920:

Brown's Job

Brown is gone, and many men in the trade are wondering who is going to get Brown's job. There has been considerable speculation about this. Brown's job was reputed to be a good job. Brown's former employers, wise, gray-eyed men, have had to sit still and repress amazement, as they listened to bright, ambitious young men and dignified old ones seriously apply for Brown's job.

Brown had a big chair and a wide, flat-topped desk covered with a sheet of glass. Under the glass was a map of the United States. Brown had a salary of thirty thousand dollars a year. And twice a year Brown made a "trip to the coast": and called on every one of the firm's distributors.

He never tried to sell anything. Brown wasn't exactly in the sales department. He visited with the distributors, called on a few dealers, once in a while made a little talk to a bunch of salesmen. Back at the office he answered most of the important complaints, although Brown's job wasn't to handle complaints. Brown wasn't in the credit department either, but vital questions of credit usually got to Brown, somehow or other, and Brown would smoke and talk and tell a joke, and untwist his telephone cord and tell the credit manager what to do.

Whenever Mr. Wythe, the impulsive little president, working like a beaver, would pick up a bunch of papers and peer into a particularly troublesome and messy subject, he had a way of saying, "What does Brown say? What does Brown say? What the hell does Brown say?—Well, why don't you do it, then?"

And *that* was disposed.

Or when there was a difficulty that required quick action and lots of it, together with tact and lots of that, Mr. Wythe would say, "Brown, you handle that."

And then one day, the directors met unofficially and decided to fire the superintendent of No. 2 Mill. Brown didn't hear of this until the day after the letter had gone.

"What do you think of it, Brown?" asked Mr. Wythe. Brown said, "That's all right. The letter won't be delivered until tomorrow morning, and I'll get him on the wire and have him start East tonight. Then I'll have his stenographer send the letter back here and I'll destroy it before he sees it."

The others agreed, "That's the thing to do."

Brown knew the business he was in. He knew the men he worked with. He had a whole lot of sense, which he apparently used without consciously summoning his judgment to his assistance. He seemed to think good sense.

Brown is gone, and men are now applying for Brown's job. Others are asking who is going to get Brown's job—bright, ambitious young men, dignified older men.

Men who are not the son of Brown's mother, nor the husband of Brown's wife, nor the product of Brown's childhood—men who never suffered Brown's sorrows nor felt his joys, men who never loved the things that Brown loved nor feared the things he feared—are asking for Brown's job.

Don't they know that Brown's chair and his desk, with the map under the glass top, and his pay envelope, are not Brown's job? Don't they know that they might as well apply to the Methodist Church for John Wesley's job?

Brown's former employers know it. Brown's job is where Brown is.*

But someone *like* Brown is out there in the marketplace. The last thing on his mind, however, is switching corporations. He's well paid, happily employed, thoroughly immersed in what he is doing. Catching his attention, and focusing it, *seriously,* on the prospect of a new horizon or another moun-

---

* "Brown's Job" first appeared in the house magazine of Batten, Barton, Durstine & Osborne Inc., with whose kind permission it is reproduced. It was written by Mr. F. R. Feland, the corporate treasurer, who might have made a great copywriter.

tain will require all the skills of an insightful, loquacious, and persuasive advocate—part barrister, part psychiatrist, part guru. In short, it will take the art and the sweet siren song of that modern Pied Piper of Park Avenue: the headhunter.

WHAT DOES A HEADHUNTER DO?

The key elements in any successful search are these:

- Eliciting from the client the job and executive specifications, and "divining" the corporate chemistry
- Researching the job market, identifying prospective candidates, and making contact with them
- Rapidly appraising apparently qualified candidates
- Referring the most suitable candidate to the client
- Negotiating an acceptable remuneration package
- Conducting the final in-depth appraisals

Each of these tasks might seem deceptive in its apparent simplicity. Let's take a look at each of them.

Eliciting the job and executive specifications and the corporate chemistry. Consider:

Job Specification

To turn somersaults, effectively interface with the other key members of the trapeze troop, and report to the circus ringleader, for a salary of, say, $100,000 a year plus a percentage of the profits.

Executive Specification

The position will require an acrobat with two years experience in another circus, with quick reflexes, and the ability to keep a smile on his face.

Seems okay? Well, yes, but the key elements of these specifications have not been included, and, because they are intangible, it is not unusual for them to be overlooked. They are: How far is the trapeze from the ground? Is there a safety net? And, what happened to the last fellow?

Answers to these questions will determine the emotional

qualifications of the candidate and reflect the corporate chemistry, neither of which can easily be put to paper. The emotional qualifications will be directly related to how well the job is *structured,* the amount of risk involved, and into whose hands the candidate will be asked to commend his spirit. The answers may also reduce the number of likely candidates and determine the remuneration package, for, regardless of what the client says he can *afford* to pay, an executive *commands* his salary by the judicious ability to share risks, and the shrewd ones to not take such responsibilities lightly.

At the very outset—at the time of drawing the specifications—I always emphasize six points for my clients:

- Is this search necessary? Or, do you already have someone who could, if the functions of several people were to be rearranged, effectively handle the task?
- Even where a star performer is required, and a search therefore necessary, the fact of recruitment, in itself, provides both an opportunity and an ideal excuse to restructure and streamline several other functions.
- Don't seek more skills than you really need. If the fellow can spin a double somersault, it shouldn't matter if he cannot also juggle.
- The laborer is worthy of his hire. And the higher you want him to fly, the greater must be his rewards. Recruit a second-rater, and the whole act will come tumbling down.
- The higher, the fewer. Or, the greater the risks, the tougher it is to fill the job.
- A candidate whose only experience has been at ground level may be unable to perform on the high trapeze. Or, it may be difficult—sometimes impossible—to recruit someone from a highly structured organization who is capable of performing what may *appear* to be exactly the same role in an unstructured environment.

I make these very basic points because it is all too easy to be diverted from the fact that, while certain skills are absolutely necessary, much of the information that goes into a job description can be a source of misdirection rather than guidance; and a certain amount of flexibility is always desirable, if the candidate is to properly fit his task and look comfortable in it—consider the words of Alan Harrington:

> I think of personnel specialists as tailors. Instead of fitting a suit to a man they tailor a man into a slot. No alterations are permitted. If his talents bulge out of the slot here and there, or if it seems that he may rattle about in it, out he goes.

This is true enough in many cases, and it is for this reason that you should be prepared to tailor the job to the executive and not vice versa. And, of course, the most vital element to a successful search is that "good chemistry" should exist between the parties. And that subject too will repay a moment's consideration.

WHY "GOOD CHEMISTRY" IS VITAL TO THE RECRUITMENT OF EXECUTIVES

John Dean notes in his book *Blind Ambition* that Bob Haldeman, when interviewing him as a candidate for employment at the White House, became visibly pleased to see that they were both wearing the same brands of wing-tip shoes, shirts, and suits: that Mr. Dean was, as it were, "one of us."

That accolade "one of us" means that, in common with my colleagues, I share values for which I might, quite literally, be prepared to die because, when you get right down to it, those values are pivotal to my psychic equilibrium.

If your calling is to be a circus acrobat performing on the high trapeze, you want to be *instinctively* assured that your colleagues are "loyal": that they share an *unlimited commitment* to your own apparently insane values. For, when the safety net is removed and you let go of your trapeze to spin through the air while the audience gasps, the shared belief of your colleagues—that *this* is the one best way to live your life—is your only guarantee that life will continue: that a pair of out-stretched hands will be in place and waiting to keep you happily employed.

The skill of a top-flight executive team is not to spin through the air but to respond with business acumen in risky and un-structured situations. Because team survival is at stake, the team requires that an individual be instinctively acceptable to all members. He may be superbly qualified, but, as with a troop of acrobats, if he isn't trusted, at an almost *primal* level, he will not get the job—or, if he does, will not survive in it.

This trust may seem to be based upon such seemingly trivial details as color of suit, tie, or teeth. But apparently frivolous prejudices often have a deeper validity on more levels than might at first be supposed.

On one occasion, some years ago, the vice-president for the Far East of a major cosmetics company was introducing to his president the candidate he had recruited through a search firm. As the candidate smiled and bowed politely, an apprehensive look suddenly flashed across the president's face, and he beckoned his vice-president outside. "You'll have to fire that man," said the president.

"Fire him, sir? But I've only just hired him. I don't quite understand. . . . "

"What you don't understand is that we're in the cosmetics industry, and that man has a gold tooth in the front of his head. Need I say more?"

While the status of a candidate's dental work might seem of minor import, the president clearly felt it reflected a serious shortcoming in an industry where fortunes turn on such ephemeral qualities as shades of color and subtleties of fra-grance. And since the president had established a worldwide cosmetics empire largely by his brilliant intuitive judgments, his assessment may well have been correct.

In the more structured lower levels of an organization, the need for good chemistry ceases to be paramount because the risks and the effects of failure are minimal. If the high-wire artist falters, his colleagues may tumble with him. But there is no risk on the ground for the clown. If he stumbles, they'll only laugh.

HOW TO ESTABLISH THE CORPORATE CHEMISTRY

How does the headhunter establish a corporation's chemistry? Essentially he needs some training in the social sciences and a keen attunement to the intangibles of corporate life. Basically the advice I give to my own staff is this:

Study the chief executive officer. The values of the leader very quickly pervade the corporation, his attitude, beliefs and expectations becoming the norm, to the point that anyone who doesn't like what he stands for will soon enough leave. Does the CEO denigrate or praise his existing staff? Is he static or dynamic? Status-conscious? Realistic? Honest?

In building an executive team, the CEO unconsciously recruits in his own image and also balances his own temperament. After that the whole thing tends to be self-perpetuating, and sometimes it can look as if *everybody* is the president's clone—and, in a way, they almost are (and usually very happy about it too).

Executives unconsciously choose one corporation over another because they identify with its values: it represents not just a paycheck but something to believe in, a whole way of living one's life. Consequently, a decision to switch can assume the significance of a religious conversion, requiring a whole new filter to reality.

The shrewd headhunter will be well aware of this fact since it is he who will often have to effect the conversion. Does this mean that he is in the business of turning people into conformists? Not really—most people *want* to conform. "You cannot," said Freud, "exaggerate the extent of man's inner instability and consequent craving for authority."

I remember a feisty international vice-president of personnel once telling me: "There's no corporate personality here. We only recruit individuals." He was a tough, street-smart New

Yorker of the "don't give a damn, just give me the numbers" variety. And so was everyone else—every last one of them a reflection of the flinty, hard-nosed, mean-spirited president, whose chief pleasure in life was kicking numbers and people around.

Study the attitude of the telephonist and receptionist. If they are surly or hostile, it is because they know they can get away with it and in a way are expected to.

Determine the corporate uniform. Every corporation has a uniform, and no uniform is a uniform all of its own. Promotion-conscious IBM executives, though they deny it, still wear dark suits and white shirts. In other corporations, you might find virtually everyone wearing brown or green polyester suits. At the other end of the scale there is a New York computer corporation where everybody, and especially the president, is disdainful of anyone so lacking individuality as to wear a tie—they *all* go open-necked or wear turtle-neck sweaters.

Get introduced to someone who was recently promoted, and try to find out why. He will very clearly reflect the prevailing expectations and precisely the virtues held in esteem by his superiors.

Pick up the corporate mannerisms, jargon, and demeanor. When I worked in chartered accounting, the most ambitious employees copied the mannerisms of the senior partner. He had a habit, before answering a question, of closing his eyes and intoning a long "Hmmm," like a doctor. This was a clue to the whole place. Seeming "professional" mattered tremendously, precisely because, although it went unsaid, accounting did not carry the esteem of medicine or law. For precisely this reason we modeled our behavior, dress, and social mores on those of our legal and medical colleagues. Maintenance of that self-enhancing behavior was vital to morale and a part of the chemistry, and on a good day an opera lover might have mistaken the office elite for players out of Puccini's *Madame Butterfly* practicing the humming chorus.

Such clues enable a well-attuned recruiter to perceive whole patterns of behavior that determine whether the chemistry of a particular candidate is acceptable. If polyester suits are acceptable, then so is the polyester mentality, which may include boots and ten-gallon hats. And the head that goes into a ten-gallon hat holds a different set of values than those to be found under a homburg.

In some corporations it may be perfectly acceptable for an executive to cap his teeth, yet unacceptable for him to cap his head with a toupee. "I just never could," said one president, "trust a fellow with a rug. I'd always feel he was covering up."

Once he has completed the task of eliciting the job and executive description and divining the chemistry, the headhunter will quickly move to his other tasks.

Researching the market. This begins with the systematic preparation of a list of people to be contacted. Since every search is unique, there is no one way to handle this task. Indeed, one urbane senior vice-president of personnel at a prestigious New York bank incredulously noted that a search firm in California offered him a paid weekend with a double room in Las Vegas and "no questions asked" if he could suggest the name of a candidate acceptable to the search firm's client. "Tacky, indeed," sniffed the banker. But then, anything, they say, goes in the wild, wild West.

At Wareham Associates we usually begin by checking our own files, and sifting various published directories. Trade associations are good places to collect names, as are specialized mailing lists, corporate reports, and the "Who's News" pages of the financial papers. Some companies specialize in sourcing candidates for search companies and charge by the hour for this service. We establish our own sources because I like to have full control over all aspects of the search.

Making contact. The point and manner of contact is vital. The executive is called and asked whether he knows anybody who would be interested in a particularly attractive position. Nowadays the question tends to mean just that, and the contact may indeed have a couple of good names. Inside a few hours these referrals can be multiplied into a hundred or more useful leads—and soon enough a likely quarry.

It's worth noting that a prime skill of the adept headhunter is to ensure, when leads are followed up, that he actually gets together with the best prospects for the purpose of seriously discussing the vacancy. It is this skill that largely determines the efficacy of a search firm. Talking to a top-caliber executive on the telephone is all well and good, but persuading him to raise his head, look you in the eye, and seriously consider your client, may take all the skill and charm of a flutist serenading snakes.

Initially appraising possible candidates. This requires rapid insight from meager data. It is not a time for in-depth questioning that might alienate. As a good doctor can "smell" disease, so should the headhunter be able to quickly sort the tap-dancer from the high-achiever.

A fruitful and relatively painless method of rapid appraisal, as we shall subsequently see, is to get together with the candidate over lunch. An hour or so across the dining table can be revealing indeed.

Referring candidates to the client. This also calls for delicacy and tact. I usually suggest a brief discussion between the parties rather than attempt to produce a full report for a formal interview. Since, in headhunting, it is the client who is approaching the candidate, the early discussion is not a good time to clumsily probe delicate areas of the candidate's psyche, nor to seek completion of voluminous forms. Experience has taught me that it is often best to move quickly when a top-caliber candidate is willing to talk to my client. If the parties mesh, then a second more leisurely interview (or series of interviews) can be arranged subsequently.

There is no hard and fast rule as to how any particular assignment may be brought to fruition. Sometimes the in-depth appraisal process will come only after the negotiation of the move has been agreed both in principle and in detail by both parties. And this, as we shall now see, can be as delicate a task as dancing upon eggshells.

15. *Secrets of Negotiation and Psychic Enticement*

It is a pitiful weakness to be resolved as to the end, and remain irresolute as to the means.

JOHN LANCASTER SPALDING

I have one case record of a man who claims he thought he was taking his wife to see the psychiatrist, not realizing until too late that his wife had made the arrangements.

ERVING GOFFMAN, *Asylums*

IT IS in the double role of negotiator *and* advocate that the headhunter can justify every last cent of his fee. He is perfectly placed to cushion confrontations and to arrange a meeting of minds.

Some clients prefer to "go it alone" at this point, believing that only they can "get the best deal." Some can but most cannot, because the ego involvement of a great man is a two-edged sword. In fact, it is not uncommon for a president to pay substantially more than necessary to "make the sale" and win a new recruit.

On the other hand, some presidents are so competitive that they derive their greatest satisfaction from belittling rather than wooing a strong candidate from a competitor corporation, and may directly or implicitly insult a candidate by treating him as though he were already drawing a company check. The best candidates have predictably strong egos, and strong egos expect to be courted. Off-hand or patronizing treatment is bound to alienate, and will generally result in the failure of the search.

Dominant chief executives develop their own idiosyncrasies. One otherwise impeccable candidate lost out on a job for which he was eminently qualified because, over a weekend of negotiations, he wore the same suit on three consecutive days.

I once knew a corporate president with such a penchant for secrecy that he insisted that his search firm be excluded from final negotiations, preferring to conduct interviews himself in a side-street restaurant from behind dark glasses, using the name Mr. X. He explained to prospective candidates that he could not trust his aides.

Such behavior, is of course, eccentric, but it is not atypical, and particularly at the close of negotiations, both parties often become nervous, tense, and touchy. A minor disagreement can sometimes see the fruit of an entire search, months of painstaking work, disappear in seconds. And when you know how easily it could have been averted, it's enough to make you weep. It's worse than a crime, you cannot help but think—it's a mistake.

Some headhunters take the view that their task is completed with the submission of a list of candidates: that inducing a possibly reluctant candidate to switch employers is akin to persuading a faithful wife to take a lover—undignified and unethical. It's a debatable point perhaps; but acquiescence in that first encounter over lunch always suggests a willingness to be courted, if not seduced. The consultant is an advocate whose skills have been retained only by one party. If a union is devoutly to be wished by his client, then that may be all that matters. If the consultant prefers to remain piously aloof, then he should not, perhaps, have accepted either the assignment or the fee that went with it.

The consummation of the union, is, of course, never assured, and the great moment of truth will come at the altar of the negotiating table, when both the parties—and sometimes the headhunter as justice of the peace—may pledge their respective vows. Such an exercise can sometimes be as enlightening for the executive candidate as it was for Alice:

> "I've had nothing yet," Alice replied in an offended tone: "so I can't take more."
>
> "You mean you can't take *less,*" said the Hatter: "it's very easy to take *more* than nothing."

Alice, of course, was engaged upon another ceremony in another world, but the sentiment and situation is, as we shall see, not entirely unrelated to the sometimes surrealistic circumstance and setting of the boardroom, where an executive and his suitor may be wrestling for their very lifestyles.

PSYCHIC ENTICEMENTS: THE MAGICAL INDUCEMENTS THAT MAKE A CANDIDATE WANT TO SWITCH RATHER THAN FIGHT

The key to understanding the apparently magical ability of some corporations to entice outstanding executives from their competitors is to appreciate the subtleties involved in the negotiation of a remuneration package. Such a package, paradoxically, may sometimes exactly represent the previous take-home income, yet be rendered infinitely more attractive through the inclusion of the most potent weapons in a headhunter's negotiating armory—psychic enticements.

"Psyticements" are particular features of the job offer that can be highlighted as potential gratifications of the candidate's suppressed, or sometimes subconscious, desires. The peculiar skill of the accomplished headhunter is the intuitive ability to reach out and touch a psyticement to that delicate part of a candidate's psyche that will induce him to switch rather than fight: to highlight that special psyticement that will seriously unsettle the executive currently settled into someone else's employ.

Psyticements are the alchemy in the executive remuneration package, the glitter on the job offer, evanescent benefits that touch at the very center of an executive's psyche, directly satisfying what A. H. Maslow has described as two of the most basic human needs: the need for self-esteem and the need for self-actualization. By enhancing, transforming even, the executive's self-esteem, by raising his perceived stature in the eyes of family, peer groups, and the business world, by holding out the thrall of a particular benefit that he especially desires, *and that he cannot either acquire for himself or obtain from his current employer,* the negotiating stance of the recruiter is significantly strengthened.

In an era which the medium is the message—and bubble reputations may last no longer than fifteen minutes—the *appearance* of success is as crucial to many people as the reality. That is why benefits such as entry to exclusive clubs, access to chauffeur-driven limousines, use of company jets, are so keenly coveted. These things symbolize success. Whether or not the success they symbolize is real is often beside the point: what matters is the reality of the illusion. In fact, it is probably true to say that the greater an executive's actual power, the less will be his concern with outward symbols. Usually it is the insecure or incompetent executive who most prizes and yearns for a *conferred* psychic satisfaction.

Perquisites often cost very little in out-of-pocket dollars— the jet, the limousines are preexistent overheads for many corporations. The true cost in making them available for a new team member is in devaluing the status attached to their exclusivity. Accordingly, the discussion of such apparently trivial items can be a very touchy subject. On the line are nobody's dollars, but *everybody's* ego. Paradoxically, then, the very discussion of items designed to enhance a candidate's self-esteem can have an opposite effect. The candidate is usually reluctant to broach these topics himself for fear that they may trivialize him, thereby diminishing his candidacy. Here, with his special skills and unique arbitrational position, the headhunter is able to "save face" for the candidate, by making it unnecessary for him to explicitly reveal his status needs to his potential new employer.

Consider, then, some of the components of a senior executive's remuneration package and how they may influence him to either stay or go, switch or fight.

Salary

Salary can itself sometimes confer psychic as opposed to monetary satisfaction, as for example where an executive makes it to "six-figure status."

But psyticements apply most particularly at the margin, where for many reasons (tax being uppermost) money loses its siren charm. The six-figure executive, when changing jobs, is primarily interested in the *margin* of increased benefit in terms of *psychic,* rather than monetary, rewards. The reason is that he places his own ego on the line when he makes a highly publicized decision to join a competitor, because the package he is able to negotiate is, at that moment, an exact measure of his market value. Thus the increment or margin is important because it provides ego-gratification; it plays to his sense of being a special person, someone deserving the very best. Also, an individual may have privately, and perhaps unconsciously, determined to be earning a certain figure by a certain age, and the increment in such a case assumes an even greater and very special significance.

Alternatively, it may simply be that a high-flyer just wants to go one better than his friends and peer-group rivals. Like Michael Maccoby's "gamesman," many high-flying executives value a high salary "not in absolute terms of becoming rich, but in comparative terms of staying ahead of others in their peer group." Adam Smith perceived the syndrome two hundred years ago when he commented that the "urge towards bettering our condition" is solely motivated by the desire "to be observed, to be attended to, to be taken notice of with sympathy and approbation."* In other words, poverty is in the pocketbook of the beholder: a man does not have to be poor to be disadvantaged; he merely has to be poorer than somebody else.

* Adam Smith, *Theory of Moral Sentiments* (New York: Garland Publishing Company, 1971), p. 109.

The shrewd headhunter, when dealing with such psyches, will advise his client not to quibble over a few thousand dollars. For, whereas the requested increment may be a minuscule item on the corporate budget, it could have sufficiently great psychic impact on the candidate to propel him into justifying it by earning it back many times over.

Corporate Status

Sometimes the marketplace status of a blue-chip corporation can provide a psychic reward all its own.

One fast-moving manager recently turned down a beach cottage, a guaranteed home loan, and access to the company jet in order to accept a counter offer, which included none of these perquisites and $20,000 less in salary. The attraction for this individual was simple: the company he joined had many high-level contacts in Washington, and he derived particular enjoyment from rubbing shoulders with the powerful as a powerful person in his own right, thereby confirming Henry Kissinger's observation that power is indeed a potent aphrodisiac.

Another executive with thrusting social aspirations—frustrated within a corporation whose community conscience stopped at subsidizing forests in Wyoming—rapidly accepted an offer from a competitor with leadership status at the Met, promising him the chance of dining frequently for the company at La Caravelle.

Felix Rohatyn's decision to become chairman of the New York Municipal Assistance Corporation is a further example of an already well-heeled executive rearranging his psychic remuneration package. His new job paid him only a dollar a year, but he was powerfully reimbursed in terms of self-esteem and self-actualization: the increased prestige and status—the chance to be more than just another banker—amply justified the move. There are many other well-placed executives on Wall Street who would similarly relish the prestige accruing from the "high profile" that Mr. Rohatyn insisted was essential to maintaining maximum political influence.

Lee Iacocca's decision, when the going got tough at Chrysler, to take a *salary* reduction of some $360,000 to one dollar a year is also interesting, precisely because he declined to forego any of his so-called fringe benefits: the perquisites obviously meant a great deal more to him than his "base" remuneration.

Office Location and Furnishing

Just as eager pilgrims in St. Peter's Square try to move close to the Holy Father, so ambitious executives want corner offices close to their chairmen. If the client can make such an office available, the shrewd headhunter will immediately draw it to his candidate's attention.

Power cannot be measured in quantitative terms, thus executives value such outward signs and symbols as office location and furnishings because they know these are often the only way their colleagues and subordinates can assess their power within the organization.

The more influence an executive *appears* to have, the more motivated are his subordinates to pull out the stops for him. For example, Dr. Henry Kissinger's White House staff regularly worked until after 10 P.M. because they enjoyed being associated with his carefully stage-managed celebrity status.

But even Dr. Kissinger (or perhaps especially Dr. Kissinger) seems to have been seduced by the whole idea of proximity to power. Woodward and Bernstein* cite a delightful example when Kissinger and General Alexander Haig fought—for possession of a particular suite in Moscow at the 1974 meeting—to the highest court of authority, President Richard Nixon.

The suite in question was adjacent to the president's and Haig had appropriated it because he maintained that, as chief

* Bob Woodward and Carl Bernstein, *The Final Days* (New York: Avon, 1977), p. 241.

of staff, he needed to be at the president's side. Kissinger hotly disputed this point:

> The summit was a diplomatic trip, he told his aides—why in hell did the chief of staff, nothing but a bureaucrat in essence, have to be close to the President? It was he, not Haig, who was to mastermind the summit strategy. It was he, not Haig, who would keep the President from making a serious error. It was he, not Haig, who would actually conduct the business when the President finished with his ritual toasts and posing for pictures. Haig knew nothing about the summit.
>
> "General Haig is out for himself and when it comes to the crunch he puts himself first," Kissinger said. . . . The battle over the suite lasted several days. . . . White House communications agents installed, removed, replaced, removed again and reinstalled special communications equipment as the prospective occupant changed again and again.

Kissinger understood that his failure to occupy the suite signaled to subordinates and to the Soviets that it was Haig, and not the secretary of state, who was at that moment closest to the president, his most powerful confidant and adviser.

And in Jimmy Carter's administration, Midge Constanza fought to retain her office adjacent to the Oval Office, not solely because she liked meeting the president in the corridors, but because she appreciated the significance of appearing close to the seat of power. John Dean gave this lust for proximity to the Oval Office a name—he called it "Ovalitis."

But Ovalitis is not confined to the White House. Any executive being wooed by a competitor tends to compare his present office location, size, and trappings against the offer of the competitor. He will predictably want a corner office with as much square footage as he can command. He will want to know how it measures up against the other managers in his peer group, paying close attention to the thickness of the carpet pile, the comfort of the armchairs, the quality of the curtains, whether the view is over Central Park or the South Bronx, and how many windows his office has in relation to other managers' windows. Windows are important for symbolic rather than practical reasons: the concern is not with the view per se, but with that unspoken and yet unmistakeable symbolic code known implicitly to any successful corporate executive, whereby the number of windows in the office signifies the place in the corporate pecking order.

Just how strong an influence symbols can exert was underlined by the behavior of a group of senior vice-presidents who were allocated spacious offices furnished in similar style in a brand new office building. When it proved impossible to give all offices window space, the chief executive suggested that the situation be resolved by rolling dice for occupancy of the windowed offices. This suggestion was unanimously vetoed by the vice-presidents, whose overriding concern was that none of their number, by accident or design, should appear more powerful than another. In consequence, they suggested that *none* of the offices should have windows. Accordingly, they each took identical interior space and gave all of the windows over to an open-plan area for their secretaries. This decision was rationalized by the explanation that VP status entailed extensive travel, and involved such hard work, that there would be no time anyway to enjoy the view. They just could not bring themselves to quietly admit their own rivalries and status concerns: to do so would have seemed childish.

Job Title

An executive's peers outside his company usually have neither time nor inclination to discover how he puts in his day, but they do pay a lot of attention to his title: general manager, executive vice-president, associate director, and so on. Accordingly, many executives advise their friends of their continuing success by sending out memos headlined "From the desk of . . . " with the name and title clearly designated. The actual substance of the job is usually known only within the company, and then only to a few senior initiates.

The experienced headhunter will accordingly advise the client that a sought-after candidate be given a more resounding title than he currently enjoys—even though the job content may remain identical—and that, if possible, he be included on the "Executive Committee." Alternatively, the headhunter may suggest that the client hold out the carrot of having the candidate's name included on the engraved corporate letterhead—another powerful inducement to switch corporations.

Perquisites

Of all the psyticements in a recruiter's armory, corporate perquisites are probably the most potent, because they provide visible and tangible evidence that an executive has, indeed, "arrived." The most exquisite pleasure for an executive gaining his first chauffeur-driven limousine is being seen stepping into it by admiring friends and envious associates. Such an act probably better than any other symbolizes his entry to the elite group who supposedly hold real power in the company. Of course, his corporate chairman may well regard the limousine as a magnet for kidnappers, and, like newspaper magnate Lord Thompson, prefer to fly economy rather than risk his life in a corporate jet, but then the chairman is granted respect by his position alone—he does not have to "prove" his success to the world, as do his line managers.

A perquisite that an executive with a particularly status-conscious wife was unable to refuse was the authority to regularly fly his family first-class to vacation with him in exotic parts of the world following the completion of company business. It will be appreciated that such a psyticement simultaneously satisfies the unspoken needs of several people at many levels.

Sometimes the lure may be even greater if the executive can travel alone, as a major computer company discovered when it announced that executives attaining 95 percent of their sales targets would be flown at the company's expense to a Hong Kong sales seminar. Executives achieving 100 percent were granted a supposedly even greater "perk": a fully paid trip for their wives also. None of the executives made 100 percent that year, although many achieved 95 percent or slightly higher.

If the headhunter can arrange for the executive to receive more—or better—perquisites than he is currently enjoying, he will generally come closer to persuading him to join the new team. A highly successful manager in the pharmaceutical industry moved companies a few years ago precisely because his new chairman was able to arrange his entry to and subsequent committee membership of a leading yacht club: the stuff, it will be appreciated, whereof childhood dreams may be fulfilled.

Such perquisites signal to both peers and subordinates, and to family, friend, and foe alike, that this is more than just a line manager under orders: this is a trusted colleague and associate; someone worthy of being treated as an equal in social as well as in corporate affairs. It was precisely this sort of recognition that President Eisenhower failed to bestow upon Vice-president Nixon by omitting to invite him to join the general and his friends at his farmhouse at Gettysburg. Nixon's status outside the farmhouse symbolized his exclusion from the president's inner circle. Similarly, if a corporate vice-president feels he has never really broached the inner sanctum of movers and shakers in his current corporation, he then is ripe for a well-phrased promise from a headhunter's client to grant him access to the power he so clearly deserves.

The Final Twist

Any one psyticement, or any combination of them, may provide a recruiter with the vital key to unlocking an apparently unattainable candidate from a competitor's employ, because these things appeal to most executives at a deep and often subconscious level. They signify his arrival in an elite club—indisputable membership among an aristocracy of achievers and power-brokers.

The final turn of the screw is to ensure that, once arrived, the executive never experiences that numbing sense of *déjà vu* immortalized by Groucho Marx when he remarked he wouldn't want to join any club that would have him as a member.

To postpone that denouement—to prevent any debasement of the psychic currency—is the consistent challenge faced by corporations that traffic in psyticements.

Somehow the corporation must hold out to its high-flying executives an ever-expanding psychic horizon: the chance to accept new promotions, occupy more prestigious buildings, share more lavish offices, enjoy more exotic vacations, dine with even rarer and more influential people—perhaps, even, one day, the president of the United States himself. Or his brother.

16. *Secrets of Executive Appraisal, or How to Build a Magnificent Management Team*

Every being cries out silently to be read differently.
SIMONE WEIL

SHORT of going aground, you never know where the bottom is until you plumb for it, and the purpose of appraisal is to plumb the waters of an executive's psyche in order to answer three vital questions. First, *can* he do the job? Second, if he can, *will* he? Third, will he be *compatible* with the existing corporate team?

The answers to those questions will be determined by personal qualities that cannot be developed on the job—work-oriented values, energy levels, motivation, resistance to stress, and innate sensitivity to others. Specific technical expertise and educational attainments are not of monumental significance, except insofar as they reflect depth of personality—or the lack of it in the case of people who lie about their qualifications.

Plumbing the psychic waters comes, essentially, down to conducting interviews, analyzing the material that you garner, and then subsequently taking pains to assure yourself that you have not been duped (as has been known to happen from time to time).

But first some prescient words of warning and advice on another matter, ere you find the long arm of some legal headhunter tapping upon *your* shoulder.

HOW TO ELICIT INFORMATION AT AN INTERVIEW
WHILE STAYING WITHIN THE LETTER AND
SPIRIT OF ANTIDISCRIMINATION LAWS

Alice would have loved America, where the federal employment laws have unwittingly created another topsy-turvy, looking-glass world.* But unless you want to lose your head, you should take notice that there are some questions you cannot legally ask a candidate directly. And sometimes they are *precisely* those questions to which you most need specific answers.

For example, it is against the law at an employment interview to ask a candidate his race, but it is *also* against the law not to employ and promote minority candidates of specific origins. Ah, the wonderful mind of the bureaucrat.

It is also, in effect, presently illegal *not* to discriminate in favor of some candidates on the basis of skin color, race, or sex. Such discrimination is called "affirmative action."

Sears Roebuck recently sued the government, claiming it has become impossible to uphold the Constitution and comply with conflicting employment laws. Sears lost. The courts held that, although there may be inherent conflicts in the law, a firm like Sears should somehow be able to cope. (Sears should perhaps study the personality of Winston Smith, who worked in George Orwell's Ministry of Truth revising the history books to reflect current political dogma.)

American dogma at the moment is that, just as always, everybody is equal, but a new perception has been added—that some are less equal than others. Consequently, implementation of the 1964 Civil Rights Act is based upon the belief that we have a "duty to redress past wrongs" in order to ensure that everyone gets "a fair share of the American dream."

Unfortunately, the laws reflecting this admirable intention are, at best, confusing. The result is that many interviewers in

---

*The very wide federal restrictions do not apply if your organization employs less than fifteen people, but you should still check with your attorney to ensure that you do not infringe local state laws.

this wonderful country are faced with at least two dilemmas that I feel bound to point out. Hopefully I can also tell you how to resolve them.

Dilemma Number 1. You must recruit the most competent individual irrespective of age, sex, race, color, or creed. However, you must also recruit a "fair" number of minority candidates who may not, initially, be as competent.

This dilemma is resolved, in theory, by systematically recruiting two streams of candidates: the competent and, perhaps, the initially less competent. The idea is that, given a chance, everybody will then achieve equal competence. Could be. Let's hope so, anyway.

Dilemma Number 2. You risk being sued if you ask some sensitive questions (such as age, marital status, or father's occupation), *but* you need answers to precisely those questions in order to properly appraise a candidate.

The conflict at an employment interview is resolved by *eliciting the answer without asking the question.* How do you do that? You do it *obliquely,* and we'll discuss exactly how to do that in a moment.

The intention of the law is to stamp out willful prejudice based upon religion, race, sex, and age, at shop-floor and blue-collar level by ensuring that only job-related questions are asked. That's all well and good.

Unfortunately, however, as it is presently framed, the law makes no clear distinction between questions that are irrelevant and, therefore, illegal at one level of employment but that may be of extreme relevance at another level, namely, that of the prospective senior executive.

It is permissible to ask virtually *any* question provided you can reasonably *prove* it to be job related. But if you are canny, you will think hard before asking even job-related questions of some people, because all it takes is one maladjusted individual with a hungry lawyer to put you to the time, trouble, and expense of defending yourself within the framework of a hostile tribunal. (Indeed, some lawyers and their clients are reported to earn a healthy living by suing unwary corporations, then exacting an out-of-court settlement in exchange for the costs, perils, and publicity of a prolonged legal battle ending, perhaps at best, with a Pyrrhic victory.)

In practice, eliciting information from an astute executive is a relatively painless exercise for three reasons:

1. He knows that information not laid out by him may, with total propriety, be gathered from a third party. For example, a credit agency can, one way or another, find out virtually anything for a corporation wanting to check out an executive.
2. He is emotionally secure in his expertise. Accordingly, he *wants* to detail all of his life because he knows that, when everything is laid out, his strengths will outweigh his weaknesses.
3. He does not want to take any position in which, for any reason, he might fail. Thus he tends to reason that candor can only redound to his advantage.

Accordingly (and I'm getting just a little ahead of myself here, but never mind), your best interview technique is to create a nonthreatening atmosphere in which the candidate feels free to talk, and then to ask him open-ended questions on values-oriented subjects—all of which, I hardly need add, is perfectly legal. For example, if you want to know (as I suggest you do) the occupation of an executive's father, you can simply ask "How do you feel about the apparently declining influence of parents on their children these days?" This should, of course, open up a wonderfully fruitful discussion.

I might add that the law recognizes that a person who can show authority on the subject of appraisal can legitimately ask questions that the dilettante cannot: *Quod licet jovi, non licet bovi,* "What is permitted to God is not permitted to an ox."

Forgetting the law for a moment and just being practical, let me make this point: If you don't understand executives, and consequently don't know what you are looking for at an appraisal interview, then no question that you could possibly ask, or any information proffered, will be of much use to you.

167

Even though at executive level virtually any reasonable question can be shown to be job related, your best tactic, both practically and legally, is to understand the significance of the information that a candidate *volunteers,* and to allow him, one way or another, to volunteer all the information that you need. This way you'll be totally within the law—and doing a fine appraisal job too.

Having touched upon the legal complexities, we can now fully look at the practicalities of executive appraisal.

The Most Common Myth of Appraisal

The most common myth of appraisal is that *you can tell how good a candidate is just by looking at him.* Of course, if you believe, from the instant you set your eye upon him, that he hasn't got what it takes, then your prophecy will almost certainly self-fulfill—competence to that extent, like beauty, truth, and contact lenses, tends to be in the eyes of the beholder.

But if you believe the opposite—that merely because he looks good he probably is good—then you may be in for an unpleasant lesson. I once had a client who called and asked if I would mind coming over and joining in a board meeting in order to "take a peek at a fellow I've just hired," to "see what you think of him and give me a quick rundown."

"Well," I said, "it's not quite as easy as that because I'd need some vital background, and the opportunity to conduct a reasonable sort of interview."

"Oh, that's a shame," said my client, "because I thought he was so good that I played my hunch and snapped him up right away as soon as I met him—I didn't want to mess around with too many questions and forms and things."

"Where did you meet him?" I asked.

"I got to know him quite well when a friend brought him out for a midweek race on my yacht. Then we got on so well at the squadron bar afterwards that I just snapped him up right away. . . ."

And fired him two months later, of course.

But, listen to me, dear reader, *this was the president of a very substantial corporation talking*. If *he* can make a mistake like that, what could be happening at the lower echelons of your organization right now?

To spare you from such embarrassment, I suggest, with all modesty, that you have these three golden rules of appraisal engraved upon a brass plate and affixed to your wall somewhere within easy sight of your interview chair:

People don't change. You might remember the story of the scorpion that asked a frog to carry it across a wide river.

> "But if I put you on my back you'll just sting me and kill me," said the frog.
>
> "Don't be silly," said the scorpion, "if I did that we'd both drown."
>
> "True enough," relented the frog, taking the scorpion onto its back and setting out to cross the river. They were half way across when the scorpion sunk its poisonous sting into the frog.
>
> "Why did you do that?" moaned the expiring frog.
>
> "Because," said the scorpion, "that's my nature."

Few of us are born with the sting of a scorpion but, genetic considerations aside, there are other compelling reasons that people don't change—namely, that the value beliefs unconsciously acquired in a person's early life, become a pivotal part of his mental equipment and *intrinsic to his nature,* thereby dictating his adult behavior.

Despite the fact that supplanting these values is virtually impossible, there still exists an undoubtedly well-meaning school of thought—led by a number of success peddlers—that maintains that people can radically change their personalities: that they can retread their old, worn, bald psyches and become as tough as a brand new, steel-belted radial tire.

Well, cast your mind back over all the people you ever recruited and try to recall even one who emerged from a lifetime chrysalis of mediocrity to become a dynamic self-starter. I bet you can't think of anybody.

The best I can do is recall the Yale undergraduate who left the following message on his bedroom door for the janitor: "Wake me sharp at 7 A.M. It is vital I get up at seven. Make no mistake. Knock until I answer." And under it he had written, "Try again at 10."

Billy Graham may claim success in turning atheists into religious zealots, but the conversion of any form of extremist to a totally opposite view is relatively simple—there is simply an exchange of dogmas, but the extremist nature of the personality remains intact. Believe that the leopard can change its spots if you wish, but don't bet on it when selecting executives. The odds are stacked against you, and the stakes are too high. Way too high.

The best guide to what an executive will do in the future is what he has done in the past. Which is why you need to find out what a candidate has actually been doing with his life. This means tracing his progress—childhood, school, college, and business career—in detail, month by month. What you'll be looking for is evidence of recurring habits (traits, to be precise), born of certain value constellations, that make the executive a really good employment risk. As you sift the facts of his life, evidence of these traits will emerge. Listen closely and your interviewee may reveal more of himself than even he is aware of.

Get him to comment on specific achievements with each employer, his reasons for joining and leaving, how he got on with his colleagues and superiors, and particularly his salary history. Salary history on its own is a remarkably accurate reflection of both industriousness in general and the capacity to make a worthwhile corporate contribution. And if by age thirty-five he hasn't already made such a contribution, then the likelihood that he is good executive material is relatively remote.

Caveat emptor. Maurice Chevalier remarked that "Many a man has fallen in love within a light so dim he would not have chosen a suit by it." This may be a useful way to begin an affair of the heart, but business affairs require a more calculating heart and a harder head.

Since you may hire your executive candidate as he is today, warts and all, you want to know all about him including the location of any job-related warts. This, in short, is exactly the time to get answers to some very specific questions about the present: Why is he contemplating leaving his present company? Does he own a house? Is he financially secure? Does he have a happy family? What does his wife think about his changing jobs? In short, obtain every piece of relevant (and, therefore, job-related) information that you can obtain.

You wouldn't invest in a $250,000 home without crawling under it—or paying someone to crawl under it—in order to inspect the piles: since your candidate may cost you a whole lot more than that, you needn't feel coy about taking a very close look at him, either—heed the words of Napoleon: "I start out believing the worst."

This is the moment—*before* you take him aboard your boat—to get your questions answered: it may be altogether too late, in more ways than one, after he has joined your crew and is sleeping soundly down below.

TEN KEY QUALITIES TO LOOK FOR

First, of course, you need to know exactly what traits and qualities you are looking for. Well, this is what I tell my most valued customers, my own staff, and myself:

Look for evidence of role-awareness. Wilde's observation that "It is only shallow people who do not judge by first appearances" is more perceptive than might at first be imagined. A candidate who presents himself for interview should be aware that *today he is onstage.* If he is at all sensitive to the expectations of corporate life, he will have chosen his costume with care and got the rest of his act together too.

If a candidate arrives in attire more suitable for a discotheque than a boardroom, then you may immediately infer that he lacks innate sensitivity and role-awareness. And if he lacks it on this particular day, you may be sure he will never have it. You may too begin to wonder about his perception of the world and his judgment generally.

Look for people with a lot of energy. The race may not always be to the swift, nor battle to the strong, but, when you are preparing to wager on what you hope will be a winner, that is the way to place your money.

The point is that some people are, quite simply, *born* with more energy than others. At an interview, or almost anywhere, they naturally exude vigor, enthusiasm, and drive. They both want and *need* to be active, up and doing. You can sense this quality in a person almost as soon as he walks into the room. It is an innate drive that puts a spring in his step and makes his eyes sparkle. Put your money on just such a person.

But beware of the inherently passive fellow who somehow got himself wound up for the purpose of this interview—or the impeccably presented tap-dancer with nothing really to commend him but a good tailor. Such an individual may look like a Ferrari, but beneath the hood may merely be the two-stroke motor of a lawn mower.

Look for people who channel their energy into their work. As well as being imbued with a high level of psychic energy, the best executive also wants to put that energy to *work*. He loves and believes in the whole constellation of values that comprise the so-called puritan work ethic: he doesn't need to have discipline imposed upon him because he carries it in his own head and imposes it upon himself.

Do not be deceived by people who *talk* about hard work, and *say* what a lot of hard work they do. To the lazy person, *everything* is hard work, and he spends much or all of his time complaining about it. One candidate who didn't get the job said in an interview, "I met a few people in my time who were enthusiastic about hard work, but it was just my luck that all of them happened to be men I was working for at the time."

Solid evidence of an individual whose superego may be imbued with the whole work ethic includes:

- Parents, heroes, or mentors who believed in hard work
- Work-oriented spare-time interests

- Willingness to take a second job
- No concern at all with hours worked—no clock-watching
- High career goals
- Completes anything undertaken
- Paid own way through college
- Rarely absent from work
- Willingness to relocate to get a better job
- Saved own money to buy an income-producing investment
- Frugal, moral, and clean

Look for inner motivation based on family destiny. It's not so much what you have or where you were born that counts, as what you did with what you had and what you make of your own life. And to determine what you did with what you had, I need to subtract what you began with from what you have now, and look at the difference.

If you went to a casino with a dollar in your pocket and went home a millionaire, you might be either lucky or shrewd. If you've been doing that all your life, you're probably shrewd enough to own the casino—possibly you do.

Determining what a candidate begins with is a matter of fixing his whole social base from birth through to leaving home or college, specifically:

- The occupation of the father
- How the candidate related to his father
- The candidate's place in the family
- The education he was given

Armed with this information, you can predict approximately where the candidate *should* now be, in terms of family destiny and within the social framework. Now all you need is some information about the present, viz.:

- Age
- Wife's occupation, or former occupation
- Father-in-law's occupation (for reasons we'll consider later.)

- Father's occupation
- Occupations of the siblings, their approximate earnings (you can guess this), and what sort of lifestyle they have achieved—i.e., are they, in the candidate's eyes, more successful or less successful than he?
- Financial situation
- The suburb of his choice
- The type of education he is planning for his progeny

Is this candidate in the process of fulfilling the typical pattern of family destiny? Do his present circumstances reflect more or less what you would have guessed him to be unconsciously shooting for in terms of the expectations of his father, siblings, wife, and peer group? If so, you know that his motivation is about average and that he'll probably be comfortable enough in the job you're considering him for if it reflects an earnings and status level slightly higher than that of his father.

But if the candidate has far outstripped the status of his father and siblings, he may be uniquely upwardly mobile—a Midex in the making, maybe.

Look for emotional maturity. People grow up three ways: physically, intellectually, and emotionally. Most executives mature physically and intellectually, but emotional maturity can never be taken for granted. Whereas you can *see* that a person is fully grown physically, and you can check his college to ensure that he is intellectually sound, badges or certificates of emotional maturity are unavailable.

Whatever his age, an immature person is, in effect, a child and operates in his child mode. But spotting immaturity—and, therefore, also maturity—is difficult because, if a person both looks and handles himself like an adult, then you are disinclined to suspect that his fully grown body is inhabited by, in effect, a child. Additionally, the immature person inevitably possesses two other qualities to mislead you: childlike charm and, as the result of long experience, the capacity to distract attention from his shortcomings.

The immature person is not a good employment risk as a

line executive because, like most children, he is essentially concerned only with his own immediate gratification and also because he tends to see his employer as a sort of Santa Claus: what he wants is to have someone to look after him just like his mommy and daddy did for him until he left home at age twenty-eight.

Conversely, *the best index of maturity is consideration and concern for the well-being of other people:* the emotionally mature executive is prepared to put the interests of the team ahead of his own, because he realizes that we can only share what we create.

Four other excellent clues to an executive's emotional maturity are these:

- *His judgment.* Has he handled himself well in his business affairs—or has he embarked upon harebrained, get-rich-quick schemes?
- *His finances.* Has he lived within his means? Is he financially secure enough to suggest that his personal, financial money-decisions are being taken with a cool, clear, adult head?
- *His domestic situation.* Has he been able to exert a mature control over his domestic life? Has he shown due respect and consideration for those who share his home, or has he given himself over to sweet pleasures of whiskey and wild, wild women—no matter what the consequences to anyone?
- *The number of his past employers and the manner of his departures from them.* Has he pursued his career in a mature and adult manner? Particularly, has he job-hopped without realistic consideration for the future of either his employers or himself?

In passing I would note that some people say the modern corporation has a duty, in the cause of social reform, to hire maladjusted executives. I think it may be better for the bottom line to give priority to the stable, the well adjusted, and the secure. Much later, from the bounty of your profits, you can hire the others. Or, better yet, give your profits to a charity that will do it for you. Much, much later.

Look for someone who can profitably channel his hostilities. You want to hire a fellow with fire in his belly, of course, but at the same time you don't want a rebel without a cause. The best executive then, while he may be mildly abrasive, tempers his hostilities with tact and channels them into the pursuit of profits. And, if he can't do that, you may be in for trouble, because *hostilities displace readily.* So especially watch for evidence of spite unreasonably directed toward previous employers and associates. Tomorrow you might be on the hate list.

Look for the need to finish a task begun. This is sometimes called a Gestalt need. It is a coupling of two qualities: perseverance and the capacity to see any task in terms of a total configuration—like a jigsaw puzzle that needs to be solved. The executive blessed with the need to take upon such a task is unhappy to leave loose ends untied, or to undertake a project that he doesn't intend to complete. Evidence of this delightful condition will be discovered simply by looking for a goal-oriented individual with a history of completing anything undertaken, as for example finishing a college degree, writing an article and getting it published or, best of all, successfully putting together a sound and profitable business enterprise.

Calvin Coolidge seemed to anticipate the Gestalt psychologists when he observed:

> Nothing in the world can take the place of perseverance. Talent will not: nothing is more common than unsuccessful men with talent.
> Genius will not: unrewarded genius is almost a proverb.
> Education will not: the world is full of educated derelicts.
> Perseverance and determination alone are omnipotent. The slogan "press on" has solved and always will solve the problems of the human race.

Look for a good reason to want to do your job. If you hire a mercenary, someone who believes in your cause only as long as the money is good, then you may be courting trouble. Such a person usually lacks any inner job motivation, and, as a result, often harbors a deep resentment of his dependency upon his employer—in consequence he will be ambivalent to a fault, *particularly if he is well paid.*

My days as an auditor provided me with a clear illustration of this point. One executive was always complaining about his employer (and my client). "But you're very well paid," I told him. "Oh, yes," he said, "they're cunning bastards. They pay you more than you can get anywhere else because that way they've got you by the ears." (I'm not certain that he said ears.)

There is, you see, no pleasing some people. They dream of sailing the world while squirreling away the money you pay them. You should allow people who really want to do something else to go and do something else. The person who will be most grateful for your money is the person with a good reason to do your job *buried deep within his psyche.* You will also want to be sure that this need is not already being satisfied off the job.

Look for loyalty to your cause. One man's freedom fighter is another's terrorist, but whatever side of the fence you find yourself on, you can always admire loyalty, even in an enemy. The sort of admiration that you'd feel for the old woman who, in time of war, started out with a poker when the enemy was approaching. When asked what she could do with her rather mild weapon, she replied, "I can show them which side I am on."

Karl Menninger would have understood exactly what she meant—he gave a nice definition of loyalty: "Loyalty means not that I *agree* with everything you say or that I believe you are always right. Loyalty means that I share a common ideal with you and that, regardless of minor differences, we fight for it, shoulder to shoulder, confident in one another's good faith, trust, constancy, and affection."

The key to loyalty, whether you're recruiting an executive or making a friend, is in finding that *common ideal,* and once again this should stem from your intended companion's deepest underlying values. If these values are not in harmony with those of your cause, then loyalty may be unattainable.

An almost perfect example is provided by Kim Philby, who, you might remember, was recruited into the British Secret Service and rose to its most senior levels. Yet all the time he was really working for the Russians. Finally, when he was revealed as a traitor, he fled to Moscow, where he was granted political asylum.

Any astute British Secret Service interviewer reviewing Philby's job application needed only to study Philby's track record to find solid evidence of potential disloyalty. First, when at Cambridge University, Philby was elected treasurer of the Socialist Society, and was, in fact, an ardent Communist. Second, Philby was, in fact, born in India, where his British father was stationed as a civil servant. It seems fairly obvious that Kim Philby had no particular reason to love England; it was not his country and, being a Communist, he did not share its ideals. Finally, and perhaps most intriguingly, his father Harry St. John Philby also forsook England—he became a convert to the Muslim religion and a devotee of the Arab cause, where he finished his career as adviser to the King of Saudi Arabia.

You can see that Kim Philby simply fulfilled his family destiny: he beat his father at the game of getting converted to somebody else's cause and country: the father embraced the Arabs and Mohammed, the son got into bed with the Russians and Marx.

Look for compatibility. Individuals make up a team, but compatible individuals make the best team. Any candidate who is unnecessarily touchy and thin-skinned at an employment interview will probably be abrasive and disruptive if he joins the team. A get-along, go-along person who also works hard is a jewel, because his shine attracts people like him. Remember too that the opposite is also true: *the bad drives out the good*. Following a fracas at the Garrick Club in London, one of the members was moved to remark that "When I joined, all the members were gentlemen." Overhearing the comment, Sir Herbert Beerbohm-Tree inquired, "I wonder why they left?"

A compatible team is a *balanced* team, and you shouldn't hire more overachievers than you need. There is a place on any team for the well-balanced, emotionally secure individual whose contribution lies in his ability to once in a while call, "Whoa, there." Emile Zola said that there have been men who have resisted kings in their glory, but there are very few men who, when all the crowd has said yes, have had the courage to stand and say no. You can use just such a person. (But just make sure the fellow is speaking out of courage and not cowardice, or you'll never finish the race.)

Recruit carefully, and you will build a magnificent management team anxious to arrive in your office on a Monday morning at 8 A.M. and serenade you in the glorious song of Ogden Nash:

> I sit in my office at 244 Madison Avenue,
> And say to myself what a good job you have
> havenue?

PRECEPTS OF APPRAISAL

Knowing what to look for isn't enough. Actually spotting talent in an interview is an art all of its own, and mistakes are easily made. You'll make fewer during an interview if you observe the following precepts:

The devil wears a halo. The halo effect is the phenomenon of scoring a candidate high on all factors simply because he is good on one, and you *like* him. He is a charming fellow, who *admires,* he says, your corporation and, best of all, he looks like your son, or the son you never had. Narcissus fell in love with his own reflection, and anybody with such a capacity (which is most of us) may discover, as did the Bard, that love can be blind:

> For I have sworn thee fair,
> and thought thee bright,   .
> who art as black as hell,
> as dark as night.

He may be cleverer than you. For no good reason we tend to assume that the interviewer is more sage than the individual on the other side of the desk. Well, tain't necessarily so. Quite apart from the subconscious capacity of the parties to an interview to fall in love with each other there is also the prospect of a Br'er Fox candidate deliberately setting out to deceive an innocent and possibly naïve interviewer. A really cunning candidate can wrong-foot, dazzle and, ultimately, dismay even a relatively clever interviewer—forget that only at your peril.

The candidate changes when you walk in the room. Werner Heisenberg's law of indeterminacy states that the process of observing a phenomenon alters it. In physics, for example, to observe atoms is to alter their position and velocity.

In executive appraisal the mere presence of an interviewer changes the candidate. Also, different interviewers evoke different responses from the same candidate, actually perceiving different facets of his personality.

The best interviewers possess innate intuition and sensitivity that causes a candidate to reveal more of himself, thus allowing more insightful perceptions to be gained.

The same phenomenon occurs in medicine where two doctors can each attend the same college, study the same texts, and graduate with the same grades yet, in practice, one becomes an infinitely better diagnostician than the other.

HOW TO CONDUCT REVEALING INTERVIEWS

Preparing for the Interview

Do your homework prior to the interview. Study the résumé. Is it internally consistent? Match the résumé against the specifications. Does it seem a good fit? Are there any special questions arising from the résumé that you want answered? If so, write them down so that you don't forget to ask them.

First the verdict, then the trial. Do your basic reference checking in advance of the interview. You probably wouldn't check a referee before a first informal discussion, but, when getting down to the nitty-gritty at a formal session, it can be very useful to have specific information on possible weaknesses because then you can sharpen your questions, and the responses too will be all that more revealing. Naturally the candidate's security takes precedence over everything but, if you've been given the names of referees, and have permission to check them, and this is a serious candidate, then you just go right ahead.

Set the stage. The aim is to put the candidate totally at ease: absolute privacy, no phone calls, and no tricks. No high chair for you and stool for him. No bright lights behind you. No asking him to sit down but not providing a chair, or asking him to smoke and purposely not providing an ashtray. You wouldn't do that to a client, and one day this particular candidate could come back to you as one . . . or as a senator. He might even marry into your family—*then* you could be unpleasant.

Into the Interview Itself

Be punctual. Punctuality is the courtesy of kings and clever interviewers. If you're not there when he arrives, he'll be agitated and restless. Be on time and be pleasant and put him at his ease. "Hello. Come in. How nice you could come. Pull up a chair and sit down and tell me *all* about yourself." Oh, and get his name right.

Establish immediate rapport. The easiest way to do this is simply to pick up on some item of small talk, like the weather, commuting, or some innocuous item from his résumé such as his golf handicap (which isn't half as innocuous as it may seem). From there, go as naturally as possible into an apparently innocent *value-oriented* topic.

Since values come in constellations, you can very quickly and accurately determine a candidate's "chemistry" and life goals by getting him to commit himself to a point of view on issues such as welfare, the family unit, changing codes of loyalty, the sanctity of the profit motive, the impact of the women's liberation movement, or whether or not Richard

Nixon should have gone to jail. Few people realize that in talking about their opinions they are, in effect, describing themselves.

Just as revealing as strong value judgments are bland or agreeable statements by which a candidate, hoping to get onside with the interviewer, agrees with whatever is said. For this reason a shrewd interviewer may push opposing opinions, apparently sincerely, on the same subject. Both the yes man and the tap-dancer are quickly exposed by this technique.

So too will be the competent and emotionally secure executive. He will pleasantly hold to his point of view, while probably starting to wonder exactly what sort of game *you're* playing.

Let him talk. You will learn more from his lips than from your own. Resist the temptation to tell him all about you. *You* may be more interesting, but this is not your day in court. Here are the key phrases:

"And what did you do then?"
"Tell me more."
"Take your time, and we'll try to cover everything."

These are your lines, and say them soothingly. Remember to:

> *Shake and shake*
> *the ketchup bottle.*
> *None'll come out.*
> *And then a lott'l.*

Shake the bottle by asking open-ended questions that cannot be answered with a simple yes or no but require ongoing discussion. Be sympathetic and understanding. Don't criticize anything and don't make disapproving facial expressions. Candidates will dodge anything that they think you don't like the sound of, so don't feed them signals.

When the candidate is on a subject that is *revealing,* smile and grunt in agreement—*especially* if you don't agree. When he gets into detail that you don't need to hear, just let it pass by with a straight face, and subtly nudge him in other directions.

182

If you find that you're not getting satisfactory answers to some questions, don't push it. File the touchy areas away in your mind and return to them later. What you will have established, even in not getting an immediate answer, is that something is being hidden. Since the truth about a man lies first and foremost in what he hides—and you now have an idea of *where* it is hidden, and he doesn't know that you know—you are strategically very well placed.

Keep him talking about himself. Don't let him trick you into a general discussion on your favorite subject, or on some triviality like what you both thought about some vacation resort. Some interviewees are extremely adroit at introducing red herrings and thereby avoiding crucial areas of their past life or present circumstances. The subject is *him, his* life, and *his* values. Gently keep him on the track.

What has he been doing with his life? Who has had the greatest influence on him? What are his goals? What does he think were his achievements? Where does he think he failed? Of course, he may not be completely honest with you, but it will be interesting to see where he puts the emphasis. An individual who said his greatest achievement was getting married (and I have heard that a great many times) might be wonderful, if you needed a professional groom. But, as an executive, well . . . you may begin to wonder.

Get real answers to your questions. If you've ever watched a politician at a press conference, you'll know that responses are easy to come by, but *answers* are as elusive as the bird of paradise. If you're not careful, you'll simply be left with a wet hen—a veritable deluge of words and a drizzle of data.

A common error is to allow the candidate to present only those facts about his past that he feels are relevant, and that, unless he is a complete idiot, will only cast him in a good light. You, hopefully, will be a better judge of what is relevant, and so it is your task to elicit all of the information you will need to predict success.

Where, for one reason or another, a candidate simply refuses to answer some highly pertinent question—such as how much he was earning in his last job—you are actually receiving an answer all of its own. For people who won't answer a reasonable question are usually hiding something. I think you can always afford to be wary of any executive who claims a pedigree but will not lay it upon the table for inspection.

Words evaporate if not trapped in ink. You'll find it invaluable to check the notes you have made, both with him during the interview and with subsequent referees whom you decide to call. Be sure to note dates, figures, and all other specific items suitable for later verification.

Contrary to popular belief, a good candidate rarely closes up at the sight of you writing down the things he is saying. Rather, he tends to feel pleased and important and, therefore, more expansive.

Penetrate his mask by not trying to. Wait long enough and, paradoxically, he may remove any mask he may be wearing. Quentin Crisp observed that "Though the strongest resist the temptation, all human beings who suffer from any deficiency, real or imagined, are under compulsion to draw attention to it."

He would love to tell you his secrets, and would do so if he felt he could do so safely. That's why you have taken care to establish rapport and a nonthreatening environment and attitude. Now all you need to do is simply wait, nodding, smiling, and sympathetically enjoying the interview. With luck, in good time, out will pop the secrets. Well, maybe.

A little stress might be revealing. When we cover up or lie, subtle physical changes occur that may be perceived almost subliminally by a good interviewer. Which brings us back to what I said before about filing away those touchy questions and delicate areas that your candidate dodged.

Now, toward the end of the interview, after you have established and sustained a good rapport and loosened the candidate's tongue, come back to those touchy areas again . . . slowly, quietly, softly. Watch his wrists, his lips, and his eyes. Do they tighten, indicating anxiety? Move slightly away from the subject, then simply pause and remain silent. Sit for a while and, without staring at him, relax in your chair and try to suggest, without speaking, that you feel he wants to tell you something more. Invariably he does and frequently he will, and sometimes it may be exactly what you need to hear.

I remember taking such a pause while interviewing a relatively poised though somewhat prickly fellow. Suddenly, apropos of nothing, he boldly announced to me, as a matter of apparent pride, that he had been fired by a previous employer. "Why," said a colleague afterwards, "do you think he told you that?" "Because he was ashamed of it," I replied. But, naturally . . .

Play your hunches. Once when interviewing an executive candidate, and for no reason of which I was aware, I heard myself ask, quietly and directly, "You have an ulcer?"

"No" he replied slowly.

"Oh," I said, looking down, and then up at him again, "you sure?"

"Well, yes," he said. "How did you know?"

I didn't *know,* but I sort of had a *feeling.* Intuition is the unconscious perception of unconscious responses that can lead an attuned interviewer to precisely those delicate areas that a candidate wants both to cover up and to reveal. He unconsciously communicates his unease by subtle changes in tone of voice, demeanor, or choice of words.

Let me give you a wonderful rule: *Nobody says anything by accident.* No matter what words we select, consciously or unconsciously, to clothe (and sometimes disguise) our thoughts, we inevitably express an idea recovered from the mind's archives—and somehow it is important enough to surface into a particular conversation, it doesn't happen by chance.

Often you will hear exactly the truth in a seemingly light or throwaway remark, and your intuition should tell you when to take a joke seriously. As when Idi Amin jokingly remarked, "I captured some of the people who tried to assassinate me. I ate them before they ate me." Later it was revealed that, indeed, the former president of Uganda *had* eaten the livers of some senior officials whom he had put to death. I suppose you could say that Mr. Amin's gut reactions helped him to survive in his job for as long as he did.

Intuition is your own visceral response to a candidate. You may not view him with a consuming fear, but you may nonetheless feel uneasy for reasons that you cannot rationally explain, like the poet Thomas Brown, who was wary of Doctor Fell:

> *I do not love thee, Doctor Fell,*
> *The reason why I cannot tell.*
> *But this alone I know full well,*
> *I do not love thee, Doctor Fell.*

Your intuition, if you are a good and sympathetic interviewer, will be remarkably accurate. But don't fool yourself. Charm is real too, and an incompetent but charming candidate can make you like him for absolutely no good reason at all.

End on a high note. You don't have to eat all of an egg to know that it's rotten, so don't feel obliged to give more time to an unsuitable candidate than is necessary. But be courteous, of course; that costs nothing. Just say that you've greatly appreciated him giving up his time and you'll need to study his résumé alongside the others being considered.

If you like the candidate, however, then take time to answer all his questions and ideally pass him directly on to whomever else he must meet. Whichever way it goes, leave him knowing where he stands, what the next communication will be, and when to expect it.

The advantage of an office interview is that it allows a more or less formal information-gathering process. The problem of such encounters, however, is that many executives are carefully prepared, and remain more or less on guard from beginning to end. Thus you may often find it useful to consider a modest investment in a quiet lunch.

17. *How to Appraise an Executive over Lunch*

The way one eats is the way one works.

CZECH PROVERB

T H E beauty of the luncheon interview is its apparent informality. Yet in a curious way it provides an almost perfect opportunity to observe at first hand exactly how an executive conducts himself in a more or less ritual setting.

The ambience of any fine restaurant imposes almost spiritual expectations upon those who choose to break of its bread and taste of its wine. And the introduction of the fermented grape, *verboten* in the office yet exquisitely appropriate to both the moment and your purpose, provides a whole new dimension to the encounter.

There is wisdom in the Latin adage *in vino veritas* precisely because alcohol is, as noted earlier, a consciousness-altering drug, and, taken midday, its effects are doubly enhanced: the inner censor becomes intoxicated and inevitably allows id tensions that might otherwise have remained suppressed to be released.

Thus the fruit of the vine may both invoke and allow you to observe responses that simply are not to be seen at an office interview. You should especially be alert to any signals of poor self-discipline, innate insensitivity, doubtful judgment, and free-floating hostility. And also watch for that greatest asset of the immature person—charm. Let the manifestation of this quality alert you to the possibility that you may be dining

187

with a child. You should immediately explore this insight by looking for the related cluster of characteristics attendant upon the immature personality. But since the luncheon table is a natural playground for such an individual, your task may not be easy; and you will need to take especial care to ensure that you actually get your questions answered. You have been warned.

The luncheon ceremony also allows you to go beyond the mere facts and figures of a candidate's life, and to probe his values, his opinions, and his tastes: those imprecise but vital qualities that constitute the man behind the mask.

Questions of a directly personal nature that may be answered tersely or perfunctorily in an office situation—that may, indeed, even cause visible offense—are ironically enough entirely appropriate in a more relaxed lunchtime setting. In fact, you might even be derelict in your social duty if you fail to ask these questions.

Similarly, your candidate is expected to respond at some length: his situation is not unlike that of a disciple of the Reverend Jim Jones—smiling gamely, he has to take his poison along with his beverage.

But unlike that last supper of Kool-Aid, the objective of this particular rite is not to bring about an ending, but to satisfy you that your companion is worthy of redemption and, all going well, to set about effecting his conversion to your cause. You want both to assure yourself that he is "one of us" and, hopefully, *make* him "one of us" into the bargain.

For this reason you should be careful not to alienate the fellow. I suggest that the dinner table is not a suitable place for questions that he might perceive to be mealy mouthed, and you will gather all that is best in the situation by ensuring that your candidate feels free to unwind and talk to you as one human being to another. You may even wish to follow suit. But you will, if you are wise, proceed with dignity and tact. "A little sincerity," said Wilde, "is a dangerous thing, and a great deal can be absolutely fatal." Exactly so. It will be your sincerity, entirely real I suggest, that may induce your candidate to reveal more of himself than perhaps he intends. But simply because you will be sincere does not mean that you should not also exploit the peculiarly rewarding opportunity inherent in this circumstance, ceremony, and setting—to closely probe the psyche of your quarry.

CHOICE OF RESTAURANT

Select a restaurant you know and, more importantly, where you in turn are known. Don't take him to your club, where business transactions of this kind may well be frowned upon and where it is assumed that members and guests will all be gentlemen. That is a point on which you have yet to satisfy yourself. Never select one of the town's most expensive restaurants, nor feel constrained to follow Lord Thompson of Fleet, who sometimes entertained his guests at a pie cart. Settle upon a restaurant with discreet good taste that specializes in catering to business clientele. Whenever possible, arrange settlement of the account with the maître d' in advance. Check-paying formalities, even with an American Express Gold Card, are inevitably distracting and superfluous. Far better just to get up at the end of the meal and casually escort your candidate to the door.

Set the meeting for around noon, so that both you and he can be back in the office shortly after 2 P.M. It is better to be prompt than early but don't be late: indirectly compliment your candidate by suggesting that you are finding time in an extremely busy schedule to devote exclusively to him. If he is more than a few minutes late, score him down a point and go straight to your table and play with your slim calculator. When he is ushered to your presence, rise to greet him wearing your normal banker's three-piece pinstripe, with white shirt, conservative tie, and a white or muted breast-pocket handkerchief—and invite him to sit with his back to the wall at your secluded corner table.

A quiet corner table is mandatory—nothing is less conducive to an executive baring his soul than a feeling that he has involuntarily joined the cast of an E. F. Hutton & Company commercial.

CHOICE OF COCKTAIL

You will usually offer your guest a prelunch cocktail, which will normally be accepted. Old hands at the game frequently have an understanding with the steward that their own drink be heavy on the mixer and light on the alcohol, to ensure their heads remain clear and unclouded.

One managing director I knew went a stage further and had an understanding with the bar steward at his favorite restaurant that when he ordered a bloody Mary he meant unadulterated tomato juice, that when he ordered a gin and tonic he meant just tonic, and so on.

A refusal of alcohol by the candidate may be of interest. It might indicate an inability to adapt and conform to the conventional business practice of drinking in moderation on social occasions. The executive who accepts only fruit juice, or refuses to drink at all, may just as readily go his own way when it comes to making other decisions that will affect, not only his own constitution, but the morale and well-being of the group he manages. On the other hand, if he immediately orders a Chivas double and on the rocks, then you might be excused for suddenly discovering in your diary a vital meeting to be attended forthwith. Not that too much should be read into an apparently simple decision. It is useful simply as a pointer, as a tantalizing glimpse at the actual human being latent within the personnel department's careful dossier.

CHOICE OF WINE AND ENTRÉE

Should the candidate—with total propriety—elect to skip a prelunch cocktail and move straight to the wine list, you will courteously suggest he make a choice. The candidate who deferentially returns the pass may be indicating, not only a lack of confidence in his talents as a sommelier, but also a general reluctance to take the initiative.

Conversely, his decision to order in the Château Lafitte

price range may or may not tell you something about his palate, but it will certainly tell you quite a lot about his *savoir-faire*—or lack of it—and his general attitude to your pocketbook. You will, after all, be picking up the tab at the end of the meal, and if he is this cavalier about spending your money before he is even on board, you can be fairly sure the pattern will continue and probably intensify once he is permanently on your payroll. If, on the other hand, he starts asking the wine steward for a Châteaubriand, you'll know you've got problems of a rather different kind. But again, any judgment should be taken cautiously. At one luncheon interview the executive candidate, sitting opposite both his potential chairman and president, was invited to choose a wine. He spoke up somewhat tremulously; after taking the order, the wine waiter nodded his head appreciatively, clicked his heels, and stage-whispered, "May I congratulate you upon your choice, sir."

"Damned good executive," murmured the president, who had already made up his mind anyway, to the chairman.

"Bloody good wine waiter," replied the chairman.

However reached, the decision on a wine will, of course, have been made in conjunction with your respective choices of an entrée: appetizers are usually best avoided, not so much for reasons of diet, but because the constant arrival and removal of dishes can frequently disrupt a candidate's train of thought—often when he is tantalizingly close to telling you something interesting. Avoid smorgasbords for the same reason: not only are they disruptive, but they tend to suggest that you do not wish to afford *à la carte*. Stick with an unadventuresome main course: fish is usually ideal. Any candidate who knows what he is up to will follow suit: he will realize that the last thing anyone at a business lunch expects to do is enjoy the food. But if such an insight eludes him and he proceeds to order himself a private banquet, then you might infer that he either lacks role awareness or, possibly, that a deeper hunger is craving to be fed: gluttony is, after all, a fairly certain signal that something is eating us.

CONVERSATIONAL GAMBITS

The real skill in handling this kind of encounter is to elicit relevant information without unnecessarily antagonizing the candidate, who may become dyspeptic if he believes his personal integrity is being questioned. It is precisely at this point that the social conventions of the lunch-table situation play right into your hands.

As in a game of chess, your opening conversational gambits should be designed to exploit the board to your own advantage. An excellent conversation opener as you pass the condiments is to comment on the length of time it takes the candidate to get to work. How long he in fact hangs limply from a lurching commuter strap will seem of little moment, and the soothing banality of the remark may well lull your candidate into a false security, potentially eliciting an expansive response to your follow-up question: "I guess you wish you saw more of your family?" (If he lives close to the office, the question may be reversed: "I guess you enjoy seeing a lot of your family?")

Although your companion should not guess it, this is a leading question. It provides you with an opportunity to chat informally in an apparently neutral setting about the one area of his life most inaccessible to your professional personnel people: the private and the personal.

At an office interview, such a question may evoke a somewhat careful response. But in a restaurant setting, his defenses are more likely to be down, and with casual deliberation you may press your advantage. Listen with close attention: feed his ego as well as his palate. If you have a Machiavellian bent and feel so inclined, you might even arrange with your waiter—as a client of mine sometimes did—to decline an imaginary phone call.

Lean forward as he tells you about his children and their plans for the future, paying particular attention to when they will all complete college, thereby relieving him of an important salary incentive. How he will handle that hiatus is also a subject that will be of particular interest to you. Probe what kind of reconciliation he has made of the perennial conflict between how much time he spends at the office and how much time he devotes to his family. Any discussion about the family leads naturally enough to where they live: this may be an ideal time to discuss the cost of real estate and in so doing determine both his status needs and his financial situation. The size of the home, when he bought it, and by how much it is mortgaged—and, of course, the status of his chosen suburb—all of these things reveal what is going on inside his head and, therefore, how hard he will be prepared to work.

You may care, after the wine has taken full effect, and if the moment is right, to innocently but slightly conspiratorily explore the question of how he regards executives who "fool around a little sometimes." The astute executive will usually turn such an apparent lapse of taste aside with a dry rejoinder: one quick response from a shrewd senior executive was that, although he personally was a family man, he appreciated that there might be truth in the adage that there is a time and place for everything. What can you say to that?

If however, your companion takes your bait and expands upon how he sometimes spends his evenings, you may be on to a fruitful field of inquiry. One executive unfortunately (for him) confessed that every month or so he and his wife sought to recapture the first fine careless rapture of the halcyon days and nights of their intense courtship by checking into a motel and "getting drunk together": a relatively mild pastime but not, perhaps, the most sensitive way to effect an introduction of one's cherished spouse to a potential employer. And, of course, other peccadillos, while they may inspire envy and a lively conversation, may possibly be interpreted to reflect both a lack of aplomb and a less than total commitment to corporate values embracing the puritan ethic. What a man does in his own time may be his own business, but just how much of that time a six-figure executive may legitimately call his own is another matter.

As you watch him partaking of his food, you might also

note whether he clenches his teeth whenever his wife's name is mentioned. Use the lunch-table situation to gauge the emotional temperature of his marriage. You might also explore his upward mobility by discussing the patterns of his home-entertainment schedule and getting him to comment upon the status of his guests. You may also discover that you have mutual acquaintances who have recently dined at his home. Such common friends may subsequently make ideal "second-generation referees" for you to follow up.

VALUES

After you sense you have gleaned as much information as he's likely to divulge on his family situation, you might toss into the conversation an apparently innocent piece of small talk like "Somebody was saying at dinner the other night that Jimmy Carter will go down as the most forgettable president in history."

Such a gambit allows you to make a fairly provocative assertion that need in no way reflect what you really think about President Carter or anything else. The more provocative the better, because your whole intent is to smoke your candidate out. The high-achiever, as we have noted, effortlessly juggles ideas, passing easily from one to the other and back again. Look for this quality. But what will interest you most is any evidence of displaced hostility (especially to an authority figure) and also of any strong personal commitment to opinions running counter to prevailing corporate values that might, in the eyes of your existing management team, invest him with all the appeal of a leper.

DARK SECRETS

As conversation ebbs and flows across the luncheon table, you will also be on the lookout for the dark side of the moon: those details about a candidate's life that he most wants to keep secret. Watch out for dates that don't match, references to companies he's never mentioned before, and, most importantly, watch his eyes and body movements, remembering that mental unease or concern often expresses itself in overt movements of the body. The candidate may suddenly begin shifting his position in his chair before replying, tightly grasp his wine glass, twist his table napkin or, most tellingly of all, unconsciously reach for a cigarette. Technically, this is displacement: his sudden flow of adrenaline has to find some outlet in overt physical activity. His voice may suddenly assume a different tone: it may become lower and more confiding, as though he had been preparing for this moment and wanted to make sure his point got across; or it may momentarily assume a higher quality, indicating a temporary lack of self-control. Most important of all, watch his eyes and his lips, looking out for any fleeting sign of embarrassment or concern.

You may not wish to follow the example of one corporate president who liked to put pressure on a candidate by questioning him on some patently important point when the poor devil had his mouth full of food, and then apologizing for having "caught him with his mouth full." Such a ploy could seem both gratuitous and a little childish: but if you ever do adopt such a tactic it would be appropriate to note whether the candidate handles the questions adroitly in either his adult or parent modes; or whether he tries to charm his way out of the situation with his child. If he chokes, you may infer that he is either mildly afraid or that the fish was not properly filleted.

COUP DE GRACE

If, as the luncheon draws to a close, there is still a niggling doubt in your mind as to whether this candidate really is the *Wunderkind* you've been hoping for, you may wish to exploit the inevitable winding down of tension that the candidate will experience as the dessert order is taken. He will assume that you apparent desire to linger with him over coffee and a small liqueur is a sign that you are now quite simply relaxed in his company. He will naturally unwind, relieved that the "testing" period has been successfully negotiated.

This is the perfect time to introduce the one last delicate question that has so far not been satisfactorily answered. "By the way, how *did* you come to leave the XYZ corporation in such a hurry again?" Don't listen to the answer, watch his eyes.

Finally, dear reader, let me say this: most of the time it will be a relatively straight-forward exercise, with the double purpose being to exchange information and establish goodwill. But, the encounter may be counterproductive if you allow a clever tap-dancer to beguile you with a canny command of restaurantese. You are playing for big stakes, and all of the money on the table is yours. This is a time for both caution and subtlety—and, on occasion, stealth.

If the exercise is successful and you do win a first-rate recruit, then one day, on the afterglow of the extra profits he has generated, you will both give yourselves over to the rich hedonistic pleasures of good food, fine wine, and lively conversation.

But the purpose of the luncheon interview is never rest and recreation. It is business—as serious a business as a visit to the doctor. Except that you are the doctor.

And now we go on to make some house calls.

18. *How to Appraise an Executive and His Spouse— in Their Own Home*

The strength of a nation is derived from the integrity of its homes.

CONFUCIUS

Young wives are the leading asset of corporate power. They want the suburbs, a home, a settled life. And respectability. They want society to see that they have exchanged themselves for something of value.

RALPH NADER

THAT a stable marriage is related to business success seems undeniable. There is a 5 per cent divorce rate among the 179 presidents and chairmen of the 100 top U.S. corporations, and 135 have been married to the same wife for at least twenty-five years.*

Most corporations taking on a senior executive are aware of these statistics and equally aware that the "invisible partner" may become either a corporate asset or a liability. Accordingly, it is not unusual for a senior executive candidate *and* his wife to be routinely appraised, as a team, in their own home.

Should you be in contemplation of such an encounter, you may care to consider the major advantages and insights to be gained from getting a first-hand look at his spouse and his home, its contents, and, in some cases, some of its more exotic cohabitants.

*From the 1979 *Who's Who in America*.

THE SPOUSE

Somebody once said that behind every successful man stands a woman—usually a very surprised mother-in-law. The remark is amusing precisely because it tends to be true. A married executive spends much of his time responding to the expectations of his wife's parents—to the value constellations that they implanted in their daughter's subconscious during childhood.

A wife influences her husband to achieve *her* family destiny along with his own: she unconsciously drives him to attain a level of success equivalent to that of her father. The corporate executive and his wife are thus a thrusting force united not just in the bonds of holy matrimony but also in the pursuit of a place—and possibly a kidney-shaped pool—in the sun.

An ambitious wife is thus a motivating force. She imposes discipline on an executive, pushing him out of bed and off to work, if need be. Macbeth, you will remember, became king in response to the injunction of his ambitious wife: "But screw your courage to the sticking place, and we'll not fail."

Similarly today in the higher levels of management, a wife who is socially at ease and able to mingle with and charm high-status clients and colleagues enhances her husband's upward mobility—sometimes not for the most subtle of reasons. I remember the president of a Hong Kong corporation explaining that in large measure he judged the caliber of an executive by the ability to marry well. Then, after a few drinks, he confided, as a man of the world, that he never asked an executive and his wife to his home unless the woman was sexually attractive. For an executive's wife to be judged unappetizing company may well represent, in such a case, a singular compliment; she may, in fact, have saved her husband, no less than herself, from a possibly embarrassing evening. But there may be other possibly more important parties to which she might also deny him access, with neither her nor her husband quite knowing why.

Equally, an appraisal of the wife will provide a further

insight into the executive's unconscious value constellations and ambitions. Ayn Rand put it very clearly:

A man's sexual choice is the result and sum of his fundamental convictions. Tell me what a man finds sexually attractive and I will tell you his entire philosophy of life.

Accordingly, on the not always erroneous assumption that an executive's wife represents his sexual choice, it will be interesting to probe *her* values in order to establish how she impacts upon her husband and to determine whether or not her expectations are in harmony with your own corporate needs. You can establish whether she is supportive of the move, and of her husband in general. The work of even the greatest recruiter may, after all, be undone by a doubtful wife in bed. One wife, when an attractive position entailing immediate promotion and a substantial increase in salary were detailed, responded incredulously, "You can't be serious—for *him?*"

But such a response is somewhat atypical, and more usually the involvement of the wife in the decision-making process should engender goodwill. The opportunities in the new position may not have been explained as persuasively as might be possible, and your salient answers to her questions or doubts may be very reassuring. Certainly you are telling her that you are taking the whole exercise very seriously, and that the security of her husband and her children, of such paramount interest to her, is no less important to you.

THE HOME

The home interview also enables you to see both the lifestyle the candidate is pledged to maintain and, if you are perceptive, some of the furnishings inside of his head. What you are looking at is *a standard of living that is psychologically acceptable* to the candidate and his spouse. Accordingly, with judicious questioning (and sometimes with no questioning at all) you can determine a lifestyle and comfort level at which the candidate may cease to go on striving: you can literally see (and sometimes smell) what it takes for homeo-stasis to be maintained. If you find that the duo are relatively happy with their nest and neighborhood, then you may infer that a comfort plateau has already been achieved and motivation diminished. On the other hand, if the executive and his wife denigrate their modest dwelling and suggest that they have their eyes upon something more grand in a more socially desirable neighborhood, you may possibly infer that the executive candidate might want to put in long hours in order to be able to afford the Shangri-la of which his loved one dreams.

It is worth noting too that high-achievers do not usually harbor the remains of cannibalized motor vehicles in over-grown, weed-infested yards. Rather they tend to be drawn to high-status neighborhoods where the barbecue parties are more likely to include socially advantageous contacts and the opportunity to keep upset with a better class of Joneses.

In such an environment the home of an ambitious executive will usually reflect both the agony and ecstasy of the puritan ethic—wide green lawns to be maintained, two or three cars to be financed and fueled, handsome children to be clothed, fed, and pushed through prestigious colleges—and so on.

Small things, as we have noted, can reveal whole value constellations. While the quality of the *objets d'art* and such trivialities as whether the wall hangings are prints or originals will be of minor interest, you may, nonetheless, be somewhat cautioned at the sight of prominently placed portraits of Lenin or Mao Tse-tung.

Items revealing of blue-chip corporate values may include a den for the candidate's evening work load and facilities reflect-ing both the capacity and the desire to entertain and impress important contacts and clients. Possibly, should you need to "wash your hands," you might even glimpse the nuptial chamber. Whether a couple chooses to sleep together or in separate beds will be purely a matter of taste and, quite possi-bly, none of your business. But if an ambitious executive and his young wife choose to occupy separate rooms, there may be a deeper reason. A corporate executive will obviously want to work harder if he is deeply pledged to the value of the middle-class family unit. Any suggestion of a spartan lifestyle may also indicate less than a total dedication to capitalism and the consumer society.

Since the whole situation will be relatively unstructured, it will also be interesting to gauge the candidate's ability to dominate a group by observing the degree of control exerted over his offspring. Drawing a child into the conversation may seem a little Machiavellian, but one executive is reported to have missed a major promotion because his eleven-year-old daughter evilly confided to a recruiter that "Daddy sat up late last night working on a case of Scotch."

OTHER COHABITANTS

Exactly who else lives in the house will also be of more than passing interest. If it is revealed that the wife's mother is a more or less permanent guest, then you might be excused for inferring that the candidate's ability to relocate is limited. On the brighter side, if you get the chance to exchange small talk with the lady, you may anticipate that the executive might be willing to sacrifice a great deal of his private time in the pursuit of overseas assignments.

Dr. McMurry relates a particularly interesting case in which a home interview revealed relevant information that had not been uncovered during the normal course of office interviewing and checking. The position entailed extensive home entertainment by the successful appointee, and one candidate seemed impeccable until, during the home interview, a rhythmic thumping was observed to emanate from the lounge-room ceiling. Since the interviewer and all of the immediate family seemed to be in the room, an inquiry was initiated as to the source of the disquieting sound.

It turned out to be a psychotic sister-in-law who, when guests came, had to be kept locked in her room: apparently the family budget hadn't stretched to private care, or, possibly for humanitarian reasons, the executive candidate and his wife had decided to keep the loved one under their own protective custody. But it was felt that the enclosure might seriously hamper the capacity of the executive to entertain corporate clients within an ambience conducive to a continuing relationship, and he missed the job.

CLOSING THE ENCOUNTER

The home interview need not take terribly long, and sometimes you will know more than is necessary to make a decision shortly upon crossing the threshold. Certainly you would not wish to unduly trespass or intrude into what an Englishman so fondly calls his castle. Where you are satisfied that the candidate is an executive of high caliber, both the time and the venue may be appropriate to suggest that, following settlement of final negotiations, a ritual luncheon with the members of the senior executive team at a truly first-class restaurant would be in order. His wife should certainly perceive that her husband is held in the highest esteem.

The departure could perhaps then be effected in a large, black, chauffeured limousine, to leave the tantalizing impression with both parties that the decision about to be reached will confer entry to a new, exciting, luxurious lifestyle at a higher stratum of society. That, in short, you are offering, not just a job, but fulfillment—a point of departure, and arrival, in style.

19. *How to Detect the Dishonest Candidate*

I went and lied; and I'm paying the price for that lack of will power.

JOHN EHRLICHMAN

GROUCHO MARX said that the best way to tell if a man is honest is to ask him. If he says he is, you know he is a crook. That may not be far from the truth, but if you really want to confirm either a candidate's dishonesty or veracity, the *best* way to go about it is to carefully and as a matter of routine verify every scrap of information that he has given you. You will also want answers to some very simple common-sense questions: Does he add up? Does he seem to make good common sense? Are there the few blemishes that you would normally expect? Or does he claim to be perfect?

The perfect executive, the polished performer with answers so good as to seem rehearsed, repays careful study. It is possible that he has attended a job-counseling session and honed his answers on video equipment. But if he has to rehearse in order to be himself, he may be nobody.

Always check out the apparently superb candidate, *particularly* if you like him. Information routinely available at the time of appraisal may not be as readily forthcoming *after* the decision to hire has been taken, and the bonds of marriage forged.

In one recent instance, the potential general manager of a Scandinavian motor distributor had gotten to final interview before, as the result of cold-blooded detective work, it came to

203

light that eighteen years previously he had gone into business on his own and six months later gone into liquidation: a fact that he had at no time mentioned during detailed discussions with the client, who saw this as a signal betrayal of trust and terminated negotiations forthwith.

Here are some pointers on how to actually check what a candidate tells you—and also a few things he might have overlooked:

VERIFY ACADEMIC CREDENTIALS AT THE SOURCE

Phone or write to the candidate's college to check whether he graduated, and in what year. Anyone who had bothered to check the illustrious alma mater of that famous forger David Begelman, former president of Columbia Pictures, would have discovered that the master's degree from Yale that embroidered his entry in *Who's Who* did not exist within the university files. Mr. Begelman had a splendid imagination, of course, an attribute to which he doubtless owed much of his subsequent success. However, he subsequently progressed from deceit to embezzlement, and so a moral can, perhaps, be drawn.

My own favorite liar is "Doctor" Bob Harris, the New York radio and television meteorologist, whose doctorate qualification existed only on his résumé and in his own head. His employer took him at his word but, upon uncovering the lie, very properly fired him. What I most admire about the dissimulating doctor is his choice of a career, forecasting the weather, because who could possibly accuse you of incompetence? *Everybody's* wrong about the weather.

INTERPRET THE WRITTEN REFERENCES

Norman Mailer's book *Advertisements for Myself* is an apposite description of most written references: only a masochist would knowingly offer a poor one. But, to the practiced eye, negative inferences may be drawn from the following:

1. Dog-eared notes from neighbors, relatives, or members of the lay clergy. (Everyone has at least three friends.)
2. Immaculate recommendations upon the engraved stationery of prominent politicians. The safe bet is that the candidate is misdirecting you to the personage and away from his employment record.
3. References from past employers that:
   - Suggest you contact the writer for further information. (Do so immediately.)
   - Are mere certificates of employment (which is all, by law, that they are required to give).
   - Praise his personality but omit mention of his work habits.
   - Mention any "unfortunate circumstances surrounding his decision to leave."
   - Say that he "chose to resign" (reflects an ultimatum).
   - Refer to an "unfortunate personality clash."
   - Are positive paeans of voluminous praise for years of service and devotion. (Find an objective source and a good reason for his "decision" to leave.)
   - Refer to his "extraordinary capacity to handle detailed work." (Usually a euphemism for a total lack of common sense.)
   - Are signed by a former peer. (His supervisor didn't have anything good to say.)

Positive inferences *may* be taken from references from a previous employer that:

- Refer specifically to "industry," "dedication," "ability to work as a team member," and *consistent* competence."
- Say that "he chose to leave entirely of his own accord and we would definitely reemploy him."
- Recommend him "totally without qualification."

But check the documentation carefully. I once noticed that a candidate had produced three glowing references from different employers each of whom had misspelt the word *conscientious*. Which is good reason, whatever the notepaper says, to call the signatory and verify everything.

INTERPRETING REFERENCES BY TELEPHONE

This too is an art. The advantage of the telephone is that your call can probe back into the past like a long, sharp needle reaching distant lands, person to person, with the operator working for you. It is always wise to contact at least two people: the candidate's immediate superior and, possibly, the chief executive.

If you are shuttled to the personnel department, it is unlikely that you will discover very much. But, those records that are available should at least be meticulous and provide an accurate verification of dates, titles, and salaries.

In speaking to a superior, you should:

- Identify yourself and your firm, and say that your candidate has asked (or at least given his permission) for you to contact the referee. To establish your *bona fides,* you should offer him the choice of calling you back.
- Confirm the referee's title and relationship to the candidate during the period of employment. This is not always easy. One candidate received a glowing telephone reference from the president of a small company who had subtly terminated the *Wunderkind*. This apparent conflict was reconciled by discovery that the referee was praising the character of his only daughter's husband.
- Begin by verifying facts—titles and dates—and then, with the dialogue flowing, try to elicit material of a judgmental nature.

You should be aware that any bias in a telephone reference usually favors the candidate. In an attempt to counter this I often explain: *"I am calling on behalf of a ruthless client who will possibly fire the candidate if he fails to make the grade and so, humanitarian reasons aside, I would greatly value your candor."*

Finally, two questions should always be asked: "Was Mr. X's work of *consistently* high standard? Would you reemploy him?"

Answers to that last question are predictable and may be interpreted thus:

- "Yes, possibly, but in another role." There are problems.
- "We don't rehire anyone." Probably there are problems.
- "I'd need to think on that." Possibly quite serious problems.
- "I couldn't really say." I'm possibly terrified to say.
- "Um. Ah. Um." I don't *know* what to say.
- "I think we possibly would." Might be okay.
- "Yes." Is okay, possibly.
- "We'd love to have him back, today." Is wonderful—perhaps.

THE SENTENCE OF DEATH

Sometimes a telephone check will reveal in an employer the mood expressed so well by Lady Bracknell.

At times such as this, Mr. Worthing, it becomes more than a moral duty to speak one's mind: it becomes a pleasure.

Subsequently the unfortunate candidate may be subjected to a withering piece of character assassination. In such cases it is *always* necessary to check another employer. There *are* genuine personality clashes from time to time, and it has not been unknown for a personal vendetta to affect the judgment and integrity of a telephone referee. However, the immediate inference is that strong words do not reflect terribly well on either party.

RUN A CREDIT AGENCY CHECK

People who have personally dealt with the candidate on a business basis can very quickly reflect the esteem with which he is regarded, whether he keeps his word, and what *sort* of person he is, as well as personal problems that he had forgotten to mention—marital separations, bounced checks, unfortunate drinking problems, possibly even periods of incarceration in mental institutions.

Presidential candidate George McGovern, you will recall, renounced his running mate Senator Thomas Eagleton when it was revealed that the senator had, indeed, been in a mental institution. Such a fact, you would feel, should have been in the forefront of the mind of a candidate for a position only one heartbeat removed from the hot button that could put us all out of business. But Senator Eagleton "forgot" to mention the fact: "My health," he said, "just wasn't on my mind. It was like a broken leg that had healed."

A minor matter to the senator, but exactly the sort of information that neighbors and friends tend to recall with extreme clarity, especially to strangers. Frankly, the "lapse of memory" on its own was hardly the mark of a shrewd politician; and surely not inspiring of trust in the heart of George McGovern.

VISIT A PAST EMPLOYER

As far as employers go, this is about the best you can do. But you should be prepared to travel to another city or even another country if the job is senior enough, because you'll be rewarded with accurate and expansive information, plus nuances and subtleties otherwise impossible to glean. If there are two people in one room, watch for meaningful glances. Don't make notes during the discussion, but do make them immediately after you leave.

Once in such a situation, a previously cagey referee informed me that the candidate was "a lazy son of a bitch who I never got to do a good day's work." I could see why.

20. *Secrets of Psychological Testing and Its Place in Executive Appraisal— in a Nutshell*

We look back now at personality testing slightly incredulous at its colonialist mentality and its banality of concepts, wondering how we could have been taken in by its promises of penetration and mastery.

THOMAS H. FITZGERALD*

FROM its zenith in the 1950s, psychological testing has fallen into the shadowy netherland of graphology, astrology, and phrenology. Yet even today some otherwise quite level-headed managers tend to be awed by the concept of "scientific" personality testing. And, paradoxically, the whole subject also tends to be invested with the inherent appeal of the occult.

In fact, most psychological tests are based upon about as much science as a witch doctor's curse; but, of course, if you believe in the power of the curse, it may kill you. We wouldn't want that to happen, and the best way to see that it doesn't is to expose some of the superstitions surrounding the subject to the bright light of day.

Perhaps the most extravagant and beguiling claim of the witch doctor is that a purportedly "objective" personality test can be administered by virtually anyone—that ticks in little boxes can be scientifically analyzed by a computer to accurately predict executive success, thus relieving management of

Harvard Business Review (July/August 1971).

the need to make a decision. (And if the fellow subsequently fails, it was, of course, the computer's fault.)

Such tests are, in fact, notoriously inaccurate and inherently susceptible to misuse precisely *because* the test is claimed to be objective and requiring virtually no interpretation. This promise—the Achilles heel of such a test—is exactly the feature that its devotees (who usually have a pecuniary interest in the sale of tests) are prone to draw attention; and it is also that which holds the most fascination for the layman. And even if the test salesman could get you to believe that the test was right more often than it was wrong, he would still be unable to prove that, in any particular case, it was either right *or* wrong. In consequence, any decision to accept or reject any particular candidate on the basis of a test score *always* carries a relatively high statistical probability of being wrong.

Projective personality tests, on the other hand, such as the Rorschach Inkblot, the Thematic Apperception Test (a series of bland illustrations), or the McMurry Sentence Completion Questionnaire, can be moderately useful when interpreted by a qualified person. These tests invite the subject to tell what he "sees" in an inkblot, an illustration, or an incompleted sentence. In so doing he necessarily records random and possibly subconscious responses that may be revealing of motivations that he himself does not fully comprehend.

For example, one recently married Englishman gave carefully bland answers (which are revealing on their own) to all but one of the questions. "My greatest fear," he could not stop his superego from recording, "is that I will be unable to father a child." It was subsequently discovered that he was a transvestite.

A projective test is, in many ways, an extension of an interview. A candidate's values are elicited, enabling his personality to be interpreted from his generalized responses. And since interpretation is necessarily a matter of judgment, the decision-making process is pushed to where it belongs—out of a computer and onto the desk of a senior executive with the courage to make a decision.

Intelligence tests present problems when it comes to appraising executives, and I am not in favor of asking an executive to take an intelligence test for three reasons. First, there is no necessary correlation between high intelligence and good judgment, and some intellectually gifted people lack any capacity whatsoever to make executive decisions. Second, you can painlessly establish how smart an executive is simply by studying his record. That he completed a *bona fide* college degree is an infinitely better guide to his level of intelligence—and his motivation—than practically any test result. From there it becomes a matter of looking at his work performance to see how well he actually handled the various assignments that he undertook. Third, the whole concept of intelligence testing is inflammatory and now has so many EEOC implications that you might just as well steer clear of the whole subject.

If you want three quick commonsense yardsticks that will help you to determine intelligence during a routine appraisal, may I suggest that you analyze all information in terms of *fact, form,* and *content.*

That a person graduated from college with certain grades is a matter of *fact* that you can go on to verify. The *form* in which a candidate presents information about himself—particularly if he has prepared his own résumé—will also allow a further insight. And the *content* of his discussion—his ideas, concepts and choice of language—all necessarily reflect his intelligence. The use of jargon is always revealing because it commonly clothes either a weak abstract intelligence, or a lack of genuine insight.

On its own, *any* form of psychological testing, however sophisticated, and whatever the qualification of the interpreter, is like trying to guess what a person looks like by studying his shadow: results vary according to the position of the diagnostician, the quarry, and the sun.

The *best* way, as I have noted, to predict what anyone will do, is not merely to study the shadow of what he says but, instead, to lift your eyes to the reality of where he came from, what he has been doing, and where he is now. This is the entire rationale behind the McMurry patterned interview procedures that Wareham Associates uses with statistically validated success throughout the world.

21. *How to Choose and Use a Headhunter*

When choosing between two evils, I always like to take the one I've never tried before.

MAE WEST

Make sure the firm you choose is capable of conducting a thorough search. This is not as simple as it sounds, because a seemingly innocuous rule of the code of the Association of Executive Recruiting Consultants precludes a headhunter from the dubious, though not entirely unknown, practice of "working both sides of the street." The code states that AERC members shall not approach the executive talent of a client for a vacancy with any other client for a period of two years after completing a search.

You can readily see, therefore, that the larger a search firm becomes the greater too must be its off-limits list, because it is denied access to an increasingly significant market sector and thus is forced to "search" from a diminishing market. Finally, it may become impossible to deliver on a claim to source and tap that one *best* candidate. It is, I think, a significant failing, and one that fetters both the big-name, large-volume operators, and also specialist houses that cover only one industry.

Gerry Roche, president of Heidrick & Struggles, a major search firm, recently confirmed that two thousand companies were "off limits" to his firm; and one of his former partners, who subsequently quit, said that "Half of the leads I should have been following up, I couldn't." Obviously, several other major companies are in a similar position.

On the other hand, such firms are deluged with unsolicited résumés from executives who are, for one reason or another, casting about. Boyden Associates, the large and prestigious organization that began the whole business under the superlative baton of the late Sidney Boyden, says that it now fills one third of its assignments from candidates who were already on file when the assignment was received. Whether or not sifting your own files constitutes a search may be a moot point, but in some cases it is the best that can be done.

It is also paradoxical that if, to gain advantage of its inside knowledge, you choose a firm specializing in your industry, you may be denied access to precisely those candidates you most want to reach. This is because "specialist" status, by definition, depends upon working for many or most of the major names in a particular industry. Thus, with the best will in the world, specialist firms, like the high-volume operators, may be precluded from making *precisely* the most vital contacts, and can only "reach in" to corporations with whom no client-consultant relationship is sustained. The best short list, as a result, can only be "best" in terms of these particular ethical—and, I can tell you, very practical—constraints.

The whole dilemma is exacerbated by the fact that some canny clients now assign each of the big-name firms one search every two years as "pirating insurance."

It was for these reasons that, early on, I determined that small is beautiful, and also made a conscious decision to service relatively few blue-chip clients *operating in diverse industries.* To those clients we also complement our search services with the *McMurry Communications Grid,* a system that subtly pinpoints incompetent executives and ticklish organizational problems.*

As a result of my decision, none of our offices has a staff of more than a dozen. In New York at the moment we operate with half that number. But don't, please,

*The grid, if you are interested, is fully detailed in the *Harvard Business Review* article, "Clear Communications for Chief Executives" of March/April 1965.

feel any sympathy at my forbearance: in every way it is a blessing to accept only the caliber of client who chooses to dine upon *haute cuisine* from an exclusive restaurant in return for his not insubstantial investment. As in sailing, the bigger the yacht, the greater the problems. The pleasures of running, on an international basis, a small, tight ship are many indeed.

Certainly we still receive a stream of unsolicited résumés for our own computer files, and often we *can* place a candidate from our file sources. Additionally, these contacts can be very useful leads to other and sometimes fatter fish for, when you really want to find a man like Brown, there's only one way to do it: follow every lead, turn every stone, shake every tree, and lift the lid on every one of your client's competitors. It's not a business for the faint-hearted and, if I were a client, my first question to a headhunter would certainly be, "Which avenues are already closed to you?"

Ask to meet the individual who will be handling your assignment. Take a long hard look at him. Imagine that you are on trial for your life and that your destiny now depends upon his silver tongue. Imagine he is your advocate about to deliver the summation of your case to an unsympathetic jury. Will he rise to the occasion? Will he press your cause with skill, subtlety, and honeyed words? Does he have the magical ability to create empathy? Will the jurors like him and want to agree with him? Or will you go to the gallows while he and they go home to an early dinner?

From the very outset this fellow will determine the fate of your search: the tone of his voice, the choice of his words, and the doggedness of his commitment will decide the number and quality of candidates prepared to toss their hats into the ring to the point of even *discussing* your vacancy. His initial failures, like those of a clumsy surgeon, will simply be buried. If he tells you that a prospect he contacted was "not interested," he may be telling the truth. However, it may also be that, *as the proposition was put,* it didn't *sound* interesting. Or perhaps that the headhunter was a dull fellow who couldn't make *anything* sound interesting. Two suitors may proffer the same blandishments in pursuit of a mate yet, for reasons that are not entirely incomprehensible, she will reward the one and reject the other.

My own experience is that, like a healthy girl raised in the cloisters of a convent, virtually all *good* executives, though they may be coy upon first encounter, are nonetheless susceptible to coaxing. Indeed, if a persuasive case is put, nine out of ten of the executives I most want to meet are able to find the time to get together either over lunch or for a drink.

This is not a matter of working magic but simply of explaining that "I'd very much like to get together with you because, even if this position doesn't interest you, I think I may have something bigger coming up very soon." Unless I'm winking at a blind horse, it is rarely impossible to get him to a drinking hole: and, once there, of course, to make him water.

Slide past the front man. The peculiarly American way of sifting search firms is to troop them in one after another and attempt to outfox some poor devil by asking him to state the weaknesses of his company. Certain clients also seem to imagine that the caliber of a search firm can be gauged entirely from the quality of its first ambassador.

Well, I don't believe that to be entirely true. In wooing a new client, the search firm will send along its *best* front man; a fellow quite commonly on first-name terms with airline captains of three continents (and who may look rather like an airline captain himself). *He,* I can promise you, will have a tongue as silver as his hair, and a thoroughly rehearsed answer for your every question. But when he leaves to sell his firm's service to one of your competitors, a blue-eyed, two-dimensional MBA may be left to pick up the pieces—your pieces.

What will you do if you are wise to take the fellow to be assigned to your search out to lunch. Ask no difficult questions—just give him three martinis, a good bottle of wine, and a decent meal. Then, over the crème caramel and brandy, casually ask about some of his clients. Zero in on exactly who was placed where and *why.* Keep it light but keep him talking.

See if he tells you more than you have a right to know. If a competitor's dirty linen is aired, then be assured that one day you too may suffer a similar fate. The more information you get, the more desperate the fellow may be for your custom, and the wiser you may be to place it elsewhere.

I tend, I must confess, to remain almost embarrassingly tight-lipped about both my clients and the assignments with which we are entrusted. Since much of that information is inevitably of an intimate nature, I tend to feel that we should keep it to ourselves.

Discover the qualification of the person who will appraise your candidates. In terms of the real world, a client places a very heavy burden on a headhunter at the end of a demanding assignment if he asks him to appraise—sometimes in effect, to shoot down—the very candidates he has so assiduously courted. But to neglect obtaining such a final assessment can generate long-term problems.

Recently, the president of a major New York securities house abruptly handed in his resignation after only a nine-month tenure. He had been unable to cope with the combined stress of his relocation from California to New York and the demands of his new job, while at the same time separating from his wife. "Why did you not say you were having marital problems when we first interviewed you?" inquired the chairman of his departing president. "Because," came the reply "nobody asked me." Obviously, for such a position, somebody *ought* to have asked him—and I think the onus for the oversight lay squarely with the headhunter.

Unfortunately, it is not unknown for appraisals to be carried out by the semiretired partner who loves to spend the autumn of his years on the golf course rather than in lengthy interviews. Such an individual is sometimes prone to that hardening of the arteries known to afflict a successful advertising agency—a stultifying sense of *déjà vu* that induces him to believe he can determine the competence of a candidate inside of five minutes. Then, depending upon how the day has been planned, he may either cut the interview short and head for the first tee, or, if he *likes* the candidate, simply tell a few stories over coffee, accept some incoming phone calls, check his watch, and suggest either an early lunch or a quick drink to celebrate.

Much potential bad blood between client and search firm would remain unspilt if more clients utilized appraisal specialists to screen the final list. I don't say this just because my own firm is called upon to provide specialist appraisal services, but because poor appraisal is probably *the* major factor in subsequent on-the-job failure.

In New York I like to see virtually every candidate being seriously considered for a key position. And if there's a doubt on anyone, we're doubly fortunate in being able to seek the second and always canny opinion of Dr. McMurry.

Of course, you may also want to rely upon the appraisal of your own personnel department. But objective advice from within your own organization is, by definition, hard to come by: and sometimes it is precisely the candidate that your subordinates *don't* like whom you should be hiring.

Ask how the search firm charges. The best, I am afraid, charge the most. And not only that, but they do not work on a contingency basis either: a fee is payable whether or not the search is terminated for any reason.

The reason for this is that you are retaining the headhunter to invest his *time.* He can only devote that time unflinchingly, and thereby cover all of the leads, if he knows that he is going to be paid for that trouble. The temptation for the contingency operator—and also, I fear, for the search firm forced to rely upon its data bank—is simply to check the files and offer you the most likely candidate available from that one source. If you don't like, or won't take, Hobson's choice, the consultant may of economic necessity have to move on quickly to an easier assignment that *will* guarantee a placement fee.

But sometimes, I have to tell you, the headhunter may conduct an exhaustive search yet still not effect a placement. Usually this will be because his client's needs have changed, causing the search to be terminated. On other occasions no suitably qualified candidate may exist—yet, paradoxically, even that piece of intelligence may justify the cost of the search.

Consider the example of a president in contemplation of closing a sick division. Is there, he wonders—before I take the last drastic decision to fire a thousand people—somebody, somewhere, with the exact technical skills and leadership ability who is prepared to risk his reputation in attempting to administer the kiss of life to my dying princess? A tall order, with about a 10 percent chance of success. But possibly, weighing the stakes against the odds, still worth the cost of a worldwide search.

Search fees are typically 25 to 35 percent of the guaranteed annual income attaching to the position being filled. They are not infrequently payable one third as a retainer at the outset, one third at the end of thirty days, and one third after sixty days. Out-of-pocket expenses are, or course, extra—and usually run to about 10–20 percent of the fee itself—sometimes more.

The "front-end retainer" is justified because much of the work is done in the first month, where determining the specification, researching the market, and initiating the most vital contacts can be handled fairly quickly. After that there can be a gestation period of up to six months—sometimes even longer—before the baby is delivered, but commonly a search is completed inside sixty days.

The cost, though, compared to the value of someone like Brown, is nothing. What would Rumpelstiltskin be prepared to pay to find someone to spin him gold? A pretty penny, I can tell you.

Choose someone you can trust. Like a doctor, your headhunter is in a position to gain insights into your corporation that you cannot always see for yourself. But such insights may require that you remove much of your clothing: good chemistry is, therefore, as vital between you and your headhunter as it is between you and your most trusted colleagues—and even more so if you want your search firm to objectively appraise those colleagues.

Sometimes, indeed, such an appraisal may be integral to the whole process. We were once asked by a *vice-president* of finance to find an "ambitious, aggressive executive capable, in time, of assuming my chair." What happened was that over lunch the *president* interviewed and hired the candidate whom we referred, and then at three-thirty fired the vice-president.

Talk to a couple of their clients. Ask to be given the names of two or three companies for whom your proposed search firm has recently completed assignments. Call and see how these were handled. Were time and care taken in developing the specifications? Did they talk to the relevant members of the existing team to determine the chemistry? Did they *really* conduct a search, or was the job simply filled from their files? Did their appraisal of the candidates seem accurate? A truly satisfied client—someone who enjoys his meal and doesn't suffer for it the next day—is the best endorsement of any search firm.

You can also tell a lot about the caliber of a search firm from the caliber of the contact, and the clients whom it offers you as referees. But you need to be careful here, because at least one New York search firm pays a substantial "referral fee" to anyone who is able to deliver a search assignment—and it has not, I regret to advise, been unknown, one way or another, for a referee to be on the payroll.

HOW TO BE A GOOD CLIENT

Be candid and expect candor. Having assured yourself that your consultant is trustworthy, you should tell him, as precisely as possible, the style of individual who would be most compatible with your organization. Detail the delicate areas, indicating both problems and pecking orders. Explain both the good *and* the bad in the position. Give the absolute top remuneration figure for a good candidate. Holding back vital information now could mean losing, or simply failing to contact top-caliber candidates who might well be interested. At the end of the road, money might not be the final enticement, but it is good bait for the hook.

It is particularly important to allow your consultant to elicit the vital information he needs to draw his specifications because these must, if the search is to be a success, reflect not merely a monochrome of facts and figures, but also the more subtle colors of your corporation's chemistry.

Such candor is, I lament, not always forthcoming. Where corporate self-image is on the line, some clients are prone to profile paragons of unattainable virtue and prowess. It may, indeed, be explained that the present corporate team comprises *only* such dynamic self-starters, ambitious almost (but not quite) to a fault. And when executive team members are present, the meeting can sometimes degenerate into an almost tribal ritual, at which the tom-toms most clearly signal a primal need to protect their own turf, rather than provide an accurate description of the vacancy.

Under such circumstances, it can take considerable tact on the part of a headhunter to determine both the parameters of the task and the profile of an acceptable personality that might actually exist this side of Saint Peter's gate. At such a moment your consultant may fear that his notes are beginning to describe the animal that is the anathema of every headhunter in the business—the dreaded wild goose. Yet he may also feel rather like an employee of Samuel Goldwyn responding to that delightful Goldwynism, "I want some one to tell me the truth—even though it costs him his job."

In such cases my own candor has not always been appreciated and has, indeed, cost me many a short-term fee. But it has sometimes been a pleasure to be called back later after some fellow with a fainter heart than mine has made promises he was unable to keep.

To get full value from your headhunter, you must also allow him to feel confident, when he begins to be in a position to refer candidates to you, that he may frankly apprise you of a candidate's flaws without evoking a kneejerk rejection of that candidate from you. For if your headhunter believes you are unrealistic in your expectations—that you are, in short, looking for unattainable perfection—then he may feel compelled to be less than utterly candid with you and hedge when giving you his professional opinion of likely candidates. And that, ultimately, would be undermining of the very relationship of mutual trust which you should both be striving to establish.

Don't expect perfection. This point can stand re-emphasis. Perfect executives do not exist on this side of your shaving mirror. The best to hope for is that the flaws in your candidate are comparatively minor and that his strengths outweigh his weaknesses. Technical expertise is important, but it is difficult to make a specialist into a generalist, whereas a highly motivated, emotionally secure executive will usually master virtually any task to which he turns his mind.

Set a realistic time-frame. The more time you have, the better. The research and the initial legwork can be handled quickly by a good operator. But getting together with candidates in order to screen them can sometimes take considerable time, simply because the *best* candidates are rarely panting to switch. The precise individual you would most like to meet will tend to value his present job and its demands way ahead of talking to a headhunter.

Such a candidate is often worth waiting to meet and, if you do not allow him the time he needs, he may gain the impression that you are *desperate,* which could make him feel even more happy with his present employer. Finding the caliber of candidate you would be happy to take as a colleague is akin to choosing a wife. It may be done quickly, or it may take time: that will depend upon the circumstances and the chemistry. But it should never be entered into lightly. *Having* to move fast is not the best way to begin any relationship. .

Don't tip your hand. Once you have employed a search firm, you should allow it to follow all leads, to contact all prospects. If you make any calls yourself, you reveal your hand and render the search more difficult. Mystery is a key ingredient in attracting good candidates. The inference that your job has already been "hawked all over town" can result from just one injudiciously placed phone call.

Don't involve more people than are necessary in the search process. I can't give you a formula for success, but I can give you a formula for failure: try to please everybody. Even a gift horse would get edgy if everyone was inspecting his teeth, or whatever.

Don't try to recruit Brown. Brown, you will remember, is gone. His wife would probably have told you that he was, anyway, a difficult and vain fellow, a fidgety limelighter whose hypermania killed him. And what worked for Brown, is one organization, might not work for you in yours. Brown, let's be honest about it, might have been a one-man woman. You and he might *detest* each other. There will be another Brown, but he will have a name and style all of his own.

Stay involved in the process yourself. Clemenceau said that war is too important to be left to the generals. In business the selection of key executives is too important for you not to be involved in yourself. Where a subordinate knows that you will inspect his final choice, he is less likely to recruit people *he* can dominate. Your involvement is also a compliment that will very often attract a higher caliber of candidate.

Don't let your own prejudices limit the scope of the search. The president of one very prestigious finance company said no to a superbly qualified candidate that I had referred to him. I was surprised and asked why. "Too short," he said. "Too *short?*" I queried, drawing myself to my full five feet nine inches: "He's the same height as me." "Ah, yes," said the president, "but I have always believed that the public should look up to anyone in finance." *He,* of course, stood six feet three inches in his long black hose.

While it is vital to have good chemistry, you should, nonetheless, hold your prejudices up to the window every once in a while. Otherwise, you may reject a possibly outstanding candidate with whom, but for a minor adjustment inside *your* head, you could have worked very harmoniously.

Sailing taught me, better than anyone ever could, that you *can* work with people from disparate backgrounds. In order to win I had to recruit people of whom at first sight I was doubtful, but who were, nonetheless, good at their jobs. And I had, I must confess, to leave a couple of very compatible colleagues on the dock. If you're sailing, you need sailors. Friends you'll have a lot of when you win.

Establish the extent to which you wish to be involved, and keep the channels of communication open. Some clients, after the specifications have been drawn, have neither time nor inclination to hear a detailed ongoing saga of the search process. They take the view that we have been retained as professionals and that we should not waste their time with small talk, but instead quietly and efficiently get on with the research, make the contacts, and screen the prospects. Only at the time of referral do they wish us to stay closely in touch, in order to bring about a meeting of the minds, to conduct final appraisals, and ultimately to tie a red ribbon around the whole package, as it were. Such an approach can work extremely well where a bond of mutual trust and respect has been established.

Other clients are like the girl in the dentist's chair who wanted to have some reasonable degree of influence over the filling of her cavities. As the dentist reached for his high-speed drill, she loosened his zipper, insinuated her delicate fingers around extremely sensitive parts of his anatomy, looked deeply into his eyes, and intoned sweetly, "We're not going to hurt each other, are we?"

I suggest that you establish your preferred style at the outset of the search. But, please, stay in touch and, if the specification changes or it *looks* as if you might possibly want to terminate the search, say so immediately.

Talk to a prospect as soon as your headhunter asks you. Asking a high-caliber candidate to cool his heels is likely to give him cold feet. Good executives don't just play hard to get—they *are* hard to get. An initial meeting needn't take more than twenty minutes, maybe less. What it does is to establish that you are serious in your courtship and that you are decisive:

by moving quickly you flatter the candidate and render him susceptible to subsequent stroking. A good candidate is like a faithful wife—very nervous about this fling, and likely to call the whole thing off at the first sign of discourtesy.

You should remember too that a really first-rate headhunter, like a pedigreed bloodhound, may sometimes catch the scent of his quarry, that one *best* candidate, in a relatively brief period of time. If he is wise, the subsequent referral will generate a psychic tempo and momentum that, like the tide, should be taken at the flood.

If, after that moment, you ask to see more candidates simply for comparative purposes—merely to assure yourself that the executive you have just sighted really is as good as he seems—then be prepared to move swiftly indeed. A beautiful woman at a masked ball will never be wanting for partners, and her gaze, once lost, may never be regained.

Nothing, believe me, is more frustrating to a headhunter than to see a superbly qualified candidate lost simply because the client wouldn't respond fast enough at a critical moment. To move at such a moment is to win the game. Failure to move may see it fade as quickly as winter twilight.

22. *How Ethical Is Headhunting?*

Grub first, then ethics.
BERTOLT BRECHT

I STARTED out thinking ethics was a place in England that retired lawyers used as a tax haven. Now I realize it is a word that inevitably heralds a doubtful practice. I am reminded of the remark that, when a dinner guest speaks of his integrity, we should count our spoons.

I shall not assail your sensibilities by pretending that ethical problems do not exist in headhunting. They do, and they are of no less significance than those that abound in law, stockbroking or virtually any field of business. But in headhunting, of course, at the very center of most ethical questions, is the whole *raison d'être* of the search firm: to promote job mobility, to subvert the status quo, to disseminate information that some people would prefer never to get out, to promote a brand of what could be called disloyalty . . . to *procure* attractive job candidates.

The persistent dilemma of the search consultant is established by the promise to his client that he will unearth the one very *best* candidate in the marketplace. In fulfilling this charter, somebody may get hurt—it may be the market competitor who loses a top executive, or the executive candidate may himself be disadvantaged by moving when he ought to have stayed put.

THE COMPETITOR CORPORATION

You need not linger in sympathizing with a corporation that loses its key executives. Indeed, should a close competitor

226

lose a key executive, you may choose to console him with the Roman philosophy: *Uno avulso non deficit ulter,* "When one is torn away, another succeeds."

As you will be aware, the headhunter is not and never was the only agent of discontent. Writing about the new breed of executive, Walter Guzzardi, Jr., observed that "The agreements between modern man and modern organization are not like the laws of the Medes and the Persians. They were not made to stand forever."

The business jungle is, after all, not the golf course, where you can always find another partner or put down another ball. But you cannot afford to be so cavalier or gentlemanly in business, where the competition is playing for keeps and may want to seize both your low-handicap partner and your apparently magical spheres as well. The best way to avoid losing anyone or anything in business is to ensure that good people are properly rewarded so that the grass on the other side of the avenue cannot be painted greener than it is. As in calling "Fore!" at golf, the shrillest cry of "Ethics!" usually comes from a president who plays an amateur game: someone who attempts to boost sagging morale with Dale Carnegie homilies and stale jokes.

Good executives quit not for money but for the *satisfaction* of sailing on a boat that looks as if it will win. To hold such executives, a corporate president must ensure that his own performance is first-rate, that *purpose and prestige* are gained from being part of his team. If the boat is a loser, serious crew members can be excused for wanting to leave, no matter how good the conditions.

THE EXECUTIVE CANDIDATE

What *is* highly questionable in ethical terms is the propriety of actively trying to make a previously happy and apparently settled executive unhappy with his existing lot.

In attempting to unlock an outstanding candidate from his present employ, the headhunter is, in fact, an active agent of discontent. By pointing out the many benefits offered by his client, he is consciously inviting the candidate to make a clear-cut—and invidious—comparison with his present employer. He is sowing what Dietrich Bonhoeffer called the "pernicious seeds of discontent," whispering softly in the candidate's ear that, not only could he be making more money, but didn't he think he *ought* to be making more money? For the purpose of enticing a "candidate" for his client—and fulfilling the terms of his assignment—the headhunter, by appealing to the candidate's pride and sense of self-respect, is consciously seeking to disturb that candidate's equilibrium and peace of mind—all in the higher interests of his client.

And even though the candidate may decide to remain with his present company, the more lasting effects of the headhunter's enticements, once proposed, cannot be easily eradicated. The consultant can move to another assignment, but the candidate is going to wonder continually and perhaps increasingly if the apparently open-handed motivations of his senior management are really so clear-cut. In short, he may be left with a lingering residue of doubt and resentment.

I remember an assignment some years ago where the client company had made it quite clear whom it wanted to recruit. I was asked to get involved because the company didn't want to risk alienating a good working relationship by making the initial phone call, and, more specifically, because it wasn't at all sure it could attract the candidate.

This company's doubts were fully justified. Dwight Hayden, as I shall call him, did not want to move. Before taking his then position as a general manager with a major conglomerate, Hayden had been with a securities firm where he had, in his own words, merely been "pushing money around." At the conglomerate he was able to sink his teeth into work that was both stimulating and substantial. He had considerable line authority, and enjoyed the interplay with his subordinates. He played golf from time to time with his president. He was constantly a first-class passenger on international flights, checking out potential acquisitions. Dwight Hayden saw no reason to move.

But my client, a blue-chip *"Fortune* 500 company," wanted him. And I accepted the assignment, believing that I could bring home the bacon where others had failed.

I set to work on my basic research. Hayden was the third child of a country storekeeper outside of Raleigh, North Carolina. He had been a very bright pupil and eventually won a scholarship to Dartmouth. At a fraternity dance he met and later married a girl I shall call Jane Talbot, a senator's daughter. The senator, after making his money on the grain market, had poured his considerable energies into his subcommittee activities, while his only daughter Jane rode to hounds, attended Fifth Avenue fashion shows, and frequently adorned the social columns. She still derived a considerable income from a trust set up by her father and, after her marriage, was well able to sustain her previous lifestyle while Dwight was out making his way in the business world.

To all intents and purposes they had a good marriage. But I found the pattern of Hayden's continual air travel intriguing. My hunch was that his frequent absences were a potential source of marital friction; that the former Jane Talbot might resent missing several of the major charity balls and private dinners while her husband was away advancing his career.

I played my hunch when I talked to Hayden about the opportunity my client offered—the presidency of a major high-status subsidiary, located in New York. I knew that status was very important to Hayden, because he had initially decided to join his present blue-chip company despite an apparently more attractive bid from a rival. I stressed the advantages of being permanently based in New York. I could tell from his tone of voice at certain moments—as much from what he didn't say as from what he did—that the position held definite appeal. But I knew too he wouldn't make the move unless I put pressure on him—unless I pushed him hard.

So, one night over dinner at a quiet midtown restaurant, I reflected to Dwight Hayden on the fate of a friend of mine who had come home one day from London to find that his wife had quietly and efficiently left him. They were holding each other back, she had written, and would both be much better off by leading their own separate lives. If the husband had only been aware of his wife's deep-seated resentment of his career preoccupations, he undoubtedly would have acted sooner to save a relationship he really cared about. From here I skillfully and systematically proceeded to play the role of Iago to the thoroughly decent, if not yet noble, American executive. Hayden did not say too much that night, but three days later he called me. He would talk with my client. Five months later he joined them.

Now I guess some of my colleagues would say that the seeds of doubt I had so carefully sown would never have uprooted Dwight Hayden if they weren't solidly grounded in hard fact. By that point of view, I was only doing him a favor by predicting in considerable detail the imminent breakup of his marriage. But I'm not so sure. Even now, years later, I could be made to feel uneasy about it.

The point I'm making is that the headhunter is playing with high stakes. He is in a unique position to influence an executive to make a decision that will change his relationship with his present employer and set him upon an entirely new road. The effect of such a decision can be monumental, and especially so in the case of older executives for whom a mistake can be costly, not just in monetary terms, but in an inability to recover an earlier position of respect or safety. Once the step of resignation has been taken, there is very little if any room to return. As soon as it becomes known that an executive has been wooed by a competitor, and *has responded,* then the bond of trust, the respect that is accorded to loyalty, may be either broken or irrevocably weakened.

This is the context in which the decision of a headhunter to "tap a shoulder" must be taken. The executive himself could be excused for not being fully cognizant of any decision to discuss an opportunity "further," but a headhunter should not be. The headhunter, to be totally ethical, must ensure that the candidate clearly appreciates exactly what he is getting into.

Once negotiations have begun, the executive candidate usually has no one with whom to discuss his loyalties other than the headhunter. It is at this point that the headhunter might be seen to face further ethical considerations, as he attempts to reconcile what is good for his corporate client with what is right in the long term for his outstanding prospect. Is it his job to be objective and to help the executive make the best possible *personal* decision? Is he to advise the candidate to weigh very carefully the costs of any decision? Should he counsel that there can rarely be any turning back from a decision to resign, and advise against even discussing the matter with the present employer? Remember that, at the time a decision is being reached, the headhunter is, very often, the only business person purporting to offer emotional support and objective advice.

It is precisely at such times in his career that the average executive is least likely to be hard-headed. This is not a "deal" that he is looking at, but his own life, his work, his career, his place in society. At this moment his judgment is very likely to be impaired, and the well-chosen words of a search "counselor" are likely to be potent indeed. At this very moment the executive needs, as a human being, good, sound, honest advice that will not disadvantage him. He *needs* to be advised by someone who cares.

What he probably needs is a combination of Henry Kissinger and Arthur Burns. What in fact he will receive are the fluent, carefully chosen words of an intelligent, articulate advocate who has been paid a substantial sum to advance a corporate client's case. Certainly, if the headhunter is a genuine professional, he will present a balanced, carefully structured case. He will endeavor to present his client's career opportunity in as objective a light as possible, warts and all, not only because he knows that he is in fact more persuasive that way, but also because he wants a good fit—and because he too has his own sense of personal integrity to think about. But if, finally, it comes down to the headhunter's choosing between failure to deliver the candidate his client most fervently desires, or recommending to that candidate that he should accept the risks and make the move . . . which way, realistically, is the headhunter going to go? The answer is that it is naïve to suppose that every headhunter will do right by the candidate when the headhunter's own livelihood depends upon a decision favoring his client.

THE NEW BREED OF EXECUTIVE

Alvin Toffler, in *Future Shock,* records that the new breed of executive has a special secret: "The very temporariness of his relationships with organization frees him from many of the bonds that constricted his predecessor. Transience is in this sense liberating."

The film *Manhattan* reflects this new liberation: when his wife leaves him for another woman, the hero, a forty-three-year-old Peter Pan with dandruff (perfectly played by Woody Allen) quits his job and finds fulfillment in the bed of a seventeen-year-old schoolgirl.

You can lament this dissolution of the old social values, or, maybe you can take them as your own, shed your own job, your wife, and your children, and make up a *ménage à trois* with Mr. Allen and his friend—I'm sure they wouldn't mind and, anyway, she was from a very good school.

Or there may be a middle ground. Simply to know that a change in the ethos now permits you a wider choice of opportunities, *should you so wish,* may, of itself, be all the liberation you need.

The role of the search firm is to ensure that, if you are good at your job, you have that choice. Shareholders are increasingly requiring that senior vacancies be filled as the result of professional worldwide search rather than, possibly, through cronyism. The result, as *Fortune Magazine* noted, is that "competent executives everywhere whose performances are underrated and unrewarded stand a better chance than ever before of being noticed and courted by someone else." And that, I think, is not a bad thing at all.

23. *How to Make a Headhunter Call You and Other Priceless Advice to the Quarry*

You think . . . that it is your part to woo, to persuade, to prevail, to overcome. Fool: it is you who are the pursued, the marked-down quarry, the destined prey.

GEORGE BERNARD SHAW

HOW TO MAKE THE HEADHUNTER CALL

T H E time to get onto a search firm's files is *before you need to*. When the cold wind comes signaling a change of climate, it may be too late. You can send in an unsolicited résumé, but shrewder executives tend to play hard to get. They want the first approach to emanate from the headhunter. Here are ten ways to make that happen:

1. Complete a bachelor's degree or an MBA, or both. If you haven't got a degree, the cards are stacked against you. It's not the education that will attract the headhunter but the credential: just having one or more establishes you as a member of an elite and gets your name onto many mailing lists. If you're really serious about a corporate career and you don't already have a degree, then my very serious advice is that you enroll today. Sacrifice three years of your life if you need to, because it's one badge you'll never regret buying.

2. Get on a select mailing list. Join all the trade associations. Subscribe to obscure trade publications. Make sure your name is in a computer with that of other high-achieving executives. Search firms commonly get mail-

list houses to run special programs that profile high-achievers. Your name should appear.

3. Get appointed to the committee of a key trade association. Make sure you are known by the pros in your profession. When they are contacted, your name will be referred.

4. Write erudite articles. One article a year will attract the attention of your competitors. You will be perceived as intelligent and industrious. Shoot for the best publication in your field. Do a good job.

5. Feature in your own corporate productions. Get your name into the annual report. Make sure your promotions are announced in the financial press. Include a good photo if you can. Headhunters religiously clip these items and you automatically become a target. Best of all, you are highlighted by your success.

6. Write a letter to the newspaper on behalf of your company. Let your wisdom shine. The letter should be serious but easy to understand. It should espouse a conventional wisdom and put your corporation in a good light. Not only will one or more search firms pick up your name, but you might even get a raise where you are.

7. Become a minority candidate. Change your name to Rodriguez—film stars have business names, why shouldn't you? Minority candidates must, by law, receive special treatment and senior management positions. Since it is against the law to ask a person his race or background, quite sane people rely upon minutiae such as surnames. If your name *is* Rodriguez, then exploit the fact. Make a noise, be seen.*

8. If you are a woman, spread the word. Get yourself interviewed as a shining example of what women can do. If you are a very feminine male, give thought to changing

*Since I first penned that piece of ironic advice, a former naval captain, one of Jimmy Carter's classmates, Robert Edward Lee, actually changed his legal name to Roberto Eduardo Leon, for the sole purpose of exploiting the present laws.

your sex. It's not as silly a piece of advice as it sounds. Dr. Renée Richards made big money on the women's tennis circuit.

9. Return an imaginary call from a headhunter. Call a big firm and say that you're returning the call of one of their consultants who wants to set up an interview. Say that, no, you can't remember his name but, if it would help to track him down *you* have an MBA and a specific background in agricultural chemicals. Another variation on this is to ask a friend to "return the call," and to say that he was asked by a consultant whose name he has forgotten to recommend an outstanding fellow with an MBA and a background in pharmaceutical chemicals. And then, of course, he drops your name.

10. Excel at the job you presently hold. Reputation will out, and in the end your good work will be rewarded. But keep pushing. Upward. Upward. Onward and forever upward . . .

WHEN THE CALL COMES

Here's what to do when the headhunter calls:

1. Close your door and listen. Unless you're very comfortable in your present job, this could be a once-in-a-lifetime opportunity.

2. Know who you're talking to before you say anything. A reputable search firm will give its name, and, if need be, you can call them back. You need to be sure that it's a *bona fide* call before you begin to play your hand at all.

3. Once you've established that you are talking to a *bona fide* search consultant (and not your boss), help him. Why shouldn't you? Even if you don't want to explore the opportunity yourself, you may well have an outstanding industry colleague who would like to know about a top opportunity—and he may be in a position to do you a favor himself one day.

4. Handle the call professionally. Even if you're not in-

terested in the opportunity discussed, it could be to your future advantage to impress the caller. Be crisp, efficient, and unfazed by the call. Your phone manner can tell an experienced search consultant more about you than you would believe possible. A good impression could bring him back later with an even more attractive opportunity.

5. Don't ask him how he got your name. Let him assume that you are frequently approached and that you are quite accustomed to such calls. It is testimony to your own high standing in your industry that a headhunter is calling you at all. If you query how or why you are being called, you are querying your own worth.

6. Don't give away confidential information. A good executive is prized for his fine judgment and his ability to handle confidences. If you so much as whisper a word about your present employer's plans, or make any criticism at all, then the consultant will have doubts about you—and rightly so.

7. If you want to explore the opportunity further, then do so in a face-to-face interview. A reputable firm will take even more care of your need for absolute confidentiality than you would yourself. Their reputation is on the line too.

HOW TO HANDLE AN INTERVIEW WITH A HEADHUNTER

A clever headhunter should be able to appraise you very quickly but, because the industry has grown so quickly, not every headhunter knows exactly what he's looking for. You could get a long way if you observe the following nine precepts:

1. Look like an executive. Wear a dark suit—not a pinstripe because everybody who is trying to impress a headhunter wears his best pinstripe—but, say, a solid gray, with a white shirt, a conservative tie, and a clean

pair of wing-tipped shoes. You can vary this uniform a little in the Midwest, but you should still look like a serious executive if you want to be taken seriously.

2. Think twice before lying about your salary. You'd be surprised how accurately a headhunter can match age, salary, and recent responsibility. If you claim to be earning more than you are, he may suspect you either of lying or of holding a job with a corporation that is overpaying you because it is unable to attract a better caliber of individual.

3. Take the interview seriously but don't try to sell yourself—not even a little bit. The headhunter is coming to you, and he wants to believe that you're happily employed where you are. Be circumspect without seeming offhand. Ask *him* for information.

4. Don't tell him that you ever left a job because of a personality clash anywhere. But if you got fired, say so. Your immediate credibility will rise, and he was going to find out anyway. But have a good reason for it all.

5. Casually volunteer information about any achievements that put you in a good light. Tell him you paid your own way through college. Suggest that you are stable, secure, well-adjusted, happy, and that you get on well with everybody, but confess that you wish you were a little less ambitious. Say that you admired your father who worked very hard; you love your wife, who is pushing you to take a new job; you enjoy your present position and admire your boss who has, unfortunately, taught you all he knows.

6. Your spare-time reading is mainly Drucker on management, and whatever other light business books you can get your hands on. Ask the headhunter if he enjoyed *Management and Machiavelli* by Anthony Jay. If he says he did, say you found it a little light and quickly mention that you balance your reading with your subscriptions to the *Harvard Business Review, Wharton Magazine,* and, whenever you are in a coquettish mood, *Fortune, Forbes,*

and *Duns Review*. Your newspaper, of course, is the *Wall Street Journal,* and you wouldn't miss a word of it.

7. You like competitive sports such as squash and skiing. You also like backgammon and chess, but you just don't get too much time to play them nowadays because you regularly put in a hard week at work, and just recently they've given you a heavier load so that you've been taking a fair bit of work home.

8. Say that another headhunter just called you last week, making five so far this year.

9. Cut the interview before he does, explaining that you've got to get back to work. But it was nice talking to him.

SHOULD YOU SEND YOUR RÉSUMÉ TO A HEADHUNTER?

It depends upon the firm. Since some of the big firms are ethically unable to call you and must rely upon their files, what you lose by initiating the approach you may gain by floating up a good résumé and getting into the computer. But do a good job. Here are seven helpful hints.

Include your salary. It's the first thing a headhunter looks for and if it isn't there he'll probably assume that you're ashamed of it, and possibly earning less than you really are. He'll also lose a certain amount of interest in you.

Include your age too. Again, it's a key item that anyone who reads résumés looks for immediately. If you're over forty, give some thought to not mentioning your age but getting your date of birth wrong by *exactly* ten years. All you want is to be interviewed and then you'll clear things up, right? I wouldn't do that myself, but I do know a fellow for whom this ruse paid off.

Make it all brief, low-key, and factual. Only so much information can be keyed into the computer. They'll call you if they're interested, and then you can produce a long résumé.

Get it laid out by a professional. But don't send in what is *obviously a "Madison Avenue" résumé.* If it looks too good the automatic presumption may be that you're being outplaced. Interest will decline.

Send only an "original." Even a perfect offset copy carries the stamp of the outplacement firm, and you just don't want to be part of that scene. Get every résumé and every letter individually typed on an automatic word-processor. You'll pay a few dollars extra, but the fact that this is an original that seems to have been typed especially for the headhunter will be worth every extra cent.

Include any unique qualifications, and be specific to your industry. Your résumé will be keyed into the computer according to Standard Industry Codes and, the more specific you are, the easier it will be for an operator to classify you.

Send a one-page covering letter. It should be individually typed and carry your personal signature in bright blue ink. Put your major selling credentials (and your salary) in the first paragraph and include enough information for a decision to see you to be reasonably taken on the basis of the letter alone. Say that you are happy with your present employer, and are not actively seeking a new job, but that you "could be amenable to discussion" if they had an attractive opportunity in line with your special skills. Don't oversell yourself, and don't use jargon.

COPING WITH TERMINATION FROM THE WRONG SIDE OF THE DESK

Henry Ford II, among other scions of industry, has beheaded some very competent executives for no apparently good reason, and so, as much as I wish, dear reader, that you will never be on the wrong side of the termination desk, there may be an advantage to be gained in looking at one subject with a cool head while you still have a cool head.

When a termination interview takes place, it should never come as a shock. There are inevitable signs that dismissal is in the air, and an astute executive recognizes them. These are some of the main indicators:

- You are asked to move into an office smaller than your last one, or to a floor with less status.
- Your car is taken away from you.
- You are transferred to an interstate branch.
- Suddenly you have to make appointments to see superiors you usually just dropped in on before.
- Your name is conspicuously absent from office memos.
- A company policy regarding expense control seems to apply only to you.
- You have to share your secretary with a junior executive.
- There is a reorganization, and your new title is "Special Duties." Or your responsibilities change from a line to a staff function.

The list is almost endless, and each firm has its favorites, sometimes subtle, sometimes not. One senior finance executive shows his hand by addressing a prospective terminee as "Mister" instead of the more usual first name.

Very rarely are there not signs that you've fallen from grace. And if you miss those signs, you probably deserve what's coming, anyway.

HANDLING THE TERMINATION INTERVIEW

Obviously you will be under pressure. The way you handle the heat may indicate your true mettle: that, anyway, is what you will be intending to communicate.

This, after all, is an excellent opportunity to leave a lasting and favorable impression with the person terminating you. With luck he may feel that you are a poised, capable, mature executive and that he has made a terrible error. He too will be apprehensive, and eternally grateful if you allow him to so execute his task that your neatly severed head falls tidily into the basket beneath the guillotine.

The decision to become an unwilling or ungracious victim,

and use this last moment to tell your employer exactly what
you think of him and his, may momentarily release your id
tensions, but it will also taint any subsequent telephone reference, which may in turn haunt your search for a new
employer.

Thus let me offer you some specific don'ts:

• Don't say anything that is in the least derogatory about
the individual effecting the termination, or the corporation. (Say it later when you are out of the place.)

• Don't ask "why?" (Not knowing may in itself be
grounds for termination.)

• Don't ask to say goodbye to your colleagues. (A person dismissed has a communicable disease and nobody
will, at that moment, want to become infected.)

• When you are happily settled elsewhere, it might be
nice to tell a couple of your former colleagues that you
have a big jump in salary, and for a lightened workload
with a thoroughly decent bunch of people. Be relaxed
about it all and suggest, one day, maybe, getting together
over a drink. Then forget them.

• Don't break down, don't argue, and, above all, don't
lose your temper. Keep your emotions under strict control.

• Don't take, or attempt to take, any company documentation with you. (If they have a mind to be nasty, it is
theft, or attempted theft.)

• Don't haggle over your final check. But study it closely
when your emotions have cooled. If you are unsure as to
your entitlements, or if you feel you may have been
short-changed, then a telephone call to your lawyer could
set you straight.

• Don't, for a while anyway, contact any former clients
to sway them away from your former employer. Wait
until you are in a position of real strength, then let out the
word. Maybe they will come to you.

• Shake hands with your former boss, thank him for the

opportunity of working for him, and wish him good luck for the future. (He'll probably need it. There is one satisfaction in knowing that all your problems at work are now his.)

- Make sure you collect all your personal effects. Or, if you can't, leave an address for them to be sent on to you.

Then don't do anything for two days. By that time you should be seeing things clearly and your approach to finding another job will be a lot more rational. Be assured you will live to regret anything you do in anger.

RESIGNATION OR TERMINATION?

Sometimes the choice of resigning is offered. Should you accept the offer? Yes, unless it is going to cost you really big money.

It always better to be able to say truthfully that you resigned. It may be a technicality at this late stage, but that technicality will be recorded on your personnel file, forever.

The other argument is to get all you can, and if you are in a position to exact a minor fortune in exchange for this terrible indignity, then, in fairness to your loved ones, you are ethically bound to demand money for your flesh.

If you are truly attuned to the situation, you will verify in advance exactly what the corporate policy to payoffs has been. If it is adequate, you may wish to have in your pocket a letter of resignation, carrying yesterday's date, announcing your resignation effective as from today.

Then, when the subject of termination is broached, with an utterly clear head firmly raise the subject of your golden handshake. If your "bonus" has already been drawn, study it closely and make sure no zeros are missing, and accept it gracefully. If the lagniappe is to be delayed until you have proven yourself a good fellow, be even more egregious. *However,* if you are being terminated by some pious puritan who, under the guise of keeping *your* money for himself, has asserted that he doesn't put gold handles on pine coffins, and you know that he won't relent, then you might, I half seriously suggest, wish to play him at his own game and beat him. As you take his check firmly in your fingers, exchange your own resignation and quietly announce that your decision to resign was taken yesterday, wish him the best of luck, and head for the bank to clear your deposit forthwith.

On the bright side, you may wish to reflect that every cloud has a silver lining and that you have been launched, albeit unwittingly, upon a new career with better prospects than the last.

PART FOUR

*HOW TO TURN
A $1,000 IOU INTO
A MULTIMILLION-
DOLLAR
CORPORATION*

24. *How to Become Established Immediately*

> *There is at bottom only one problem in the world and this is its name. How does one break through? How does one get into the open? How does one burst the cocoon and become a butterfly?*
>
> THOMAS MANN, *Doctor Faustus*

FOUR AXIOMS FOR ASPIRING TYCOONS

THE early metamorphosis of an aspiring tycoon is usually effected in a low-overhead environment within the protective green chrysalis of Other People's Money (OPM). The emergent butterfly is characterized by a cluster of predictable traits: high profile, cool nerve, wide smile, unbounded optimism, and the unyielding pursuit of someone to love—a client. But, for the unwary, there can be many a slip betwixt the cocoon and the client; and the tycoon in contemplation of the flight from emergence to eminence might, with advantage, apprehend the wisdom inherent in four profoundly simple axioms:

Axiom 1: If your outgo exceeds your income, your upkeep will be your downfall. The fact is that new businesses most frequently fail for simple lack of initial capital. It always takes longer than you think, which makes low overheads as comforting as a rich uncle because they allow time for the pursuit and subsequent conversion of unwilling clients.

Axiom 2: Appearance is the only reality. To others you are what you seem, and the essence of turning a $1,000 IOU into a million-dollar corporation—or a prince into a frog, or a frog into a gourmet dinner—is the manipulation of that amorphous

247

jumble of symbols, sounds, shapes, colors, and impressions that is thrown, kaleidoscopically, into a pattern on the screen at the back of the human head.

We consciously apprehend only the pattern. The individual colors are absorbed unconsciously, subliminally, on many cerebral and emotional levels.

A doctor's cure lies in more than his words or his six years in medical school—it's in the tone of his voice, the hue of his office, the color of his gown, the authority of his stethoscope, that white blur and red seal of the certificate on the wall behind him.

Success in almost everything you could think of is largely based upon nonverbal transmission of powerful abstract messages. Life imitates art, reality is a concept, our world a set of images: images for which hard-headed corporate executives are prepared to pay top dollar over on Madison Avenue. Such is the power of art to shape life that, if Botticelli were alive today, he'd probably be working for *Vogue*. Shelley, an incurable romantic, would possibly be writing copy for vaginal sprays.

In New York, because I now have an established organization, I can afford to work at a small spartan black table. But when I was an aspiring tycoon, my first desk was enormous and had to be assembled in five great pieces inside my office.

Perhaps I was simply an aspiring megalomaniac, but still, as through a glass darkly, I seemed to perceive that a desk, if you are an aspiring tycoon, is not *just* a desk. It is a symbol, an altar of your intended success. It is at just such an altar that the archetypal New York banker puffs the incense of his fat cigar, robed in a three-piece pinstripe and immersed in heavenly Muzak. To become a priest of business, then, you would be wise to follow his example. Sounds a little too simple? People wouldn't take you seriously, you say? Well, if you feel like it, why not prove the advice for yourself simply and without great expense: invest in an organ to grind and a monkey on a chain holding a tin cup for you—I'll bet you don't collect anything but nickels and dimes, but you *will* collect, because people will believe that you are what you seem.

But it needn't cost you a fortune to take a more daring route and, from your very first day in business, project the image of an already up-and-going enterprise that has been around for years. This can be easier than you might think. You don't after all need acres of office space to command a good address on your stationery, or an imposing brass plate on a solid timber front door. My first office, as I mentioned, at the start of this voyage was not premier space. But I covered the ratholes with tin, the walls with mahogany veneer, and the floor with thick golden carpet. At the windows I installed rich opaque silk curtaining that caught and enhanced the natural light, then framed them with a regal blue shantung, and, like a bridal gown, it all touched the floor.

Conscious of Machiavelli's advice that a stranger judges a prince by the bearing of his ambassador, I hired an attractive, well-groomed, well-spoken secretary. The wall between us was so thin she could have pushed her finger through it— certainly we never had a communication problem. Nonetheless, I installed an intercom unit on my desk and also on my secretary's. There were five buttons on each set. Some callers thought my organization occupied the whole floor. In a way, it did.

Whenever the phone rang my secretary would positively sing our name. But getting through to me was always made marginally difficult. You had to be announced. Then, when I came on, I would say "*John* Wareham speaking," to distinguish me from all the other Warehams in the office: "How can *we* help you."

Axiom 3: You become what you seem to others. Like the New York banker, the shimmering priest attends his altar with incense and heavenly choirs. It affects the congregation, but just as certainly it *affects him too.* Any top sportsman can tell you he plays a better game when dressed for the part.

I would not for one moment be so immodest as to suggest that my appreciation of symbolism accounted for my early success. A lot of the credit must go to my capacity for enjoying what I was doing. Rolled-up sleeves and long hours are powerful symbols too.

But, once people perceive you as a tycoon, they will help to make you one. An entrepreneurial friend of mine went on to become famous, bad-tempered, ulcer-ridden, and very, very rich. He employed a small staff of five, yet his entry in the telephone book took the entire page, listing some dozen departments and divisions. If you had ever gotten to see his switchboard, you would have observed that all of the calls were answered by the same operator, and most of them went to Mr. Big. He said the "big image" helped him to raise public money for his ventures.

Aristotle Onassis became a shipping magnate although his envious rivals said he owned only the smoke above the tankers that bore his name. Which was true—it was all done with OPM. People were prepared to back Ari because of his self-fulfilling *reputation*.

As long as we *believe* in the wizard of Oz, we invest him with magical power and he really becomes a wizard. Helena Rubinstein understood that women buy dreams, not smells—not grease, but beauty. When we believe there is magic in the bottle, we create the genie.

Axiom 4: The first transition is in your own head. "From the sublime to the ridiculous," Napoleon remarked upon his exile and imprisonment, "is but a short step." So too is the journey back the other way. Keeping a hold on reality is a luxury you can rarely afford when you set out to become a tycoon. Believing you are special when the only evidence of this state exists within your head commands a higher priority—and you must also be capable of communicating this new reality to your clientele.

I first met "The Galloping Gourmet," Graham Kerr, in a dingy set of rooms above a winter-bleak corner of windy Wellington in New Zealand some twenty years ago. We were both hustling for business with very little in sight. He had given up his evening to address some thirteen "Jaycee-ettes," and I was in a back room on the committee of a three-man fund-raising team. Through the thin door I could hear him pull out all the stops, talking to those housewives as if they were the worldwide television audiences he was later to command. In a way they were, though at that time his television debut was still a dream. At the close of the evening we shared a drink. My subsequent recollection of Graham was of a very friendly, totally natural individual who believed he was going places. Listening to him, I believed it too.

"Imagination rules the world," said Napoleon. "It is like the Danube: at its source it can be crossed in a leap . . . I abandon myself to the most brilliant of dreams."

Actually deciding that you really are in business to *stay,* or that you are not just a doctor but a *great* doctor, not just an advertising man but *the* advertising man, not just a politician but an *emperor,* requires the clear head of a madman. Like the decision to win a beautiful woman, it is not to be taken solemnly, but with gusto and passion, for that is the only way she will succumb.

Advertising tycoon David Ogilvy records that the day he began in business he made a promise to his small staff: "Agencies are as big as they deserve to be. We are starting this one on a shoestring, but we are going to make it a great agency by 1960."

That peculiar brand of humility is the stuff of great people. An internalized belief in their own worth guides their actions, shapes their world, and invests that of their followers with a *special significance.* Their world changes because they are prepared to move to the sound of their own music. And, like the Pied Piper, they inevitably attract a following: sometimes children, sometimes rats—it depends upon the personality of the piper. If you want to become great today, you need only to hear the music in your head and then arise and commence to dance the Tycoon Tango.

Thoreau put it nicely: "If one advances confidently in the direction of his dreams and endeavors to live the life which he has imagined, he will meet with a success unexpected in common hours."

25. *Two Short-cuts to Get You Moving Faster than the Competition*

No man can cut out new paths in company. He does that alone.

OLIVER WENDELL HOLMES, JR.

WHEN I was eight years old I sold football badges for the big game in my home town. So did 108 other eager beavers anxious to earn a twopenny commission on a badge that sold for a shilling—today that would be about ten cents on an investment of sixty. The reward for the boy who sold the most badges was twenty shillings . . . one whole pound—an enormous sum to a small boy accustomed to sixpence worth of weekly pocket money.

When I first set out to sell, I stood on a dusky Friday evening with two friends at the main intersection where thousands of people passed and we all shouted, "Football *Soo-*vin-*ears!*" In half an hour two people stopped to buy and we fought for the sale. Being smallest, I missed out both times.

It then occurred to me that I was standing in the worst possible place to sell anything, first because I couldn't buttonhole hurrying passers-by and, second, because if anyone did stop, I only had once chance in three of getting the sale. So I took to the bars. Even though it was against the law, I trudged into every saloon in town. I would sight a circle of people, duck between the legs, arise into the middle, and go into the pitch I had created and rehearsed.

I was a source of amusement and bewilderment. Someone

would say, "Give the kid a shilling." I would retort, "Give the kid nothing! Support your team, and all buy a badge." I was never happy until I had sold everyone, and then I would hurry on to the next group.

My parents, had they fully recognized the nature of my wanderings, might not have appreciated either the short- or long-term significance of this work, but I won the one-pound first prize for every match. More than that, my commission came to almost five pounds and my tips anywhere up to ten. At the age of eight I was, I thought, a millionaire, and this first fortune, though quickly squandered, taught me two short-cuts that I have assiduously applied to the art of wooing clients:

Separate yourself from your colleagues. I've always been wary of any association that purports to sell both my services and the services of a colleague. A professional association can certainly do a good job advancing the overall professional standing of its members, and this is a laudable pursuit. Personally, however, I have tended to the rather expedient view that he travels the fastest who travels alone, and have joined only associations whose requirements for membership include *bona fide* academic accomplishment.

Go where the best prospects are. If you're selling football badges, the best prospects (1) are in bars and (2) have already been softened for your soothing advances by the terrifying effects of demon alcohol. In business it's better to go to the ethereal chamber of your intended angel—his heavenly office—and catch him stone-cold sober, and prepared to do business at 10:30 A.M. on any weekday except Monday, when he might just be nursing the demon.

26. *How to Win Clients*

We are confronted with insurmountable opportunities.

POGO

Four Errors to Avoid

ATTRACTING the eye of a well-heeled client is not too different from romancing an aristocratic woman—vulgar overtures tend to go unrequited.

So, before you set about your courtship, please allow me to suggest four no-no's that might save you from disdain:

Don't advertise. Not in the press, that is. Media advertising is great for a clarion call that, by its nature, commands the mass market. But for a professional—*never*. Advertising is what a so-called professional does when he doesn't know who to talk to: clear advice to any shrewd executive that his clientele is, at best, limited; that some may be fleeing; that he has been reduced to begging in public.

Don't make cold calls. Cold canvassing chills the soul. The odds of reaching a good contact are low, and if you do you will have to spell your name and *explain yourself,* which almost inevitably will make you sound like a diamond trader or an insurance salesman. Even if and when Mr. Angel gets your intended message, your cold call may still persuade him you have no existing clients, or are absolutely *desperate* for more. When he puts down the phone, perhaps earlier than you might wish, there is a good chance you will feel like a teenage suitor who gave the candy and flowers but never got kissed. Don't chance it.

Don't think a brochure will get you clients. The myth that a brochure will entice droves of clients is perpetuated by public relations people who get paid to produce brochures. In fact, a brochure will rarely sell anything unless you have already established your credentials, and this will require more than your pretty face and fancy words on glossy paper.

Ultimately, serious prospects will ask to "see your material," and then you may need a brochure. But if it comes unsolicited, your best hope is that the front page will get a glance as it travels to the file under the desk. In fact, I'd almost bet five dollars that not one person in three would be any the wiser if you took a competitor's brochure, pasted your own logo on the front cover, and passed the whole thing up as your own.

Don't expect anything over lunch except indigestion. Hope makes a good breakfast, a dyspeptic lunch, and a poor supper. Yet some people, surveying the many packed restaurants of business communities, really do believe you can get a client by buying him an expensive meal. I fear they may be engaged in wishful thinking. However *haute* the cuisine, it is difficult indeed to enjoy your food while trying to sell someone something. You mention your services just as a fish bone gets stuck in his throat or, worse, your own. And, since you will probably have little to celebrate, the arrival of the check may be even more discomforting.

I was spared such embarrassment one evening at the Casa Brasil restaurant in Manhattan's Yorkville when my wife and I were dining with the New York president of Canada's DHJ Industries, Chuck McCrae, and his wife. At 11:40 P.M. I said, "Chuck, is it snowing outside and have you seen any wild moose in the street?"

"No," he said, "not at all, and it's summer."

"Then we are in trouble," I explained, "for there are men in this restaurant wearing ski masks and carrying sawed-off shotguns."

255

At that point they overturned our table, spilling an excellent bottle of Château Graud-Larose (they were desperate men). After explaining that this was a stick-up, which I did not doubt, they threw Chuck against the wall and took his loose change and credit cards, as well as cash from the register, the patrons' jewels, and my wristwatch.

It was all over in a flash and suddenly, as an optimist always can, I found that the cloud had a silver lining. The glazed eye of my shaken guest locked mine as he intoned: "I will never forget you or your firm for as long as I live."

But it's difficult always to make that sort of an impression, and perhaps the most appropriate time for dinner is after the deal has been consummated and you are prepared to unwind. But be warned, nonetheless: an ongoing professional relationship should always be conducted with the advice of Machiavelli in mind—your friend may one day become your enemy.

If you can't get to prospective clients by advertising, cold calling, sending out brochures, or buying lunch, how *can* you open that essential first conversation with your putative client?

Solving this dilemma requires, *before* any telephone call or other form of solicitation, becoming:

- An acknowledged authority
- Recommended by people who matter
- Attractive to deal with

HOW TO BECOME AN ACKNOWLEDGED AUTHORITY

Know thy subject. As I have said, it starts in your own head. Get the books and study them; read the technical publications; join the trade associations and attend all the seminars. In short, *absorb all the material* in your field of expertise. This won't take as long as you might think. In any specialized field it doesn't require all that much time to have read *all* of the books.

A college degree might be a help but the absence of any formal training in naval architecture didn't seem to bother the world's current number one yacht designer, my countryman

Ron Holland, whom I first had the good fortune to meet during Cowes Week. At the time he was on the threshold of world fame, but you would never have guessed it. Still in his twenties, he was unpretentious, happy-go-lucky, wore blue jeans and cowboy boots. Next year he knocked his stuffy, long-established, blue-blooded New York competitors from the roost that their credentials had commanded for more than twenty years. How did he do it? Simply by designing yachts that *sailed faster than the competition*.

The world then beat a path to Ron Holland's studio, and, at the time of writing, the top ocean-racers of England, America and Greece are all his designs.* And it's the same in any field: build a better mousetrap, and you'll never need to deal with vermin again.

It was for this reason, some ten years ago, that we at Wareham Associates gained the jump on our competitors by installing a computer and collating information on executives by industry, suburb, qualification, age, and salary, plus a myriad of biographical data. The intention, then dimly perceived, was to determine factors common to executive success, and also to provide instant information on salary levels by industry and qualification. Over the years, as we updated our methods and equipment, we were able to look at appraising executive potential by analyzing data fed into the computer, until we could predict personality traits and levels of motivation from hard life data. When we became able to link our computers worldwide, we were able to gather and analyze, from any country, a priceless electronic intelligence network.

Look as if you know your subject. I said earlier that "to become established you must do all one can to be established." So, *from the outset,* wherever I have gone I have endeavored to project the image of:

---

* Actually, another of my compatriots also pulled off the same trick. Bruce Farr, a twenty-four-year-old radical designer, literally revolutionized the ocean racing world from a sleepy office in Auckland, New Zealand. The world authorities reacted by changing the international rules of ocean-racing yacht design.

- An already well-established market force
- A trusted, respected, and reputable organization
- A knowledgeable, worldly, and wise approach to our business

Building this delightful image is one task, of course. Getting it into people's heads is another and perhaps an even tougher challenge. Let me tell you how to do it.

Give something away. Most people chasing business put the cart before the horse and ask for money before they themselves give anything. Instead, I suggest you follow the advice of Ecclesiastes and send your bread upon the water. (In New York you may have to send a cart full of bread and maybe your horse too.)

After starting out in New York, we arranged a series of business luncheons at the Waldorf, flying in exotic speakers from far-off cities and countries. It was a small price to pay for the pleasure of inviting key executives to share a first-class meal at a legendary hotel and hear an authoritative speaker give a serious address on executive appraisal, or some allied subject. It is, of course, non-U to solicit at your own dinner table, but some quite useful messages can be communicated with relative dignity on such occasions.

Get the small details right. I said not to advertise, but your letterhead is just that—an advertisement. Whether the message is good or bad depends on what you can do with paper, art, and ink. A letterhead is your first ambassador, and as such it should subtly establish your name, your expertise, your good taste, your *savoir-faire*. Get it laid out by an artist and printed by a craftsman. Make it unobtrusively impressive. A good letterhead is like a custom-tailored suit—it suggests that you know what you are about; that you are to be taken seriously; that you have already given such valuable service to your clients that their appreciation has enabled you to afford a good tailor.

Letterhead colors are more persuasive than you might guess. High-achievers, according to the psychologist David

McClelland, are attracted to dark blues and regal reds. And psychiatrist Ainslie Meares says that a corporate logo should resemble a phallus. Meares argues that such symbolism will influence people to categorize your corporation as a thruster. *Really?* Yes, really. Reflect upon the E-type Jaguar, a classic of automotive design some fifteen years ahead of its time when it first appeared in the early fifties and virtually remained unchanged for two decades. What does it cost? How did it sell? What does it look like? What more need I say?

Your corporate name is likewise worthy of contemplation. It should be distinctive, memorable, short, and prestigious. I probably stayed with my family name because I am egotistical. But it also derives from an Anglo-Saxon heritage (I think we were smugglers) spanning back to the seventh century A.D., and I also like to pretend it has a Wall Street flavor. If my name had been Grubb, Runt, or Toady, I might have felt differently.

A good address too can both enhance a letterhead and inspire confidence. Few people may visit you, but everyone who matters to you (with luck) may know and be impressed by your address. Also, remember that you don't need to own the building to take advantage of its international name. So if you can choose a name that is widely known, then you are onto a good thing; nothing succeeds like address.

Claim the expertise. If you sound and look like an expert, then people may believe you when you make the claim. What *is* an expert, anyway? Some people would argue that he's someone who knows more and more about less and less until finally he knows everything about nothing. If you are unsure of a field in which to claim your expertise, then consider being a marketing or public relations consultant. Nobody knows what these people do, anyway, except work exclusively on retainer. You can do that too.

HOW TO GET RECOMMENDED BY PEOPLE WHO MATTER

The first thing is to meet them. David Mahoney, chief

executive of Norton Simon, said he spent vital hours of his youth lingering at the 21 Club in New York, sipping soda water and striking up conversations with the rich and famous.

You could do a lot worse than become a fixture at a place where the eminent gather, although I wouldn't suggest actually eating there because it can be terribly expensive. But a glass of milk costs very little, and an order like that will get you remembered as mildly eccentric and therefore rich. Give the bartender outrageously generous gratuities (you can afford to on glasses of milk), and he will then allow you to call him Freddie and introduce you by name to his wealthy clientele. In that setting, on those terms, the automatic presumption that you are a "someone" will allow you to seize whatever opportunities fate puts before you.

I met my British Commonwealth chairman Sir Arthur Harper in the course of my first consulting assignment for the Dutch International Philips corporation. He was chairman of the subsidiary I was setting up, had a lot of other directorships, and used his office only intermittently. Philips assigned me his desk for my own work, which was to take some four months.

I'd hardly spread myself out, Goldilocks-like, in the fat chair at the oversized desk, when Sir Arthur returned. Unlike Goldilocks, I was not asleep, but nonetheless I was young and innocent. He was wise and thoughtful. He looked at me and lifted the phone: "We'll have to get another desk," he said. It was installed, and, to my great surprise, I was to experience the unique pleasure of sharing the office of a powerful man who would become both a fine friend and a fountain of helpful hard-headed advice.

Some two decades ago I met Doc McMurry in my hometown and asked him home to dinner. Sitting around the fire that evening with a cold, black, southerly wind beating at my timber walls, I could never have guessed that he would return the favor so handsomely in a land so far away. His name, commendation, friendship, and support have been invaluable, and it would have been difficult indeed to establish myself in America without his help.

And Rupert Murdoch, who as I mentioned earlier parlayed a small-town newspaper into a publishing empire operating on three continents, also helped me greatly. I called on him following his takeovers of *New York Post, New York Magazine* and the *Village Voice,* which established him as a tough, shrewd and daring operator in this town of lions. (Even ousted *New York Magazine* publisher, the imperious Clay Felker, was subsequently reported to remark, "What can you say? The man's brilliant.")

Mr. Murdoch welcomed me very warmly in Dorothy Schiff's old office at the *Post* and was immediately appreciative of my situation. I wanted to include his high-profile name in a special promotion to establish that my clients, like Mr. Murdoch, with whose international organization we had placed a number of executives, were hard-nosed corporate leaders who expected results. Would he mind writing me a letter for inclusion in our promotion?

He moved to the typewriter at his desk and immediately typed a personal note on his corporate stationery. It was a rich favor that did a great deal to help establish my credentials here.

"The best of luck," he said passing over the epistle with the ink still drying on his signature. "It's a great town."

BEING ATTRACTIVE TO DEAL WITH

> *Everyone secretly would like to prove that he is absolutely irresistible, but some people give up too easily, while others do not give up when they should.* ERIC BERNE

> *Man with long face should not open shop.* CHINESE PROVERB

A smile will open a lot of doors. Whether they stay open may depend upon the color of both your shoes and your teeth, and whether the shine is in your eyes or your pants.

When I started out and only had one suit I used to get it

pressed on the way to visit a client while I hid behind a curtain. An aspiring tycoon should look like a tycoon. Wear a five-hundred-dollar suit, even if you have no money in the pockets. Suit first, money later. Polonius knew it before any of us were born:

> *Costly thy habit as thy purse can buy,*
> *But not expressed in fancy; rich not gaudy;*
> *For the apparel oft proclaims the man.*

If you look like a derelict, you'll collect nickels. Look like a millionaire, and you'll possibly get the best table in the house. And if you can get that, you *must* be a tycoon, and people will want to patronize you. Hey, *presto!*

I once met an American holidaying in my ancestral village of Wareham in Dorset, England. We struck up a conversation when I observed that he bore a positively uncanny resemblance to Richard Nixon.

"Yes," he said, "I do. But more than that I live at San Clemente, and often, if I eat unannounced at an expensive restaurant, they rush to give me the best table, *and then they don't bring the check.*"

"Do you then tell them who you really are?" I inquired.

"It would be unfair to disillusion them," he said.

It was a positively *uncanny* resemblance.

And, of course, in addition to looking good, you need to be a great conversationalist. This begins with the ability to listen. Usually it ends there too.

I once called on a fellow who had an enormous swordfish mounted on the wall behind his desk. "Ever go fishing?" I asked innocently. Three hours later we discussed his assignment for half an hour, and I left with a contract to mount on my own wall.

The chairman of a construction company sat in front of seven huge color photographs of seven children flanking even larger portraits of himself and his wife. "You're a family man, I guess?" I inquired casually. Four hours and the life stories of seven children later, his chauffeur took me back to town with an assignment in my briefcase.

The key to being a good listener is to actually *be* interested in people, and I must confess that I don't find this difficult—to me the lifestyle and background of prospective clients is always fascinating.

They too are often relieved to put off their masks, forget the rigors of business, and relax for a while in the company of a sympathetic listener. These conversations are part of the pleasures of business. As well as making you attractive, an attentive ear is a sure receptacle for cash and checks.

Lord Chesterfield advised his son to take his tone from the company in which he found himself, and this is a fine rule. I was cursed with a youthful countenance, but Professor Daniel Levinson, who gained fame with his book *Seasons of a Man's Life,* said that I was "precocious," explaining that it was a compliment indicating special wisdom and insight. Who was I to argue with such a perceptive eminence?

But I wasn't always so sure. When newly in business I attempted to enhance any latent machismo with a moustache. Alas, it only served to highlight my pubescence, leaving me wispful. I was not slow to remove the growth.

One other time, when calling upon the deteriorating chairman of a giant corporation, I sprayed my shock of brown hair with silver from an aerosol can. Did it work? For the first time in my life a very attractive forty-year-old woman sat herself next to me and offered her address. Then later, the chairman spoke to me about the problems of "men of our age"—and I had an inkling of what he meant.

Be yourself is the worst possible advice you can give to some people but, now that I have a few gray hairs of my own, I think the best course for most of us, if we can find out who we are, is to serve the dish *au naturel*.

The particular advantage of doing business in another country is that an out-of-town accent tends to be attractive. I learned this when I took up public-speaking many years ago and saw the almost hypnotic effect that broken English can have on an audience.

In Britain, where hesitancy connotes the fashionable confusion that comes with an upper-class education, some Englishmen, when attempting to get elected to Parliament, affect a stammer. I was blessed with one, but too much exposure to the public platform is spoiling it. When I had the good fortune to win my hometown oratory competition, which the crown prosecutor had failed to do in six attempts, he was piqued. "That stammer," he told a friend, "is a trick to win audiences—and it works."

In New York I first worried that a British accent might be a disadvantage but, in fact, it opened many doors. Likewise, Henry Kissinger's dense pronunciation is usually taken as the hallmark of an international. Actually, I wouldn't advise imitating Henry, but maybe you could develop a lisp—it's been a positive boon to Barbara Walters.

I said that you should have attractive offices, and you may have thought I was drawing the bow a bit long. But a skilled negotiator once told me that, in his experience, the most productive meetings are held in pleasant, bright, airy conference rooms.

It is valuable, I think, to invest your life with the flavor and opulence of ritual. People laughed at the Englishman who dressed for dinner in Africa, but I think it enhanced the meal—at least until he found himself on the menu.

It's also worth giving a little thought to the furnishings inside your head. I went off health foods the day I saw that the advice, "You are what you eat," was coming from the vegetarian Tiny Tim. But we do become what we read: New Yorkers are spoiled by having the *Times* available on their morning doorstep, and the cleverer ones tend to savor the Op-Ed pages more than breakfast. I have always endeavored to read a couple of good nonbusiness-related books a month.

HOW TO GET TRIPLE-A PUBLICITY

We are all dancing in the same ballroom, but the tango of

the tycoon requires special panache, gusto, and practice. A rose between your teeth may make you noticeable to some, but nothing will command a serious audience as quickly as the radiant sheen of the spotlight. You can dance into it, or, if you have money in your pocket, you can possibly use some of it to catch the eye of the man who directs the spotlight. Best to get your act together first, though.

Of course everybody in this country knows the value of publicity: I don't think the bullet had even gone cold when Arthur Bremmer, the would-be assassin who put presidential aspirant George Wallace in a wheelchair for the rest of his life, asked that typically American question: "How much do you think I'll get for my autobiography?"

America is *the* great celebrity society, where a jail sentence can be parlayed into a talk-show fortune, a third-rate burglary into an entire Watergate industry. Publicity here is the sweetest of all deodorants, and obeisance is to the talk-show host.

The particular advantage of publicity, if you are an aspiring tycoon, is that it can very precisely help you achieve three critical goals:

- Create awareness of your name.
- Establish your authority.
- Render you an attractive *cause célèbre*.

People who ignore advertising devour news. It becomes part of the collective consciousness and forms the basis of serious discussion over lunch. David Ogilvy shrewdly acknowledged this fact when he advised that an advertisement should be disguised to look like a legitimate news story.

The mass media have an insatiable appetite for people and personalities, comings and goings, ups and downs. Journalists depend for their livelihood on being able to report upon the lives of experts and idiots in all walks of life. With a little thought you should be able to arrange that your name figures in this gallimaufry. But, please, not as an idiot.

I was momentarily tempted when a wide-eyed and utterly serious New York PR man told me that he would guarantee me a picture and story in the world press. It would all come about as the result of an address I would give to a business audience on the art of baring an executive's psyche. While telling the story I would divest myself of my clothing. The removal of my pants would mark the climax of my address. Naked but, if everything worked out, still vitally shielded by the podium, UPI flash bulbs would light my élan.

"It will be a *great* campaign," said my erstwhile practitioner of media magic. It was the last thing I remember him saying.

One fellow who actually paid for and accepted similar advice was a New York headhunter of German extraction. He was purveyed by his public relations advisor as a former SS officer and a proponent of Gestapo-type "stress" interviews. A glossy magazine took the story and ran it, including a photo of the Eichmannian interrogator in his office with a searing spotlight behind him. The deadpan body copy explained that he interrogated executive candidates with studied insults and demeaning questions, alternatively delivered with guttural intensity and syrupy charm. Finally, he dimmed the lights, flicked a switch and studied the responses of his quarry to the exposure of pornographic movies. These reactions, according to his unique *Weltanschauung,* would reveal an executive's stress threshold, and hence his likelihood of job success.

It was great publicity in terms of column inches but dubious image building, attracting as it did a certain measure of *Schadenfreude* and good-natured banter among his professional colleagues.

I did once myself score a doubtful coup by telling a Rotary audience that it should be grounds for divorce that a man's wife was hampering his career. Today the story line would be the same but the sexual roles reversed. *Plus ça change, plus c'est la même chose.*

Another time I drew bold headlines with the tongue-in-cheek suggestion, during the course of an address to the British-American Chamber of Commerce, that unwed, live-in corporate couples were rendering corporate chairmen ambivalent, anxious, envious, and uneasy: as a result, I concluded, executive menopause is arriving earlier. This was a little outrageous, perhaps, but it touched a psychic nerve, which is the key to much publicity. "If you want an audience," Marlon Brando observed, "give them blood. It's the *ultimate* hustle."

But chasing headlines can sometimes find you impaled upon a double-edged sword. Sometimes better than being the meat in a hungry reporter's sandwich is to slice your own. Business and trade magazines are always in search of specialist articles, and, because good material is hard to come by, the *Harvard Business Review* actually solicits manuscripts. (And rejects them too, I can tell you.)

It's a lot of work to get an article placed in a major publication, but the results can sometimes be surprising. I once wrote a longish piece for the business section of the *New York Times* that the computer kindly relegated to the front page, and my phone ran hot with cranks for almost two weeks. But a couple of new clients also called. So did four publishers to see if I was interested in writing a book. When they generously pressed me with money, I was embarrassed to refuse.

HOW TO SORT THE WHEAT FROM THE CHAFF

Michelangelo said that, even before he began to work on a fresh block of marble, he knew there was a masterpiece in there. All he had to do was chisel it out.

In the same vein, one thing you can do is get a telephone book and survey it page by page—your clients are all listed. If they only knew what a wonderful fellow you are, they would be calling you. All you need is a sharp chisel and a lot of patience.

Your chisel and your patience both will wear better, however, if, instead of the phone book, you obtain through a good direct-mail house three finely honed lists, as follows:

1. A small list of those prospects whose custom you most
fervently desire, and upon whom you intend to manifest
the magnificence of your physical presence.

2. A large list of marginal prospects who might just use
you but who would not repay intensive wooing. This list
should be extended to include people of eminence who
are opinion leaders. Such individuals are often sought out
for their advice, and they like to be marketplace insiders.
If you can deliver a subtle communication to such people,
you may effect some seeming miracles.

3. Nonprospects whose money is good but whose custom
may be unsuitable.

However hungry you may be, the courage to walk away
from some prospects is the key to building a stable of satisfied
clients. In the final analysis, the quality of your base list of
prospects reflects your own personality, the quality of your
service, and your future. So let the first bite of your chisel
eliminate the dead wood.

I have a particular set of criteria for selecting nonprospects.

1. We don't accept an assignment for a corporation unless it is providing a valuable service to the community.
It's not that we are idealists, just that it's difficult to
recruit good executives for questionable clients.

2. We don't recruit for corporations that are dying.
Some quite large international corporations are held together by creditors and rubber bands. Again, any shrewd
executive is likely to be or become aware of this fact,
leaving us to recruit second-raters. Such people are simply more dead weight, as a consequence of which they
are very likely to be fired—with the blame assigned to
Wareham Associates. Thank you, but no.

3. We don't accept assignments from clients who want to
pretend that we are paid employees. I turned down a
major corporation in New York that wanted to both
supervise us and assign some of their own staff to actually

work alongside us—and using *our* name. Their suggestion was that they could do the job as well as, if not better than us—that we were just an extension of their personnel department. You don't hire a brain surgeon and want to hold his scalpel, nor a barrister and write his summation. A happy marriage may be solidly established upon a bedrock of mutual distrust, but successful consulting is generally a more intimate relationship requiring the mutual respect of both parties.

4. We don't need clients who expect us to agree with all of their foibles and prejudices. W. C. Fields said that, when people asked for his advice, he listened carefully and then advised the inquirer to do what he wanted to do. That's a tempting course, but in the consulting business you would wind up either broke or broken-hearted. I find it better to dig in and deliver the sometimes unpalatable truth. This can be expensive, of course. I lost a major cosmetic king simply because he refused to accept my advice that the best man available was already working for him. The key to the headhunting business is the word *available*. There were, certainly, better executives on the market, but there was, I was certain, nobody who would be able to suffer the president's bizarre moods and whims. This I delicately explained, and we parted on cool but fairly amicable terms. A competitor accepted that particular assignment but was unable to arrange a marriage.

5. I am wary of a prospect who tells me he has used everyone else in town without success. I know that most of my colleagues and competitors take their work seriously and *want* to do a first-rate job. If several of them fail with the same client, I tend to suspect, as did Hamlet, that something may be rotten.

6. I don't like a client who denigrates his entire executive team. Some people in any organization inevitably fail, but if everybody is second-rate, then so is the organization—and its emperor.

HOW TO APPROACH YOUR PRIME PROSPECTS

Assembling your hot list will present you with few problems. In New York I simply selected what I regarded to be the premier corporations in each industry. We ended up with only 297 names.

We enjoyed the advantage of already having recruited elsewhere in the world for some hundred of the greatest *"Fortune* 500 corporations." But, wherever I've opened a new office, I have seldom been handed work on a platter just because a particular organization has retained us in another city or country. Mind you, I'd be lying if I said it hadn't been a help virtually everywhere except New York. Here the *haut monde* genuinely *do* believe that the out-of-towner knows nothing about anything, and in such a setting I was keen to boast neither my fundamental humility nor my unpretentious origins.

Our back-up list of marginal prospects included a further 2,314 names, and the response to the steady stream of propaganda that we loaded onto the postman's back yielded some excellent leads. Burdening the mailman is itself an art akin to filling Santa's sack, requiring a keen perception of human nature. The eye of a jaded child can be easier to satisfy than the brain above the hand that holds the blunted scalpel that slits envelopes.

In 1970 I flew to San Francisco to collect an international direct-mail advertising award that Wareham Associates had won for an expensive promotion of our services. On the Big Day I suffered from jet lag, overslept, and sheepishly collected the trophy in New York a week later. But I still remember enough about the subject—based upon countless failures, culminating, finally, in heartening success—to spare you some of my own mistakes.

There are two major advantages of direct-mail advertising:

1. It is flexible as Silly Putty, thus enabling you to reach a carefully selected audience of one or of one million. Actually, *any* letter that puts your name before any client

or prospect is a piece of direct-mail advertising, and this you should always remember.

2. You can precisely tailor your message to your audience. Direct mail is an *intimate* medium. Marshall McLuhan would call it "hot." If it is good, it *involves* the recipient by commanding his attention.

My own award-winning, five-color, four-shot, high-cost campaign, looking back on it, was, in my opinion, *hopeless,* because it trivialized a serious subject.

I should have put into practice Marilyn Monroe's insight that "Men are always ready to respect anything that bores them." Instead I let our ad agency persuade us that *humor* was the key to getting the attention of the man at the top. But, when you are selling a serious service, you must engage the serious interest of the recipient. The approach can be unique, compelling, attention-getting, urbane, but it should *never* be trivializing.

The story is told around New York of a marketing wizard who conceived a unique promotion to sell personal jets. To test his conception, a carrier pigeon, in a box, was hand-delivered to the president of a famous New York bank. A message on the box offered the president a glass of champagne and a seat on a special demonstration flight. Whether or not he chose to accept the invitation, the beauty of flight, said the invitation, would be revealed when the pigeon was set free carrying the president's reply, which should be attached by him to the pigeon's leg. A small hole in the box provided the opportunity to affix the said reply to the said leg.

What happened was not quite according to plan. The president accidentally opened the box. The terrified bird flew out and, quite without appreciation of the corporate pecking order, defecated upon the president's hand-tailored, banker-blue suit. Trapping the feathered fury in order to release it down on Park Avenue proved a task requiring the help of other well-dressed colleagues, who were similarly befouled.

I persuaded that very same president, with whom I had

neither met nor previously spoken, to twice call my office for the sole purpose of discussing our services, merely by writing him a courteous letter. No messy bird. No Madison Avenue hype. Just a clear, simple, dignified message. What could be nicer? The moral, of course, is that you must give serious thought to the tone, tenor, and medium of all presentations, else the dropping that you land upon a president's desk may reflect neither your sentiment nor your intentions.

To be effective, any piece of direct mail you send must:

- Arrive
- Get opened
- Get read
- Get your message into the recipient's psyche
- Attract a favorable reaction

Here are my rules for making your direct-mail campaign a success:

1. A personal letter from you to your prospective angel should:
    - Give no clues that it is part of a campaign.
    - Address him by his correct name. (Obvious, you might think, but it doesn't always happen.)
    - Contain, in the first sentence, a benefit, a hook, and a summary of what is going to be said.
    - Be individually typed with a *fabric* ribbon. (The proliferation of word-processors has rendered "perfect" form letters suspicious and a sizeable mailing should therefore look marginally imperfect.)
    - Address him as one gentleman might speak to another in a club when they have only recently been introduced: the tone should be friendly but not familiar; the message intriguing while not allowing the wheels to show; the style never stilted, pompous, or apologetic. Take as many or as few words as you need to tell your story in a *persuasive* manner.

- Be personally signed in ink or broad felt-tip pen. The recipient should feel that the letter has been written personally for him.
- Contain a postscript offering a benefit, and a reason to take some action. The postscript is often looked at first, and certainly it will be read last.

2. Accompanying the letter could be a piece of propaganda that does not look like a piece of propaganda. Our own best material is contained in our *Harvard Business Review* reprints, which:

- Offer specific information that a prospect will *want to read.*
- Establish our own expertise and reputation.
- Suggest we are taking the person we are writing to very seriously.
- Effectively provide a third-party endorsement of our services.

Compared to the above approach, a brochure has practically zero credibility, and will probably be read by no one but your competition.

THE NOT-SO-GENTLE ART OF SOLICITING ANGELS

If you take my advice, then your prospect, before you ever call him to set up an appointment, will:

1. Know the name of your firm
2. Appreciate your expertise
3. Be aware that important people think well enough of you to quote you, recommend you, publish your stories, or ask you to address noteworthy audiences

With any luck, your prospect may already *want* to meet you—indeed, *mirabile dictu,* may even have called your office.

But life is rarely that easy, so let us proceed on the assumption that your prospect has not yet gotten around to placing that call, and that, to alleviate his workload, you have decided to take the impetus in arranging a meeting. This will involve a letter and a telephone call. You can skip the letter if you like, but if it's an important contact you might want to drop your name and letterhead by him again.

The letter. It can be useful for this missive to emanate from a secretary with a grand title, the chief advantages of this indirect approach being:

- The writer can, with as much subtlety as the truth will allow, describe you as a genius
- You avoid the risk of a direct rebuff
- You can follow up later with your own letter if need be

This communication should:

- Be impeccably typed, addressed, and spelled
- Refer to a mutual acquaintance who has suggested that contact be made, or to some news item about the recipient that you have gleaned from the paper (guaranteed to catch his attention, and a good reason to subscribe to the *Wall Street Journal)*
- Include yet another interesting article you have written
- Refer to an intriguing possibility for discussion
- Advise that you will very soon be calling to arrange an opportunity to get together. The advantage of this suggestion is that he may feel obliged to keep your letter on his desk pending your call

The telephone call. I would suggest that you get an articulate ambassador to set up your appointments, for the reasons listed earlier. Additionally, your emissary can afford to be pushy: indeed, would be derelict in his duty to be otherwise. His *job* is to arrange this appointment, and anyone attempting to put him off must, very properly, be harassed. However, if *you* do get on the phone, and you don't get through, or your calls don't get returned (as can happen now and then), then both you *and* your organization have been rejected and demeaned.

Should you decide to make your own call, an excellent ploy is to place a person-to-person call from another country. Such calls are flattering and rarely fail to track down even the most elusive quarry; and, of course, the detective work is included in the price of the call. Calling person-to-person from another city can be quite effective too, but never as effective as from overseas. If you can't get abroad, then consider having a colleague call from another country.

Another very useful way to gain the attention of a senior executive is to become a free-lance journalist. When I hadn't long been in New York, I wrote a piece about economic recovery that required me to personally interview Peter Engel, then the head of Helena Rubinstein; David Mahoney, chairman of Norton Simon; and Colin Marshall, at that time chief executive of Avis.

I met Colin Marshall at 7:30 A.M. on a midweek morning and we had a long and very pleasant discussion. Near the end of our talk he asked whether or not Wareham Associates had an international charge account with Avis. When I confessed that we did not, he arranged the matter on the spot, thereby confirming my belief that a chief executive always knows the value of a client. And gently one-upping me too.

Incidentally, when that article appeared in six countries, I received personal thank-you calls from my illustrious interviewees—and a couple of very good clients.

Five other points are worthy of note:

1. *Establish a bond of intimacy with the secretary.* Woo her a little. But judge your target, remembering the advice of Alfie: "Get a married woman laughing, you've got it made. Get a single girl laughing, and it's all you'll ever get."
2. Refer to your previous correspondence with *número uno* as though you have been writing to each other for years. Sympathize with his secretary that he is always in such demand. Acknowledge that she is the person who really runs the place (very true, since she runs his sched-

275

ule). Enlist her as an accomplice in helping you get an appointment. If you get on her good side, you will soon be talking to Mr. Angel whether he likes it or not. At worst, she just may point you to a genuinely more helpful contact, which enables you to tell *that* individual that Mr. Angel has *instructed* you to get together.

3. Never say you want to *introduce yourself.* Say you have something quite unique to show him that will require Getting Together. Of course, if someone else is calling on your behalf, the advice can be that you have just flown in from Brussels—or, better yet, will *soon* be flying in from Brussels—and need to set up a brief appointment. The advantage of this ploy is that it focuses upon a suitable date rather than the subject of your meeting. Perhaps, in similar vein, you could paint your house white and say that you will be coming direct from the White House. Obfuscate a little. The goal at this stage is merely to get in.

4. Rarely give your name or ask for the Angel to return your call. Explain that you are very busy and will probably be out. Politely apologize on behalf of your caller that *he* is out, and ascertain when he'll be expected back, and make an appointment to call him back. It's a Byzantine business, but top people do receive hundreds of crank calls every day, and their secretaries automatically want to—and are paid to—shield them from unfamiliar voices.

5. Be prepared for the unexpected. I can confirm that my expatriot countryman, Keith Crane, president and chief executive of Colgate, is inclined to sometimes answer his own phone, as are a number of other senior executives who like to stay in touch with their public.

Into the heavenly chamber. It is important, once in the presence of an angel, to have an answer to the inevitable question: "What good reason is there to use you in preference to our existing firm?"

Frankly, the question is a red herring. There is no good

reason and every good reason. The angel will make his choice for emotional reasons rather than as the result of your compelling logic.

Choosing any professional service is like buying a yacht: people buy romance and dreams. I have seen normally sane people literally fall in love with the alluring lines of forty feet of dry rot, and then invent all sorts of rational reasons to justify the large dents made in their wallets.

But the Catch-22 is that you must still adduce something sound for your Angel to hang his logical hat upon, and this should be done with a straight face. In New York my answer was simple: "Any firm is only as good as the consultant handling your particular assignment."

Everyone always agreed. I paused and then proceeded: "In New York *I* will be supervising your work and, as founder of an international organization operating on three continents, I have particular ego-involvement in seeing that you get the very best service available. Can the consultant who presently handles your work point to the same motivations? Or is he anxious to finish work at five and get home to his family? Does he *care* about you? Is he *really* trying as hard as he used to? Do you even *know* who is handling your work?"

A frown would cross Mr. Angel's face at this point, and on we went: "But the *best* reason to use Wareham Associates is that we service only a small number of select clients in disparate industries (especially true at the time of my visit). This enables us to scour the market and tap the shoulder of that one *best* executive wherever he may be: *to approach any and all of your competitors unfettered.*"

By now I had usually captured his attention. "Mr. Angel, the big New York search firms just *cannot,* with the best will in the world, offer you the same guarantee. Sometimes, as a result of this peculiar industry, they find themselves *in bed with your competition.*"

This somewhat romantic approach yielded some attractive clients. I remember being called at 5:15 P.M. on a bleak winter Friday to the executive offices of a major banker. The chairman was furious to have discovered, after my call upon him two weeks earlier, that indeed his big blue-chip search firm *had* robbed Peter to pay Paul and poached one of his key executives. I walked out with a substantial five-figure retainer in my pocket, and a client whose custom means more to me than the affection of some of my own relatives.

Sometimes I would depart from my prepared message. Once when I called upon Pfizer Inc., said to be the largest manufacturing employer in this greatest city in the world, I was surprised to find myself agreeing with expatriate Australian Neville Smith, the former director of international manpower planning, that executive search was like pimping. We both laughed at that one.

I also enjoyed a laugh with George Green, president of the *New Yorker,* who listened very carefully, then, when I finished, applauded my performance and made me a gift of the famous Steinberg poster that shows where the world ends—at the edge of the Hudson. One of the great pleasures of living and working in Manhattan is blending with great institutions like the *New Yorker* and urbane companions like George (or is it the other way around?). When we discovered we were near neighbors, it was a pleasure to ignore my own advice never to befriend clients or entertain them at home.

Our other major service is contained in Dr. McMurry's unique Communications Grid, and the key to selling this service is often to suggest no more than the truth to the chief executive:

As corporate president you are a victim of the Looking Glass Syndrome. The memos that reach your desk, the reports, the board meetings you attend, all reflect your own image and very little else. Before you were promoted you could survey the corporate psyche through many windows. But now that you are on the other side they have become mirrors. Your staff can still see you, but their faces and words only reflect *your* expectations. And your *key* executives, those you actually pay to give you the truth, have a vested interest in withholding bad news, partly because they fear to bring it, but sometimes because they stand to gain if you fail. They mightn't push you into an abyss, but if they see you innocently stumbling towards one they may simply avert their eyes.

Appealing to a chief executive's paranoia is valuable because the *only* way he can discover what is going on is to hire an outside agency (such as Wareham Associates) to conduct the McMurry Grid. This involves subtle polling techniques and unique field-survey appraisals that enable key executives to be painlessly appraised and corporate problems that otherwise would never have seen the light of day to be precisely pinpointed.

And now, gentle reader, before you rush to the perhaps justifiable conclusion that my methods seem a trifle desperate, please reflect upon a Greek proverb passed on to me by a tycoon whom I met while sailing in the Aegean: "First secure an independent income, then practice virtue."

Recall that I was a hungry and haunted country boy struggling to survive in a jungle of silver-tongued Manhattanites. I was Gulliver among the Brobdingnagians, Alice in the Red Queen's garden, very much in contemplation of losing my head. In Her Majesty's United Kingdom I would have behaved differently. But in America I took my tone from John Wayne, who once remarked of the American Indians:

> I don't feel we did wrong in taking this great country away from them. There were great numbers of people who needed new land, and the Indians were selfishly trying to keep it for themselves.

THE REAL SECRET OF GETTING CLIENTS

A client is like a friend. You don't make friends by tricking them into liking you. They come to you because they, no less than you, want a trustworthy comrade, someone with whom to share the burden of trying to make it in a tough world.

It's when you've been around long enough for people to have forgotten when you began, and have established an image that has become your reality, that a reputation is built. There are clients out there who would love to give you their work. What they need to be assured of is that they can rely upon the integrity of your reputation: that you can be *trusted*.

A fool and his money may soon be parted, but rich fools are becoming a scarce breed, and, anyway, a *good* client is *never* a fool, and will count his money carefully. Good clients deal with good people. What you need is to be worthy of your client, and that will take patience and sincerity.

The real secret, I must confess, is that it is upon ourselves, and not our clients, that we must do the most work.

John Wareham is founder and president of an international executive search and management consulting firm headquartered in New York.

He studied psychology to complete his degree in commerce at Victoria University of Wellington in New Zealand, where he was born. He is also qualified as an economist and a chartered accountant.

A spare-time ocean racer, he also plays squash and chess, and enjoys an interest in theater, opera, and classical music. Mr. Wareham lives in New York City with his wife, Margaret, and their four children.